From Beneath the Altar

*A COMMENTARY ON THE REVELATION,
WITH QUESTIONS
AND SPECIAL STUDIES*

By Carl McMurray

www.spiritbuilding.com for study helps

SPIRITBUILDING PUBLISHING
15591 N. State Rd. 9, Summitville, Indiana, 46070

Spiritual "equipment" for the contest of life.

FROM BENEATH THE ALTAR
1st printing 1992, 2nd edition 2007
ISBN: 0-9774754-2-5

© SPIRITBUILDING, 2007, All Rights Reserved.
No part of this book may be reproduced in any form without the written permission of the publisher. Printed in the United States of America.

Scripture taken from the
NEW AMERICAN STANDARD BIBLE®,
© Copyright 1960, 1962, 1963, 1968, 1971, 1972, 1973, 1975, 1977 by The Lockman Foundation
Used by permission. (www.Lockman.org)

Archaeology photos in special studies section by Kyle Pope
Used by permission.
© Copyright 2003, Ancient Road Publications ™
http://kmpope.home.att.net

Digital art used throughout by Duncan Long
Used by permission.
© Duncan Long, All Rights Reserved, http://duncanlong.com

COVER: Angel watching over cemetary in Cleveland, OH., Photography by Sarah McMurray. For info or to contact about photography email: Sarah@Spiritbuilding.com.

Preface to the first edition

"And when He broke the fifth seal, I saw underneath the altar the souls of those who had been slain because of the word of God, and because of the testimony which they had maintained; and they cried out with a loud voice, saying, 'How long, O Lord, holy and true, wilt Thou refrain from judging and avenging our blood on those that dwell on the earth?' And there was given to each of them a white robe; and they were told that they should rest for a little while longer, until the number of their fellow servants and their brethren who were to be killed even as they had been, should be completed also."

Revelation 6:9-11, NASV

From the thoughts in the above passage comes the title of this commentary. The picture presented in the beginning of the book is one of the saints persecuted, wondering, and waiting. It proceeds to a presentation of the church victorious and glorified. The unseen spiritual battle requiring the perseverance of the saints and the promises of the Lord that leads from humiliation to glorification is the message of the Revelation and the point of this book.

This effort is an evolution of class material that has been presented numerous times with many additions and changes. It is intended to perhaps fill in the gaps where other knowledgeable men failed, in the author's opinion, to either remain consistent in their interpretation or deal with certain interesting aspects of the vision. Hopefully it will allow the student to read the Revelation and relate it to other passages of scripture as a means of certain interpretation. In view of the many speculative and sensational doctrines being advocated today based upon this book, this seems to be an imperative for the Christian desiring to be able to "give answer to any man that asketh you." If this work helps one believer to stand fast and be encouraged against the strong winds of false doctrine, its purpose will be accomplished. May God bless you in your thoughtful consideration of this important book.

Carl (Mac) McMurray
December 29, 1992

Author's Comments

In the first printing of this volume I gave great thanks to my secretary, Alayne Hunt, for her many, many hours of proofing and correcting. I would not take that away since this second volume also would not be here without her help.

Additionally, since the first volume I have collected another proofreader and corrector. It seems sometimes that people are waiting in line for the job of correcting me. Alas, it is sorely needed. I have continued to teach and add to the original material and so I need to give great thanks to another helper that the Lord gave me who has continued the tedious work of proofing this material in addition to everything else she does for me. I cannot say thank you enough to my companion in life, my wife Lorna.

I need to say thank you to my beautiful daughter, Sarah Grace. She is the one who originally requested the teaching of this material, over and over, when it was not taught promptly. She has always complimented my work by asking for and preferring her father's classes. And in any endeavor she has happily contributed her photographic efforts to encourage me and help out.

Lastly, I must say thank you to the three men who have meant more to making me who I am at this writing than anyone else could possibly know. By their influence they have shaped my studies, my writings, and my teaching efforts. To my Granddad "Mac" whose label I wear and who set me on his knee and began giving me spiritual directions as he first taught me the authors of the New Testament. To my father, Carl Sr., who never pushed me to preach or teach, but modeled self-control (in dealing with a rebellious son) and real faith in practicing in our home what I heard taught from the scriptures. He has always been ready to listen and encourage me in my work. And to my son, Forrest, who at every stage of life has far surpassed his father at the same age and who has gone far beyond my expectations of nobility and character in manhood. He is a mans' man with a love for God. I have always felt the eyes of these three upon me and have tried to act in a manner to make them as proud of me as I am of them.

To all of the above, and more, I say thank you, and I would like to dedicate this volume to you.

Carl (Mac) McMurray
July 2007

TABLE OF CONTENTS

Page No.

Introduction to the Revelation 9

Propositions Concerning the Understanding of the Revelation 12

Section One (chapters 1-11) **The Struggle on Earth**

1. Chapters 1-3 (Christ in the midst of the lampstands) 15
2. Chapters 4-7 (The book with 7 seals) 45
3. Chapters 8-11 (The 7 trumpets of judgment) 79

Section Two (chapters 12-22) **The Deeper, Spiritual Struggle**

4. Chapters 12-14 (Woman and the man-child persecuted) 111
5. Chapters 15-16 (The 7 bowls of wrath) 143
6. Chapters 17-19 (The fall of the great harlot/beasts) 159
7. Chapters 20-22 (The judgment upon the dragon) 189

Map of the seven churches 214

Special Study #1 - The Time of Fulfillment for the Revelation 215
Special Study #2 - The "Comings" of the Lord 219
Special Study #3 - Ephesus 222
Special Study #4 - Smyrna 225
Special Study #5 - Pergamum 227
Special Study #6 - Thyatira 229
Special Study #7 - Sardis 231
Special Study #8 - Philadelphia 233
Special Study #9 - Laodicea 234
Special Study #10 - Premillennialism in the Book of Revelation 236
Special Study #11 - What About Total Annihilation? 239
Special Study #12 - The Caesars and Persecution of the Saints 240

Footnotes 244
Bibliography 246

INTRODUCTION TO THE REVELATION

You are about to enter into a study of the book of the Revelation. This book is also known as the Apocalypse. The term apocalypse is from the Greek word "apokalupsis" which means... "an uncovering."[1] Apocalypse is a transliteration of this Greek word, similar to our word "baptism" being a transliteration of the Greek word "baptisto" or our word "deacon" being a transliteration of "diakonos." The actual translation of "baptisto" is "immerse." The actual translation of "diakonos" is "minister" or "servant." And the actual translation of "apokalupsis" is "revelation." The book is the "revelation" or uncovering of a mystery which is unknown until it is revealed.

"There are three most distinct plans followed by various commentators. Substantially they may be stated as follows:

(1) **The Preterist System**, which applies the visions mainly to the Jewish nation and pagan Rome, with most of them placed before the destruction of Jerusalem.

(2) **The Futurist System**, which makes the main part of the symbols yet to be fulfilled. This usually includes the return of fleshly Israel to Palestine, the rebuilding of the material temple, and the personal reign of Christ upon David's throne here on earth for a thousand years.

(3) **The Historical System**, which teaches that the different series of symbols show the future events of the church from soon after John wrote till the final states of men are reached."[2]

There are many additional ideas besides these 3, but these are the main interpretive plans that are usually followed. Out of man's dealings with this highly symbolic book flow many contradictory, conflicting, and sometimes blatantly false ideas and teachings. These misunderstandings should not be a reason to avoid the Revelation, but on the contrary should encourage us to meet it squarely and study it deeply. "The book begins and ends with a blessing pronounced upon those WHO HEAR AND KEEP the things that are written therein"[3] (Revelation 1:3; 22:7). The symbols should not remain a mystery to Christians because symbolic language is common in both the Old and New Testament.

No claim for originality in this guide for study is made. The writer has gleaned much of his material from Hendriksen's MORE THAN CONQUERORS and

Hailey's REVELATION, but numerous other sources were also consulted and considered. Hopefully, credit is given where due by the use of footnotes. The writer believes that the Revelation is just that, an uncovering. It is not a mystery that we cannot fathom. By an open study and with much comparison within the scriptures we can receive much encouragement from the book. We will be using, more or less, the Historical System with a "parallelist" interpretation. By doing this and staying inside the boundary lines set up by understood scriptures, we believe that we can establish the truth. The text most commonly used in preparing this material was the New American Standard Bible, although much comparison is made with the King James Version for the easier study of some more traditional students.

Never shall we be able to understand the book of Revelation unless we interpret it in the light of contemporaneous events. We should always ask...How did the first readers understand this book? We should make an earnest attempt to understand the conditions and circumstances out of which this prophecy arose. The Apocalypse has as its immediate purpose to gird the wavering hearts of the persecuted believers of the first century with strength unto calm endurance and unflinching loyalty to Christ. Hence, every paragraph of this glorious prophecy is filled with significance, instruction, and comfort for the seven churches of Asia. This book is an answer to the crying need of that particular day and we must permit contemporaneous circumstances to shed their light upon its symbols and predictions. True, most emphatically true: this book has a message for today, but we shall never be able to understand what the Spirit is saying to the churches of today unless we first of all study the specific needs and circumstances of the seven churches of Asia as they existed in the first century.

We find accordingly that the Apocalypse is replete with references to contemporaneous events and circumstances. Believers were being persecuted severely, bitterly. Their blood was being poured out, 1:9; 7:14; 6:10; 16:6; 17:6; and 19:2. Some were pining away in dank dungeons or were about to be imprisoned, 2:10. They had been suffering hunger, thirst, and famine, 6:8; 7:16. Some had been cast before wild beasts. Many had been beheaded, 20:4. At Pergamum, Antipas had been killed, 2:13. John had been banished to the Isle of Patmos, 1:9. The Roman government encouraged persecution. Its emperor-worship inspired false religion and its capitol was the center of lust, 13:7, 15; 17:18. False teachers and sects were troubling the churches, 2:2, 14, 20, 24. Nevertheless, true believers were causing the light of Christ to shine in the darkness of superstition and unbelief. Philadelphia was given "an open door" for this very reason, 3:8.

All these things were real. They were facts—many of them hard facts—for the church of that day and age. These believers were not interested in Hitler, a war in the Balkans, the N.R.A., or the 1948 presidential campaign. They were intensely interested in the struggle between light and darkness, the church and the world, Christ and the dragon, truth and error. It was to those people that the Revelation was primarily written. The Apocalypse is an answer to the crying needs of those persecuted, sorely afflicted believers. When we have learned what God gave them to help them and give them hope when it seemed there was no hope on earth, we will have learned much that will help and sustain us also.

PROPOSITIONS CONCERNING THE UNDERSTANDING OF THE REVELATION

PROPOSITION I: The book of Revelation consists of 7 sections. They are parallel, each spans the entire new dispensation, from the first to the second coming of Christ.

PROPOSITION II: The 7 sections may be grouped into 2 major divisions. The first major division (1-11) consists of 3 sections. The second major division (12-22) consists of 4 sections. These 2 major divisions reveal a progress in depth or intensity of spiritual conflict. The first major division (1-11) reveals the church —indwelt by Christ—persecuted by the world. The church is avenged, protected, and victorious. The second major division (12-22) reveals the deeper, spiritual background of this struggle. It is a conflict between the Christ and the dragon, in which the Christ—hence, His church—is victorious.

OUTLINE OF THE APOCALYPSE
from Propositions I and II

THEME: The victory of Christ and His church over Satan and his helpers.

I. **THE STRUGGLE ON EARTH,**
   THE CHURCH PERSECUTED BY THE WORLD, THE CHURCH AVENGED, PROTECTED, AND VICTORIOUS. Chapters 1-11

   1. (chapters 1-3) Christ in the midst of the lampstands.

   2. (chapters 4-7) The book with 7 seals.

   3. (chapters 8-11) The 7 trumpets of judgment.

II. **THE DEEPER SPIRITUAL BACKGROUND,**
   THE CHRIST (and the church) PERSECUTED BY THE DRAGON (Satan) AND HIS HELPERS. CHRIST AND HIS CHURCH ARE VICTORIOUS. Chapters 12-22

   4. (chapters 12-14) The woman and the man-child persecuted by the dragon and his helpers (the beast and the harlot).

   5. (chapters 15-16) The 7 bowls of wrath.

John's Revelation

6. (chapters 17-19) The fall of the great harlot and of the beasts.

7. (chapters 20-22) The judgment upon the dragon (Satan) followed by the new heaven and earth, new Jerusalem.

PROPOSITION III: The book is one. The principles of human conduct and of divine moral government are progressively revealed: the lampstands give rise to the seals, the seals to the trumpets, etc.

PROPOSITION IV: The seven sections of the Apocalypse are arranged in an ascending, climactic order. There is progress in eschatological emphasis: the final judgment is first ANNOUNCED, then INTRODUCED, and finally DESCRIBED. Similarly, the new heaven and earth are described more fully in the final section than in those proceeding.

PROPOSITION V: The fabric of the book consists of moving pictures. The details that pertain to the picture should be interpreted in harmony with its central thought. We should ask two questions. First, what is the entire picture? Second, what is its predominant idea?

PROPOSITION VI: The seals, trumpets, bowls of wrath, and similar symbols refer not to specific events, particular happenings and details of history, but to principles - of human conduct and of divine moral government—that are operating throughout the history of the world, especially throughout the new dispensation.

PROPOSITION VII: The Apocalypse is rooted in contemporaneous events and circumstances. Its symbols should be interpreted in the light of conditions that prevailed when the book was written.

PROPOSITION VIII: The Apocalypse is rooted in the sacred scriptures. It should be interpreted in harmony with the teachings of the entire Bible.

PROPOSITION IX: The Apocalypse is rooted in the mind and revelation of God. God, in Christ, is the real author. Hence, this book contains the purpose of God concerning the history of the church.

(from Hendriksen's MORE THAN CONQUERORS)

From Beneath the Altar

> **Revelation 1**
> 1. The Revelation of Jesus Christ, which God gave Him to show to His bond-servants, the things which must soon take place; and He sent and communicated it by His angel to His bond-servant John,
> 2. who testified to the word of God and to the testimony of Jesus Christ, even to all that he saw.

THE REVELATION
chapter 1
Section I, 1 (see page 12)

1. Whatever is written here is given by God to Jesus Christ. This is why it is "the Revelation of Jesus Christ." It is also a revelation of Jesus Christ because it is a revelation of His glory, rule, and execution of judgment. The Revelation of Jesus is given for the servants of Jesus Christ. The way it was "communicated" (NASB) to them was by His angel to John. The KJV uses the word "signified" here. One of the meanings of the original is that which is given in signs, or made known by symbols. This fact separates Revelation from every other New Testament writing. Where all the other New Testament messages are given in words to communicate the message of the author (that author being God), this book was given in a series of signs, symbols, and pictures that John was told to write down. It is not the words specifically that communicate the message of this book, but the pictures that John describes. Therein will be found the message from God. Though overlooked by many, the time period for the prophetic visions to be fulfilled is given here, i.e, "must shortly take place." This must limit our interpretation in spite of those who consistently try and apply the visions to our future. (See Special Study #1.)

2. John was one of 13 "witnesses," 1 John 1:1-4; Acts 1:8, 21-22; 2:32; and 3:15. In accordance with the preceding scriptures, the term "witness" is a peculiar term that applies accurately only to the apostles. A witness is one who has personally observed something. To use the term "witness" today to describe a sharing of the gospel with another is to misuse the term. One might be a "witness" of what he believes the Lord has done personally in his own life, but since our walk is a walk of faith, not sight, there can be no true witnesses for the Lord in our age. There are no "witnesses" today since none living today have 1) seen the Lord personally, or 2) been chosen specifically by Him for that task.

> 3. Blessed is he who reads and those who hear the words of the prophecy, and heed the things which are written in it; for the time is near.
> 4. John to the seven churches that are in Asia: Grace to you and peace, from Him who is and who was and who is to come, and from the seven Spirits who are before His throne,
> 5. and from Jesus Christ, the faithful witness, the firstborn of the dead, and the ruler of the

3. "He who reads" refers to the reader in those early public assemblies. "He" is singular while "those who hear" is plural. Manuscripts of Scripture were valuable and hard to come by at that time so the same practice was adopted among Christians as was practiced by the Jews in the synagogues. An individual would read to the whole group from perhaps the only copy of Scripture a congregation might possess. This was because each copy had to be hand-printed. "Blessed" can be translated happy or fortunate. It is absurd to think that one can be made happy by simply hearing without understanding what he hears. However, the one who "heeds" what he hears (understands and acts upon) will be blessed (happy or fortunate). "For the time is near" provides strong motivation for obedience, because the things to be revealed (woes, fears, battles, and the one hope) were in the *near future*. (See Special Study #1.)

4. Asia was the richest of all Roman provinces, located in the western part of modern Asia Minor. The number 7 is used too many times in both the Old and New Testament to ignore. It is used in some manner 54 times in the Revelation. The number 7 symbolizes completeness, the whole, and even perfection probably taking its primary meaning from its connection to Creation and Deity. Here it represents the whole church in every place, the complete body of believers, or all congregations together, by these 7. Peace is a result of God's unmerited favor (grace). Grace is provided by the Father, dispensed by the Spirit, and merited for us by the Son, hence the mention of all three, John 14:25-27.

5. Jesus is referred to in 3 senses here: the faithful witness while He was living, the first-born in His resurrection, and the ruler of the kings in His present state on His throne. The first refers to His personal knowledge of those things which He taught and held up as a goal for all of God's children. See 1:2 for notes on "witness." The second is *not* a description of "origin," but a description of "position." Jesus was not born first from the dead. Others had been resurrected (i.e., Lazarus, the widow's son, and those who left their tombs at His crucifixion and went into the city) before Him (though they died again whereas He defeated death). The point, however, is that He is the "first-born" in "position" or prominence. Just as in Colossians 1:15, He is the "first-born of all creation," not

> kings of the earth. To Him who loves us and released us from our sins by His blood--
> 6. and He has made us to be a kingdom, priests to His God and Father--to Him be the glory and the dominion forever and ever. Amen.
> 7. BEHOLD, HE IS COMING WITH THE CLOUDS, and every eye will see Him, even those who pierced Him; and all the tribes of the earth will mourn over Him. So it is to be. Amen.
> 8. "I am the Alpha and the Omega," says the Lord God, "who is and who was and who is to come, the Almighty."
> 9. I, John, your brother and fellow partaker in the tribulation and kingdom and perseverance which are in Jesus, was on the island called Patmos because of the word of God and the testi-

the first created being, because He was not created at all. Instead, He is the head over all creation, having the preeminence in creation is the message of the verse. The third appellation has reference to His position presently, whether recognized and honored as such or not. Psalm 2:9 describes the fact of "the nations" being given to Him as His inheritance upon taking the throne after His resurrection. Our Lord is King of Kings. He rules the disobedient with a rod of iron and He rules His kingdom with a scepter of righteousness.

6. "Made us to be a kingdom" is in the present tense for John and his readers. The kingdom was in existence then (and continues now), and Christians were priests then (as Christians continue to be now), not sometime in the future. See also 1 Peter. 2:5.

7. Here we see the announcement of Christ's coming. "Clouds" may not refer to fluffy vapors in the sky here. Instead, consider that He is speaking of clouds of heavenly hosts. This would be a great crowd of beings that will accompany Him at His return. NOTE: *with* the clouds, not *in* the clouds. He will not come in secret (Jehovah's Witnesses doctrine) but rather "every eye" will see Him. "Those who pierced Him" refers not only to those who hung Him on the cross, but also to those who crucify Him afresh. The mourning will be by all those wicked of the earth who will dread His coming.

8. "Alpha and Omega" are the first and last letters in the Greek alphabet. They are the beginning and the end. Thus Christ is the beginning and the end, the first, last, and everything in between. I believe it is Jesus who is being called "Lord God" here because of chapter 2:8. If so, then the same descriptive terms used of the Father in verse 4 are used of the Son here, showing His relationship and equality.

mony of Jesus.

10. I was in the Spirit on the Lord's day, and I heard behind me a loud voice like the sound of a trumpet,

11. saying, "Write in a book what you see, and send it to the seven churches: to Ephesus and to Smyrna and to Pergamum and to Thyatira and to Sardis and to Philadelphia and to Laodicea."

12. Then I turned to see the voice that was speaking with me. And having turned I saw seven golden lampstands;

13. and in the middle of the

9. John was on Patmos because of the word and testimony of Jesus. In other words, for publicly claiming his Savior and sharing his knowledge with others. "Patience" (KJV) here means steadfastness or perseverance, especially related to trial (NASB). In his ECCLESIASTICAL HISTORY, Eusebius declares that the apostle was exiled to the Isle of Patmos by Domitian, p.101. Once more we point out that John was *at that time* a partaker with other Christians in the "tribulation" and "perseverance" which was in Jesus. He was also *at that time* a partaker in the "*kingdom.*" It was in existence at that time and continues until now. The kingdom is not something to be looked for in the future.

10. "In the Spirit" means Holy Spirit guidance and influence for the vision. "Lord's day" was the first day of the week (modern Sunday) since this was the day that 1) traditionally Jesus entered Jerusalem like a king on a colt, 2) Jesus was proven to be the Son of God by His resurrection from the dead (Romans 1:4), and 3) Jesus established His church/kingdom upon, since the day of Pentecost (Acts 2:1) always fell on the first day of the week. If the Lord has a day, this most certainly must be it. The voice John heard was "loud" and "like" a trumpet. The trumpet sound was used to call God's people together, Exodus 19:19; Leviticus 25:9; Joshua 6:5; Isaiah 58:1.

11. John's charge to write and send. See verse 1.

12. In the Old Testament, Solomon's temple had 1 stand with 7 lights. Here we see 7 stands, each one a candle (more accurately a lamp or light). We see the independence of each stand or congregation as well as their similarities; they are all golden.

13. In seeing "Him" who was in the midst of them, John saw the close proximity of Christ to His churches showing intimate knowledge and personal handling. This was the same Jesus that John had walked, talked, eaten, and slept with, but He was changed. Thus he says this being was "like the Son of man." The garment and girdle represent royal dignity that belongs to priesthood and kingship.

> lampstands I saw one like a son of man, clothed in a robe reaching to the feet, and girded across His chest with a golden sash.
> 14. His head and His hair were white like white wool, like snow; and His eyes were like a flame of fire.
> 15. His feet were like burnished bronze, when it has been made to glow in a furnace, and His voice was like the sound of many waters.

NOTE:

Let us try to see it thus: Notice that the Son of man is here pictured as clothed with power and majesty, with awe and terror. That long royal robe—that golden belt buckled at the breast—that hair so glistening white that like snow on which the sun is shining it hurts the eye—those eyes flashing fire, eyes which read every heart and penetrate every hidden corner—those feet glowing in order to trample down the wicked—that loud reverberating voice, like the mighty breakers booming against the rocky shore of Patmos—that sharp, long and heavy great-sword with two biting edges—yes, that entire appearance 'as the sun shines in its power,' too intense for human eyes to stare at—the entire picture taken as a whole, is symbolical of Christ, the Holy One, coming to purge His churches, 2:16, 18, 23 and to punish those who are persecuting His elect, 8:5ff.

(Hendricksen, MORE THAN CONQUERORS, p. 71)

14. White usually carries an idea of holiness and/or purity. One can just imagine eyes "like a flame of fire"—burning in the intensity of their zeal for the church/kingdom (John 2:17) and their love for each member—a piercing gaze able to "discern the hearts of men" and see into a heart without guile, John 1:47. The one upon whom John looked was a changed person from the one that had walked the earth simply as a man. No longer would Isaiah's prophecy of the Messiah's appearance apply, i.e., *"no stately form or majesty...nor appearance that we should be attracted to him," Isaiah. 53:2.*

15. There is an idea presented here that is reminiscent of God's promise in Malachi 4:3. "...His feet like...it has been caused to glow in a furnace" makes one think of something that is purified because of fire. Perhaps feet that are pure and walk in the way of righteousness. His voice was like standing in the presence of a great waterfall. It is thunderous, deafening, and all other sounds are pushed aside. There can be no ignoring its power.

> 16. In His right hand He held seven stars, and out of His mouth came a sharp two-edged sword; and His face was like the sun shining in its strength.
> 17. When I saw Him, I fell at His feet like a dead man. And He placed His right hand on me, saying, "Do not be afraid; I am the first and the last,
> 18. and the living One; and I was dead, and behold, I am alive forevermore, and I have the keys of death and of Hades.
> 19. "Therefore write the things which you have seen, and the things which are, and the things which will take place after

16. Assumptions about the 7 stars are unnecessary since they are explained later. "Countenance" (KJV) here is "face" (NASB). In the two-edged sword proceeding from his mouth, we see a representation of the word of God described in Hebrews 4:12 in a similar way. *"Living and active and sharper than any two-edged sword, and piercing as far as the division of soul and spirit, of both joints and marrow, and able to judge the thoughts and intentions of the heart."* At the same time we can also see a two-edged sword from the standpoint of these early Christians. In the same way that we see firearms as an authoritative tool of the modern day policeman, the two-edged sword would have been a symbol of power since it was the most common weapon of the Roman soldier. It would represent a serious type of authority.

17. Overcome with awe and fear, John grew weak and fainted. Not an uncommon reaction when confronted with Deity. Note Isaiah 6:5; Ezekiel 1:28; Daniel 8:17, 27; and 10:8-10. Although it naturally did so, the vision of Christ was not meant to terrify John; therefore, "Do not be afraid...." Jehovah used the same title, Isaiah 41:4; 44:6; and 48:12.

18. Jesus has the keys (power, authority) of death and Hades. Hades literally is the "place of the unseen," the waiting place of the soul after being separated from the body until judgment. Until the last day, death is always followed by Hades, Revelation 6:8; 20:14.

19. Another order to write, but with more detail.

20. 7 stars in His hand are the 7 angels of the churches. Since the lampstands are the churches, the supporters of light, viewed externally, the stars may well represent the inward life or spirit of the congregations addressed by Jesus. This position seems to be confirmed by the letters themselves. Jesus addresses each letter to "the angel of the church...," and concludes with the appeal, "He that hath an ear, let him hear what the Spirit saith to the churches" (KJV). Whoever

> these things.
> 20. "As for the mystery of the seven stars which you saw in My right hand, and the seven golden lampstands: the seven stars are the angels of the seven churches, and the seven lampstands are the seven churches.

is addressed is to hear—the angels are addressed—the churches are to hear. It follows that the angels are that part of the church addressed which is to hear; this would be the spirit or active life of the churches (Hailey, REVELATION). This would also follow since the stars are in His hand. The life of the congregation is in His hand and it is up to Christ to determine whether a congregation lives or dies.

QUESTIONS ON CHAPTER 1

1. Where does the name "Apocalypse" come from?

2. What does the title of the book (i.e., the Revelation) imply?

3. What is a number one priority to understanding Revelation?

4. When was the Revelation written, by whom?

5. Whom does this book bless?

6. Why is the church called a "kingdom," and why are Christians priests?

7. What might the "clouds of heaven" be in this picture?

8. Why will "all the tribes of the earth" mourn?

9. What does the name "Alpha and Omega" mean?

10. Why was John on Patmos?

11. What is the "Lord's Day," and why is it called that?

12. How was John "in the Spirit"?

John's Revelation

13. What does the number 7 imply?

14. Who are the 7 churches, literally and figuratively?

15. Where is a similar description to verses 13-16? Who is it?

16. What would be implied by a two-edged sword?

17. What does "having the keys" mean?

18. Who or what are the 7 spirits?

19. What are the 7 lampstands? The 7 stars?

20. Name 8 ways that Jesus is described in this chapter.

21. What message do you see in the picture of this glorified Being walking among the lampstands holding the stars of the churches in His hand?

> **Revelation 2**
>
> 1. "To the angel of the church in Ephesus write: The One who holds the seven stars in His right hand, the One who walks among the seven golden lampstands, says this:
> 2. `I know your deeds and your toil and perseverance, and that you cannot tolerate evil men, and you put to the test those who call themselves apostles, and they are not, and you found them to be false;
> 3. and you have perseverance and have endured for My name's sake, and have not grown weary.
> 4. `But I have this against you, that you have left your first love.

THE REVELATION
chapter 2

1. For comments on the "angel" of the churches, see 1:20. The fact that Christ "walked" among the lampstands points to His ability to be active in the affairs of His congregations as well as the fact that He is in the "midst," i.e., near to each one. (See Special Study #3.)

2. Deeds (works) can be either good or bad. Here they appear to be good, and we have the assurance that Jesus is aware of good works, even though it seems sometimes that no one else ever is. Toil indicates strenuous labor. Perseverance (patience) is enduring steadfastly in that labor. They are commended for not enduring evil men. It seems that "tolerance" is not just a problem of our century. Although lovers of peace will never find confrontation a pleasant thing, the church should never tolerate those who refuse to submit to the will of Christ. These brethren had also tested false apostles and rejected them. The testing of those claiming to teach and lead is always laudable and is accomplished by close examination to what God has spoken. Comparison to "what we have always done" or to our traditions is not the real test nor is it the one that is commended here, 2 Timothy 4:1-4; 1 John 4:1.

3. In spite of opposition and false teachers with their false doctrines, these had shown stamina (perseverance, patience) and remained strong for His name's sake, that is, because of their love for Him they wore His name (Christian) and walked worthy of it.

> 5. `Therefore remember from where you have fallen, and repent and do the deeds you did at first; or else I am coming to you and will remove your lampstand out of its place--unless you repent.
> 6. `Yet this you do have, that you hate the deeds of the Nicolaitans, which I also hate.

4. All the good in the world will not cover the stain of wrongdoing. They were doing the right things but not for the proper motivation. Both attitude and action, motion and motivation are important to our Lord. Was it the motivating love for God and His word that they had shown in their burning their books of sorcery? Acts 19:19-20. Was it the fellowship of love for God's work manifested in their sorrow at Paul's leaving? Acts 20:36-38. Or was it the relationship of love they showed one for another? Ephesians 1:15. Maybe it was a combination of these, maybe none of them specifically, but some type of love (active concern) was missing and they needed to get it back.

5. Even though they had done good works, they had fallen. Repentance is a two-part function. First, one must have a change of heart or mind when the human will submits to God's will. But changing one's mind is not all that there is to repentance. They were also to "do the deeds that they had done at first." Action *must* follow attitude. There needed to be a change in this congregation, not just an acknowledgment that something was missing. Jesus' coming would not be in sudden wrath, but simply in a removal of the lampstand out of its place. Can there be any sadder description of one of Christ's churches than this one, that its light no longer shines in that place. It is quite possible that people might still be holding services of some kind, but our Lord's attitude is that the salty savor is gone and such a congregation is of no more spiritual value than something thrown out to be trodden under men's feet. There is no faithful church in Ephesus today...only ruins.

6. Both the church and the Lord hated the deeds, not the individuals. It is impossible to *love* righteousness without *hating* wickedness. Those who try are doomed to a tepid, milksop of spirituality. We have no positive proof today as to who the Nicolaitans were exactly. It is believed that they were probably another sect of those who were developing into the Gnostics of the second century. It is thought that they practiced all sorts of immorality in the name of Christ. They believed that the body could sin in order to gain a true knowledge of sin, but that sin did not affect the soul. They believed body and soul were not connected in any real way. The end result of this type of thinking is very similar to those today who teach that once one is saved, it is impossible for that one to be lost.

> 7. `He who has an ear, let him hear what the Spirit says to the churches. To him who overcomes, I will grant to eat of the tree of life which is in the Paradise of God.'
> 8. "And to the angel of the church in Smyrna write: The first and the last, who was dead, and has come to life, says this:
> 9. `I know your tribulation and your poverty (but you are rich), and the blasphemy by those who say they are Jews and are not, but are a synagogue of Satan.

No matter what the sin, salvation is assured we are told. Solomon was correct. There is nothing new under the sun. The Nicolaitans of the first century have given rise to the Calvinists of our own century. Our salvation, received by grace through faith, is not to be taken lightly. It is worth our constant defense and the rejection of every sin in our lives.

7. The charge to hear is made to all who will listen to spiritual things. The letter is not just for the church at Ephesus—it is what the Spirit says to "the churches." "Overcomes" is from the Greek word which means *to conquer*. To the one who conquers is given the privilege of eternal life and being close to God.

8. Christ can say "be thou faithful unto death" (2:10) because He has conquered death. "Unto death" means...up to and even including death if necessary. (See Special Study #4.)

9. Christ was aware of the trials and persecutions of His saints. To be a Christian in Smyrna meant ostracism, poverty, want, etc. Jesus knew this but admonished them to be faithful because they were laying up treasures in heaven that could not be taken away, James 2:5. Those who said they were Jews but were not were people born into the nation of Israel who had rejected God by rejecting His Son. Physical Israel had been replaced by a spiritual nation, or kingdom—Christians. These so-called "Jews" would naturally persecute the Christians. They were not being led by God to do this, but were in fact led by Satan. NOTE: The fact that these Jews still had the power to persecute Christians might lend some strength to the argument that this book could have been written before 70 A.D. and the destruction of Jerusalem, the temple, and subsequent loss of strength of the Jewish religion. This author still leans toward the later date of writing, but this point is acknowledged in the interest of fairness. The other side of this argument, however, is that tradition has it that the Jewish persecution of Christians here was worse than the Roman, even after the destruction of Jerusalem. It is said that the Jews here gathered wood on the Sabbath so that they might burn Polycarp.

> 10. `Do not fear what you are about to suffer. Behold, the devil is about to cast some of you into prison, so that you will be tested, and you will have tribulation for ten days. Be faithful until death, and I will give you the crown of life.
> 11. `He who has an ear, let him hear what the Spirit says to the churches. He who overcomes will not be hurt by the second death.'
> 12. "And to the angel of the church in Pergamum write: The One who has the sharp two-edged sword says this:

10. They were not to let fear overcome their faith. "Prison" here would probably include fines, exiles, arrests, tortures, etc., as well as imprisonment. These things stand on our horizon in this culture today also when the Christian stands against homosexuality, advocates biblical discipline of children, church discipline of erring members, the scriptural role of women in the home and/or church leadership, or even holds up the priority of worship. Lawsuits, fines, threats of locking church doors over some of these issues have already gotten the attention of fearful elderships in some places. Do not make the mistake of reading this simply as an historic document. The same forces are at work in every age. While the devil tempts one to lose heart through threats and suffering, God is testing or proving us. This *should* make us stronger if we have been making our faith strong to begin with. "Ten days" implies a certain length of time, set and measured, as well as a full period of suffering. Then it would end. "Faithful unto death" does not mean faithful up to the point of death. It means...faithful even if it brings death upon us. There are 2 uses of the word "crown" in the New Testament. Here it is the crown of victory, i.e., victory wreath, worn by athletic and military victors. See 1 Corinthians 9:25; 2 Timothy 4:8; James 1:12; and 1 Peter 5:4.

11. There are only 2 alternatives, the crown of life (eternal life) or the second death (lake of fire, the destiny of the wicked). No middle ground of purgatory or limbo is mentioned here to spend time suffering in before moving on to heaven.

12. Once again, sharp two-edged sword is a symbol of power and authority. Jesus has the power, not Rome, seems to be the message that these Christians needed to learn. The same is true today. The Christians' court of appeal is not the Supreme Court of this nation; it is the Supreme Court in the heavens where our King sits as Chief Justice. It is to Him we must answer. (See Special Study #5.)

> 13. `I know where you dwell, where Satan's throne is; and you hold fast My name, and did not deny My faith even in the days of Antipas, My witness, My faithful one, who was killed among you, where Satan dwells.
> 14. `But I have a few things against you, because you have there some who hold the teaching of Balaam, who kept teaching Balak to put a stumbling block before the sons of Israel, to eat things sacrificed to idols and to commit acts of immorality.

13. Why is Satan's throne here? Perhaps for any/all of the following reasons:

- Aesculapius (God of healing) was worshipped here under the symbol of a snake entwined about a rod (symbol of physicians today). The snake is represented by some as having represented Satan to early Christians.

- Pergamum was the capitol of the province so there was a great deal of emperor worship here. People were led to confess, "Caesar is Lord," an abomination to early Christians.

- It was also the center of worship to Zeus. He was the head of the gods and also addressed as "savior." An awesome monstrosity of a temple was located here for him that would have dominated the city buildings.

Antipas was put to death for doing what several were doing, i.e., holding fast and refusing to be unfaithful to the Lord.

14. "Few things" stands in opposition to their great commendation. These erring individuals were probably in the minority but needed to be pointed out. Some there were encouraging a "spirit of compromise," like Balaam in the Old Testament, Numbers 23; 24; 31:16. Although Balaam served God at first, he constantly was seeking ways by which he could gratify his materialism. He finally succeeded and remains a testimony to all today that seek "loopholes" in their spirituality by which they might satisfy their worldliness. Balaam says, "keep looking" and you will find what you seek. Our Lord says to beware of such compromisers. Through fornication and idolatrous practices some were being led astray and others were likely making excuses for them, thus again, compromise. Another lesson from Balaam that we can make application of here is that though he could not curse Israel outright, he instigated a stumbling block in front of them, and they fell themselves. Jesus warned that it would have been better for such a one that a millstone be tied around his neck and he be cast into the sea. Such is the attitude of our Lord toward those who cause others to sin.

John's Revelation

> 15. `So you also have some who in the same way hold the teaching of the Nicolaitans.
> 16. `Therefore repent; or else I am coming to you quickly, and I will make war against them with the sword of My mouth.
> 17. `He who has an ear, let him hear what the Spirit says to the churches. To him who overcomes, to him I will give some of the hidden manna, and I will give him a white stone, and a new name written on the stone which no one knows but he who receives it.'

15. For Nicolaitans, see comments at verse 6.

16. Both groups needed to repent—those who were active in their sin (Nicolaitans and Balaamites) and the members of the church who put up with them, showing a compromising attitude. Else the Lord was going to war against them. He did keep His word here and it was complete "destruction" for them. The Lord did not just war against them with His word, but it is to be noticed that neither of the above two groups have left any definite trace in history, in continued teachings, disciples, documents, writings, etc. The only way we know of them at all is through the scriptures here and tradition.

17. Lord's "hidden manna" stands in contrast to the meats offered to idols, John 6:27-35. It is that which gives us eternal life. There are several good ideas on the meaning of the stone here, but one seems to blend more easily with other passages in Revelation and in the Old Testament than the others. I believe the writer may very well have reference to this so it is presented for your consideration.

   White is the color of holiness and purity. It describes the hair and head of Christ (1:14), the garments of the elders (4:4), Christ's horse (6:2), the cloud (14:14), the second horse, as well as the heavenly army on white horses (9:11, 14), the throne (20:11), saints (3:4, 5, 18) and martyrs (6:11), as well as those coming out of the great tribulation (7:9, 13). The new name is the name of Christ (3:12; 14:1; 22:4) or "Christian." See also Isaiah 62:2; 65:15. No one but the child of God will know what a great blessing it is to wear the name of Christ. The idea of a stone implies perhaps the lasting quality of this state. This would fit well with the type presented in the Old Testament of the high priests wearing the name of Jehovah on their forehead (Exodus 28:36ff) because they are specially consecrated servants of Jehovah, as all Christians are consecrated priests now.

> 18. "And to the angel of the church in Thyatira write: The Son of God, who has eyes like a flame of fire, and His feet are like burnished bronze, says this:
> 19. `I know your deeds, and your love and faith and service and perseverance, and that your deeds of late are greater than at first.
> 20. `But I have this against you, that you tolerate the woman Jezebel, who calls herself a prophetess, and she teaches and leads My bond-servants astray so that they commit acts of immorality and eat things sacrificed to idols.
> 21. `I gave her time to repent, and she does not want to

18. Fire, quite often in the Scriptures, is linked to divine anger. He is ready to trample and burn to ashes all those wicked who corrupt His flock. (See Special Study #6.)

19. "I know" because *nothing* is hidden from eyes like a flame of fire. Jesus recognized spiritual growth in this church. Their deeds were greater than at first. Contrast this with the admonition to Ephesus to repent and do the deeds they had done at first. Our deeds never can seem to remain stagnant. We are either growing and progressing in our spiritual growth or regressing.

20. Jezebel is a name synonymous with seduction to idolatry and immorality, 1 Kings 16:31; 18:4, 13, 19; 19:1-2. This was probably a woman in the congregation of great influence and perhaps even teaching ability. Because of her influence, once again, some were being persuaded to compromise with the world and commit fornication (perhaps spiritual or perhaps sexual, committed in the idols' temples) and eat things offered to idols. Some think it might have been a segment or cult within the church, but a single woman of influence seems more reasonable to this writer. The church is rebuked for "suffering" (tolerating, putting up with, refusing to stand against) the error to continue within the body. There are some strong lessons in this part of the book for those who sit back and think that they will not be accountable for what goes on in the church. The Lord's church does not have a spectator section.

21. God's grace toward the sinner is seen here in the opportunity to repent, 2 Peter 3:9. We also see the strong hold sin has on us in the phrase "she does not want to repent...." This is why sin should be defeated as soon as it appears, not allowing it to sink its roots into our hearts and harden our conscience.

> repent of her immorality.
> 22. `Behold, I will throw her on a bed of sickness, and those who commit adultery with her into great tribulation, unless they repent of her deeds.
> 23. `And I will kill her children with pestilence, and all the churches will know that I am He who searches the minds and hearts; and I will give to each one of you according to your deeds.
> 24. `But I say to you, the rest who are in Thyatira, who do not hold this teaching, who have not known the deep things of Satan, as they call them--I place no

22. "I cast her" does not imply violence, but one who is forced to lie in a bed. There are not two different punishments here. Her followers were going to share her fate if they did not repent. They were all going to endure punishment from the Lord. The translators of the NASB have added that the bed she/they were going to share was one of "sickness." This may be a figurative type of sickness since "pestilence"(disease) is the fate promised to her spiritual offspring. We will not rule out actual physical sickness tied to the practice of immorality, however. The number and power of sexually transmitted diseases makes this a real alternative to be considered here.

23. Her spiritual offspring will be destroyed also. They are the result of individuals following after her and leading others astray (verse 22). What will happen to them will so obviously be a judgment from the Lord that all would recognize it as such and acknowledge the justice in such action. The justice is seen in the Just One being able to read the mind and heart, not to be fooled by excuses and empty philosophies.

24. The ones who have not given in to this influence and teaching are left alone to carry on and do their best. Notice, the Lord does not think that their teachings are "deep things," but that is what the sinners themselves have deluded themselves into believing. Very often those in rebellion to God try to convince themselves that their knowledge and experience in sin is a good and profitable thing and that they are much wiser because of it. Scientology reigns supreme in this regard today as it uses the ravings of a science fiction writer to make an appeal that it claims is superior spirituality for enlightened minds. It finds fertile soil to grow in Hollywood not surprisingly. Christians are often mocked as naive and lacking in understanding. Nothing could be further from the truth. Avoiding sin and its resultant tragedy, consequences, and guilt is the pinnacle of wisdom. Paul verifies this in 1 Corinthians 2:6-8. The wisdom of divinity is available for those who are truly mature, not spiritual children who are playing at being "grown-up" by engaging in the "passing pleasures of sin."

> other burden on you.
> 25. 'Nevertheless what you have, hold fast until I come.
> 26. 'He who overcomes, and he who keeps My deeds until the end, TO HIM I WILL GIVE AUTHORITY OVER THE NATIONS;
> 27. AND HE SHALL RULE THEM WITH A ROD OF IRON, AS THE VESSELS OF THE POTTER ARE BROKEN TO PIECES, as I also have received authority from My Father;
> 28. and I will give him the morning star.
> 29. 'He who has an ear, let him hear what the Spirit says to the churches.'

25. Remain steadfast. 2 Corinthians 15:58.

26. Overcome = conquer. We note that there are most certainly deeds or works that we MUST do or "keep" until the Lord returns. "Authority over the nations" is continued in verse 27.

27. This thought, which begins in verse 26, clearly has reference to Psalm 2 where the Father promised to raise the Son up to sit on His throne and rule the nations. They are His inheritance that He rules with a rod of iron, crushing and breaking them as He pleases. He rules His people, on the other hand, with a scepter of righteousness. We reign (Romans 5:17) in a secondary sense with Christ in that by our lives and words we judge the world, much as Noah did, Hebrews 11:7. By Noah's actions he demonstrated the wisdom and acceptability of obedience. This blessing of glory will be more exactly realized when we ascend to sit with our Lord, but in a certain sense it is a fact now! When we are in communion and fellowship with the King, we are sharing in that kingship. As He has been given authority, He is able to promise/give it to His people.

28. Jesus *is* the morning star. Revelation 22:16; 2 Peter 1:18-19.

29. We are warned here and it is true everywhere, do not take lightly what is said by the Spirit of God.

John's Revelation

QUESTIONS ON CHAPTER 2

1. What, to you, are the single most noteworthy points, good or bad, about each congregation?

    Ephesus -

    Smyrna -

    Pergamum -

    Thyatira -

2. Explain "faithful unto death."

3. Who was Antipas?

4. What is Balaam remembered for?

5. Give several synonyms for "perseverance."

6. What is a synagogue of Satan?

7. How would one leave his first love?

8. Explain what a "witness" is.

9. Define tribulation.

10. How was tribulation coming?

11. Explain the "second death."

12. What is Jezebel remembered for?

13. What two things were the Ephesian church commended for?

14. What lessons are there for us in the above answer?

15. What can we do to avoid the second death?

16. Who were the Nicolaitans?

17. According to what will we receive our reward?

John's Revelation

> **Revelation 3**
>
> 1. "To the angel of the church in Sardis write: He who has the seven Spirits of God and the seven stars, says this: `I know your deeds, that you have a name that you are alive, but you are dead.
> 2. `Wake up, and strengthen the things that remain, which were about to die; for I have not found your deeds completed in the sight of My God.

THE REVELATION
chapter 3

1. The one speaking is the one with the "seven spirits" or the "spirit without measure," John 3:34. The Spirit of God is a life-giving spirit and should appeal to those who are spiritually dead. In 5:6, the seven spirits are equated with the seven eyes of God, which go out into all the earth. The reference there seems to be to the Spirit's omniscient power. That would agree with this introduction of Christ as the one who controls and directs the Spirit so that He is able to "see" through their "name" or reputation to their true selves or character, which was "dead." For info on the seven stars see notes on 1:20. The stars represent the inner life of the congregation and Jesus holds this in His hand. Once more He *knows* the inner life of each church He addresses. "Name" is *reputation* here. Their reputation was of men, but Christ was not fooled. He knew their true character. (See Special Study #7.) Congregations today who are more concerned about the "name" they have among their brethren than the inner character which Jesus looks upon can learn a valuable lesson if they will give ear and heed.

2. Because of their city's history, the Christians at Sardis should have understood what it meant to "wake up" or "be thou watchful." The city had fallen twice because the inhabitants thought their cliff walls unassailable. Though Jesus refers to them as "dead" (verse 1), He also mentions here some "...things which remain." There was still hope for these Christians if they would get up and get at it. "Perfect" here is ...*complete*. Their service to God was not complete and they should not have been sitting upon their reputation and acting like it was.

> 3. `So remember what you have received and heard; and keep it, and repent. Therefore if you do not wake up, I will come like a thief, and you will not know at what hour I will come to you.
> 4. `But you have a few people in Sardis who have not soiled their garments; and they will walk with Me in white, for they are worthy.
> 5. `He who overcomes will thus be clothed in white garments; and I will not erase his name from the book of life, and I will confess his name before My Father and before His angels.
> 6. `He who has an ear, let him hear what the Spirit says to the churches.'

3. We prefer the rendering in the newer translations here, i.e., "...*what* you have received" as opposed to "...*how* you have received..." No matter *how* they had received the gospel, they were being told to remember *what* they had heard and received (2 actions) and do it again. What little remained of righteousness they were to keep doing. What had been allowed to slip away they were to repent of. Jesus' coming here is one of judgment and discipline on his brethren/enemies.

4. Judgment will always ultimately fall on an individual basis, not congregationally. In Pergamum and Thyatira, a small element had fallen into temptation and sin. Here in Sardis a small element had kept themselves pure. Often we have heard this passage used over the years to justify one who continues in a congregation as that church goes into error. Keeping silent and doing nothing while a congregation disregards the word of God is not what is being discussed or commended here. The one whose robes are white is the one who continues in his walk of righteousness, including his stand against sin whether in the church or out, and his defense of the gospel. Spinelessly going along with the crowd while claiming to still walk with white robes is nonsense. White once again represents purity, holiness, and sanctification.

5. "...not erase his name..." (Exodus 32:33; Psalm 69:28; Malachi 3:16). There is no chance of being lost if we will run the race to the end. The way to overcome evil is with good, Romans 12:21. If we confess Him with our life, then He will confess to the Father that we are His, Matthew 10:32-33.

6. The charge here is for all to hear.

7. Keys represent power and authority (Isaiah 22:22; Matthew 28:18) and Jesus claimed to have them. Being "of David" implies that this authority is especially concerned with God's people since that is whom David and his lineage ruled over. The description of Him as holy and true is in contrast with the lying, false

John's Revelation

> 7. "And to the angel of the church in Philadelphia write: He who is holy, who is true, who has the key of David, who opens and no one will shut, and who shuts and no one opens, says this:
> 8. `I know your deeds. Behold, I have put before you an open door which no one can shut, because you have a little power, and have kept My word, and have not denied My name.
> 9. `Behold, I will cause those of the synagogue of Satan, who say that they are Jews and are not, but lie--I will make them come and bow down at your feet, and make them know that

Jews of verse 9. Christ claims here to be able to shape events for His pleasing. He can give opportunities (open doors) or take them away (close them). Jesus certainly does have the "key" or "all authority" now since His rule includes heaven and earth (Matthew 28:18), angels and authorities and powers (1 Peter 3:22), the church (Ephesians 1:20-22), the kings of the earth (Revelation 1:5), and death and Hades, Revelation 1:18. (See Special Study #8.)

8. The deeds of the church at Philadelphia were good. Jesus was aware of them and was going to reward them accordingly. "Little power" is generally understood to mean that the group of Christians there was small in number, though it seems not so in faith. Strength is not measured in numbers on God's scale. It seems that they had used the opportunities that God had given them so they were being rewarded with more of the same. An "open door" may very well imply an opportunity to teach the gospel or wield some influence for the Lord to be glorified. This blessing is being promised by the one who claims the power to give such blessing. This writer believes this same principle is at work today. If we do not use the opportunities that we have, we will never receive the greater blessings. If we will step out in faith upon the opportunities God gives us, our reward will be continued opportunities for service. We may dream of being faithful in great things, but if we are not faithful in the small opportunities given to us, then we prove ourselves false, Acts 14:27; 1 Corinthians 16:9; 2 Corinthians 2:12; Colossians 4:3.

9. "Synagogue of Satan" would be those Jews in the flesh who had rejected the gospel of the Messiah. True Jews would have been those who, like their father Abraham, had faith in God's word so they could receive the Lord gladly, Romans 2:28-29. In some way, these stubborn rejecters of the faith and persecutors of Christians were going to learn that God, in fact, blessed the ones they persecuted. "Bow down at your feet" does not imply that they would literally bow down to Christians, but that they would bow down to God openly or in front of these faithful saints. The saints would see them humbled.

I have loved you.
10. `Because you have kept the word of My perseverance, I also will keep you from the hour of testing, that hour which is about to come upon the whole world, to test those who dwell on the earth.
11. `I am coming quickly; hold fast what you have, so that no one will take your crown.
12. `He who overcomes, I will make him a pillar in the temple of My God, and he will not go out from it anymore; and I will write on him the name of My God, and the name of the city of My God, the new Jerusalem, which comes down out of heaven from My God, and My new name.

10. Patience = perseverance = steadfastness = endurance, 1 Corinthians 15:58. Whether He would "keep them from the hour of testing" by *immunity from* or by being *brought safely through* (1 Corinthians 10:13) is not clear. Both options are certainly open to the Lord. The word "earth" is used 81 times in this book with a variety of meanings. Often it is used as metonymy for the world or realm of sinful, unregenerated men. In places, the "redeemed" are distinguished from "those that dwell upon the earth." The term here may simply refer to the "whole world" as they knew it, i.e., the Roman Empire. Whatever the exact meaning of the Lord is here, the implication is one of watchfulness, security, and care for His people. "Hour" here is used to mean a season or period of testing. Obviously it is a measured time shorter than a "day," year," or "age."

11. Exhortation to steadfastness, 1 Corinthians 15:58. Please note the danger, even with these good brethren, of losing their crown (salvation). This denies the doctrines being taught by many today of "once saved always saved" or the "impossibility of apostasy." "Crown" implies victory, Revelation 2:10; 2 Timothy 4:7-8. There is no implication of any gain to the taker of the crown, only loss to the loser. Once again, please note, He is not referring to a final, all-encompassing judgment day...His coming was going to be *quickly*. Though it may not be strictly according to the early pattern of Christianity, it should be noted that there are those calling themselves Christians in Philadelphia today. (See Special Study #1 and #2.)

12. A pillar is a permanent fixture as shown from the fact that "he would not go out" anymore. This was the blessing that David sought, Psalm 27:4. The victor will wear 3 names. The name of the Father, the Son, and the city of God (new Jerusalem). Wearing the name shows that he belongs to all 3 just like a wife wears the name of her husband when she belongs to him. New Jerusalem is the church spiritual... more on this later.

John's Revelation

> 13. `He who has an ear, let him hear what the Spirit says to the churches.'
> 14. "To the angel of the church in Laodicea write: The Amen, the faithful and true Witness, the Beginning of the creation of God, says this:
> 15. `I know your deeds, that you are neither cold nor hot; I wish that you were cold or hot.
> 16. `So because you are lukewarm, and neither hot nor cold, I will spit you out of My mouth.

13. Once more, a charge of *all* to hear.

14. "Amen" is from a word meaning *to be firm or steadfast*. It is akin to the Hebrew word for truth. It is used to express certainty. If Christ is the "amen," then He is the "certainty" of God's promises, 1 Corinthians 1:20. Three things are necessary for one to be a witness:

   a) He must have a first-hand knowledge of that which he testifies; he must have seen it with his own eyes.
   b) He must be competent to reproduce and relate it for others.
   c) He must be willing to make it known faithfully and truthfully.
   Jesus fulfills all these prerequisites.

"Beginning of creation" does not mean that He was created first (Jehovah's Witnesses doctrine). It means that He is the source of all created beings and things. In the beginning God created..., but the Word was the means. Christ was the means through whom all things were made that have been made, John 1:1-3. He was before all things, Colossians 1:15-17. Being the creator of all "things," the "things" which were giving the Christians at Laodicea their sense of security would pale in value next to Him. (See Special Study #9.)

15. Those that are spiritually cold (those without knowledge of the gospel, completely cut off) can often be worked upon to see their need. So also those who are "hot" (humble hearts, willing hands, living good lives but outside the gospel also). But the ones who think they're something when they are nothing have deceived themselves and being self-deluded end up apathetic. The lukewarm, complacent, and self-satisfied are difficult if not impossible to work with. They simply do not care enough about spiritual things to trouble themselves.

16. Not necessarily a fact, but a warning. The term that is translated "spew" (KJV) or "spit" (NASB) here is not the "spit" that one might think of when he considers tobacco chewers or little boys showing off. It might be rendered more accurately "vomit." Jesus was saying they were sickening in their present condition.

> 17. `Because you say, "I am rich, and have become wealthy, and have need of nothing," and you do not know that you are wretched and miserable and poor and blind and naked,
> 18. I advise you to buy from Me gold refined by fire so that you may become rich, and white garments so that you may clothe yourself, and that the shame of your nakedness will not be revealed; and eye salve to anoint your eyes so that you may see.

17. This congregation, like many today, seems to have had material prosperity. They lived in a wealthy, prosperous area and seem to have imbibed the attitude of the city they lived in. They were wealthy enough not to have to depend upon anyone (they thought), not even God. By developing this attitude of independence they had fallen into a trap that many fall prey to. They had equated external privilege with God's favor. We must learn what they forgot, the external view *does not* always, if ever, represent true spiritual condition. The church at Smyrna was poor, but actually rich. This church was rich, but actually poor. They were, it is sad to say, satisfied! Hosea 12:8; Luke 18:11ff. Being satisfied with what and where they were spiritually, they would never be able to grow, improve, or do better. Their progress in the gospel had stopped.

18. "Counsel" or "advice" is given to get them interested in seeking after pure (refined by fire) spiritual riches rather than material gain. Wisdom and knowledge are spiritual riches, Colossians 2:3. The Laodiceans were known for a glossy-black garment they wore. Christ demands that these people become different. The Lord is more interested in the "white garments" of a pure soul than the latest fashions. He desires that His people be different, pure, and holy. These who were spiritually blind are exhorted to humility and reverence so that they might be able to see truly. These three remedies could only be received from Christ. If there is a single congregation in the seven that speaks directly to the modern culture, Laodicea may be it. Modern men and women have plenty to eat, warm homes, jobs, education, health, comfortable transportation, and instant communication. We amuse ourselves with electronics and hobbies, and even the poor among us are often overweight and given fashionable handouts from charity. All the while worship attendance falls, Bible study drops off, and we find ourselves avoiding the confrontation of naming our Lord publicly.

19. Reproof is the language of correction. "Discipline" is defined as *treatment suited to a disciple or learner*. "Zealous" means literally *to be on fire, excited*. Correction, whether harsh or gentle, always comes from Christ because of love, Hebrews 12:5-13. They are admonished to repent or turn from the path they are on.

> 19. 'Those whom I love, I reprove and discipline; therefore be zealous and repent.
> 20. 'Behold, I stand at the door and knock; if anyone hears My voice and opens the door, I will come in to him and will dine with him, and he with Me.
> 21. 'He who overcomes, I will grant to him to sit down with Me on My throne, as I also overcame and sat down with My Father on His throne.
> 22. 'He who has an ear, let him hear what the Spirit says to the churches.'"

20. In spite of their haughty attitude, the Lord seeks admittance to lives which had excluded Him. The picture presented is not the "irresistible grace" picture of a forced entrance, not to be denied because God has chosen them. Instead, it is one of pleading admission. There must be action on our part to establish this communion or fellowship. Jesus has done all that He can as example, teacher, prophet, leader, and sacrifice. We must open the door to our hearts and lives for Him to enter.

21. The one who can conquer his own self and the materialistic attitude that can surround one is shown in victory with Jesus Christ who also overcame this world in His way. It is a great victory to be able to do so. The assurance of this promise is seen in the fact that Christ was glorified before us.

22. Continued reminder and charge for all to hear, learn, and profit.

QUESTIONS ON CHAPTER 3

1. What is one's "name" and why is this term important?

2. Why would "come like a thief" have special significance for Sardis?

3. Explain how a "few people" could walk in white while a congregation dies.

4. What can we learn from the reputation of the church at Sardis?

5. White always seems to have what type of meaning?

6. Explain "key," especially "of David."

7. Which church had an "open door"? Explain what this is.

8. What are some of our "open doors"? (in the context of a congregation)

9. What can we learn from the first commendation of the Philadelphians?

10. How could Jews be "false Jews"?

11. What does the promise of a "crown" mean?

John's Revelation

12. What is the "new Jerusalem" that comes down out of heaven?

13. What is meant by being spiritually "lukewarm"?

14. Can you think of any symptoms of "lukewarmness"?

15. Why is the Lord so harsh in rebuking the Laodiceans?

16. What is the literal meaning of "zealous"?

17. What aspect of Christ's love do we hesitate to embrace?

18. Thought question: How does the Lord accomplish verse 16 today?

19. What is the most noteworthy point about each congregation, good or bad?
    Sardis -
    Philadelphia -
    Laodicea -

20. Looking at each of these congregations, how do you think they might have been influenced by the cities in which they were located?

21. How could Christians today be influenced by society?

> **Revelation 4**
>
> 1. After these things I looked, and behold, a door standing open in heaven, and the first voice which I had heard, like the sound of a trumpet speaking with me, said, "Come up here, and I will show you what must take place after these things."

THE REVELATION
chapter 4
Section I, 2 (see page 12)

INTRODUCTION:

John (and through him the churches) has just been given a general picture of the church soon after it was established, i.e., how it stood in his day (chapters 2-3). He has also been given a hint of what is to come, the judgments to be rendered in this life, and the final judgments to be rendered eternally. This was all very fine and good, but the trials that first century Christians were going through made it important for those suffering saints to know more than just how things stood at the present time. For this reason we will move, with John, a little deeper into the spiritual realm so that we might understand with those early Christians that more is going on than just what we happen to see around us. Chapters 4 & 5 show us that the throne of God is in control of all things. These chapters are one picture. I agree with several others that chapter 4 is saying, "Believe in God," while chapter 5 follows up with Christ saying, "Believe also in Me." The point for those saints (and us) to remember is that God's throne remains in heaven. It is not in Rome, America, or anywhere else on the earth, and GOD STILL RULES. This is not just a picture of heaven. This is a picture of "the entire universe from the perspective of heaven."[4] All things are governed by the throne occupant; therefore, the picture of the throne (chapters 4 and 5) precedes the picture of trials and tribulations (chapters 6 and 7) to show that even these things are "under control." They should not be a reason for discouragement but a reason to strengthen self and continue to grow stronger as one ever looks toward that glorious throne and its occupant.

1. It seems that for some length of time John was returned to his normal state of mind and being. He then sees another vision. This is not a vision of the "next dispensation" as some premillennialists would have us to think. It simply means that the scenes John observes in this vision followed the ones in chapters 2 and 3.

> 2. Immediately I was in the Spirit; and behold, a throne was standing in heaven, and One sitting on the throne.
> 3. And He who was sitting was like a jasper stone and a sardius in appearance; and there was a rainbow around the throne, like an emerald in appearance.

There is no trumpet, once again, but a voice "like" a trumpet. This seems to be the same unidentified speaker as in 1:10 and he tells John again to "come" and see.

2. Once more, John finds himself "in the Spirit" or "in spirit." "Paul earlier could not tell whether he was in the spirit or not (2 Corinthians 12:2), but John knew."[5] "Throne" is used 17 times in these 2 chapters, showing its importance. Keep in mind as we start this section that John did not really see heaven; he saw a vision of it, meant to impress a message on his sight. He does not see the throne of God but a vision of the throne. The message is in the picture. There is no reason to suppose that these things described are what it will look like in heaven. In most scriptures, the truth is impressed upon the mind by way of words. It is thus "seen" with the mind. In the Apocalypse, truth is impressed upon the sight. We are left to discern the message from the vision. Therefore, John does not literally see the actual things that he describes in the book, but he sees a vision of the things arranged in such a way so as to get a message across. One sitting on the throne is obvious terminology for God (7:10), and He is called that henceforth. He is the one from whom all authority ultimately procedes.

3. The description here is not a description of the person God, but of His radiance and His glory, Ezekiel 1:26-28. The names of many gems in antiquity are quite different from their modern names. Many conclusions that are drawn are just educated guesses based upon what limited research is available. Jasper stone is quite possibly a diamond (21:11), and a sardius is thought to have been a stone of fiery red color. The crystal-clear brilliance immediately brings to mind an impression of God's holiness, righteousness, and purity. The sardius would make one think of His justice in divine judgments. This view would certainly be justified in the picture the Psalmist paints in Psalm 89:14-15. The "rainbow" has been a sign of God's mercy and forgiveness since the days of Noah as defined by His own actions. Likewise, many feel that the emerald color, or soft green, the "living color" represented mercy. "If these suggestions are correct, then these verses describe the holiness and righteousness of God's character 'dwelling in light unapproachable' (1 Timothy 6:16), and the justice of His divine judgments encompassed and tempered by His infinite mercy."[6]

4. Around the throne were twenty-four thrones; and upon the thrones I saw twenty-four elders sitting, clothed in white garments, and golden crowns on their heads.	5. Out from the throne come flashes of lightning and sounds and peals of thunder. And there were seven lamps of fire burning before the throne, which are the seven Spirits of God;

4. Out of the MANY ideas to be found on who these 24 elders are, there are two main lines of thought that seem to make more sense.

- The first is that the 24 represent the 12 Old Testament patriarchs and 12 apostles. This is because those before Christ received their inheritance through Christ (Hebrews 9:15) like all (Jew & Gentile) do today. One group receiving it by faith in a Messiah to come and the other receiving it by faith in a Messiah who came. In both Jewish and Christian systems "elder" was a term for those looked to as leaders; and therefore, the terminology would fit in well with those on 24 thrones, secondary to God, 21:12-14.
- The other idea that seems to bear some consideration is that these 24 elders represent the "royal priesthood" or church. "The '24 elders' are royal. They are dressed in white garments that are the righteous deeds of the overcoming saints, 2:4,5; 19:8. They wear the crown of overcomers (stephanoi). They are 24 in number, which is the number of the courses of the priests in the Old Testament. See 1 Chronicles 24:7-18."[7]

Although the picture of a royal priesthood is definitely an aspect of the new covenant and our relationship with Christ, this writer prefers the first interpretation of the two, mainly because of the passage in Revelation 21:12-14. There in this same book is a picture that specifically ties the Old Testament patriarchs together with the apostles in a relationship with the kingdom. The term "throne" (NASB) is a better rendering of the Greek word *thronous* or *thronoi* than "seat" (KJV), unless you think of it as being a seat of authority or power. Crown means victory and white again indicates holiness.

5. Lightning and sounds and peals of thunder emphasize awesome majesty and glory as God is on His throne. Seven is the whole or complete number once again, so the lamps burning before the throne show us the Holy Spirit present and active in all His ability and in His work of illuminating or revealing. The number seven would also imply the fullness, power, deity, etc., of the Spirit since we see the Spirit here in such close proximity to the throne.

6. and before the throne there was something like a sea of glass, like crystal; and in the center and around the throne, four living creatures full of eyes in front and behind.	7. The first creature was like a lion, and the second creature like a calf, and the third creature had a face like that of a man, and the fourth creature was like a flying eagle.

6. As the court of the earthly temple had its laver of washing, aptly named a "sea" for its large size (2 Chronicles 4:2-5), so here John beholds a sea before the throne. The purpose of the lavers before the tabernacle and the temple was for the ceremonial cleansing of the priest and the anointing of the altars, etc., Exodus 40:7-13. Certainly the idea here is one of separation. Just as the cleansing water separated the priests from the temple, the throne of God is set apart or *separated*. Though they are not identified as such, I believe that from the similarities in description we can say that the four "living creatures" are cherubim. Notice: "living creatures," Ezekiel 1:5. "Four in number," Ezekiel 1:5. "The likeness of their faces," Ezekiel 1:10. "They are associated with the throne of God," Ezekiel 1:26. "Full of eyes," Ezekiel 10:12. "Rainbow encircles the throne where they are," Ezekiel 1:28. They are identified as cherubim in Ezekiel 10:20. Cherubim are a class or kind of celestial beings like angels, etc. They do not represent another group or class of beings, just like angels do not represent another kind of being. They themselves are a kind and seem to find their responsibility around the throne of God. They could be considered as the "defenders of God's holiness."[8] One stood guard between Adam and the tree of life after God had spoken. They stood over the ark of the covenant gazing down at the law within and the "mercy seat." "These creatures are the judges of all who enter the presence of God."[9] They appear in 1 Chronicles as the chariot upon which God rides in judgment. See also Ezekiel 1 and 10. The high priest could not sprinkle the mercy seat with blood without passing by them. They are ever watchful and concerned about God's character, thus "full of eyes and around and within," and they seem here to surround the throne of majesty. The picture is that this mighty one on His throne simply cannot be approached without being under the watchful eye of these bodyguards and champions of every word and aspect of holiness of God. Without ceasing they magnify the ALMIGHTY.

7. The four forms represent various aspects of creation that are ready to carry out God's purposes. The lion speaks of power and/or nobility. The calf or ox addresses strength and the ability to render service. In God's scheme, the face of man seems to indicate intelligence (no matter how often our foolish actions deny God's intention). The eagle speaks of swiftness.

> 8. And the four living creatures, each one of them having six wings, are full of eyes around and within; and day and night they do not cease to say, "HOLY, HOLY, HOLY is THE LORD GOD, THE ALMIGHTY, WHO WAS AND WHO IS AND WHO IS TO COME."
> 9. And when the living creatures give glory and honor and thanks to Him who sits on the throne, to Him who lives forever and ever,
> 10. the twenty-four elders will fall down before Him who sits on the throne, and will worship Him who lives forever and ever, and will cast their crowns before the throne, saying,
> 11. "Worthy are You, our Lord and our God, to receive glory and honor and power; for You created all things, and because of Your will they existed, and were created."

8. These creatures have the power and ability to go everywhere and see into all things; therefore, they can truly appreciate the one whose presence they are in and they show their awareness by continual worship.

9-11. Their worship is the signal for the 24 elders to also worship and pay homage to the Father, the one who sits in majesty upon the throne. "Cast their crowns" indicates that they recognize that it is due to God that they have overcome; therefore, their crowns are really His. "Existed" and "created" is explained in that all things existed in the mind of God before they were created and were brought forth by an action of His will. Please note that since the worship of the cherubim is the signal for the elders to worship and the cherubim worship without ceasing... the elders worship here in this vision is also unceasing.

QUESTIONS ON CHAPTER 4

1. What is the focus of this second vision of John's?

2. What might be represented by referring to the occupant of the throne as a "jasper stone"?

3. What would be represented by the term "sardius" in the same context?

4. What was in sight like an emerald around the throne?

5. What might that which is mentioned in #4 represent?

6. What do the 24 elders represent?

7. What do the 7 lamps signify? What does this picture say to you?

8. What would this throne scene say to oppressed Christians?

John's Revelation

9. What would the four aspects of the living creatures represent?

    A. lion -

    B. calf -

    C. man -

    D. eagle -

10. What might these living creatures be, in actuality?

11. How did the 24 elders refer to the one sitting on the throne?

12. When, exactly, did the cherubim offer up praise and worship to the one sitting on the throne?

13. When did the 24 elders cast their crowns and worship the one on the throne?

14. What do you think the answers to the above 2 questions might indicate?

Revelation 5	
1. I saw in the right hand of Him who sat on the throne a book written inside and on the back, sealed up with seven seals. 2. And I saw a strong angel	proclaiming with a loud voice, "Who is worthy to open the book and to break its seals?" 3. And no one in heaven or on the earth or under the earth was able to open the book or to look into it.

THE REVELATION
chapter 5

1. John saw a book laying in (Greek - on) the open right hand of the Father. A "book" here is not a flat object made up of pages bound together, as we now have, because there was no such thing at that time. It was actually a "scroll" written "inside and on the back." Being written on both sides would show that there was a wealth of information that was contained in the scroll. It was lacking space to contain all the information on just one side. "Seals" were wax or some sort of soft substance the writer would stamp with his insignia. This kept the scroll from being tampered with or opened before the proper time. The scroll has been described as containing a variety of things by various writers, i.e., the destiny of man, the providence of God, His eternal counsels, and even the eternal justice of God. I believe it would be best to sum all the above up as "God's eternal plan for all ages." This is best argued by the fact of who among all is able to open the scroll and reveal its contents. The fact that it is sealed means that the plan is *un*revealed and *un*executed. To be able to open the scroll by breaking the seals would not only mean revealing the plan but also carrying it out. For there to be seven seals might show the connection of the scroll with deity. It also may be an indication that it is completely sealed, or a complete mystery. This would also explain why no one in heaven or earth would be able to open the seals except deity.

2. Challenge for a worthy one goes out into all creation.

3. Back from all creation comes the answer...no one is worthy! Here the word "worthy" literally means *of sufficient weight*, i.e., of moral character and ability.[10]

> 4. Then I began to weep greatly because no one was found worthy to open the book or to look into it;
> 5. and one of the elders *said to me, "Stop weeping; behold, the Lion that is from the tribe of Judah, the Root of David, has overcome so as to open the book and its seven seals."
> 6. And I saw between the throne (with the four living creatures) and the elders a Lamb standing, as if slain, having seven horns and seven eyes, which are the seven Spirits of God, sent out into all the earth.

4. John's weeping is understood if we consider the fact that the scroll being opened means the execution of God's plan and the revealing of it to His saints. In this particular time of persecution and trial, they/he would feel a need to know what (to some extent) God has in store for them. John is being shown these visions so that he and the churches might understand that all is not lost. If the scroll is not revealed, then the plan is not carried out and they do not receive understanding.

5. Not an angel, but one of the elders speaks and tells John to stop weeping. This is one who has experienced first-hand the redeeming power of the Lamb of God. "The Lion" evidently refers to Genesis 49:9-10. The ruler from the lineage of David and the tribe of Judah, the one with the strength of a lion who would bear the scepter of righteousness over God's people and speak peace or rest to all men has come. He has overcome Satan and wrested the keys of death and Hades from him in the process, 1:17ff.

6. John looks to see this "Lion of Judah," a symbol of strength, majesty, and power, but instead sees a Lamb. The Lamb has the appearance of being slain though it is now standing and very much alive. The "slain" appearance may indicate the sacrificial neck wounds of the offered Lamb. Jesus had overcome and received the power to open the book, not by force of kingly might, but by His sacrifice through love. He truly was/is the only one of proper moral character (worthy) to open the book and reveal the plan of God. Worthy is the Lamb. The Hebrews used the term "horns" to represent power (Deuteronomy 33:17; 1 Samuel 2:10; 2 Chronicles 18:10), and seven of them would imply complete or all power, Matthew 28:18. Seven eyes would imply omniscience or full and complete knowledge. He is also omnipresent through His seven spirits (Holy Spirit, in all His ways and influences) who are sent out into *all* the earth. His presence is everywhere. John is looking at a vision of Deity standing center stage, between the throne and the elders and the creatures.

7. And He came and took the book out of the right hand of Him who sat on the throne. 8. When He had taken the book, the four living creatures and the twenty-four elders fell down before the Lamb, each one holding a harp and golden bowls full of incense, which are	the prayers of the saints. 9. And they *sang a new song, saying, "Worthy are You to take the book and to break its seals; for You were slain, and purchased for God with Your blood men from every tribe and tongue and people and nation. 10. "You have made them to

7. The Lamb ascends to the throne and takes the scroll. This happened when Jesus ascended to the throne after His resurrection and was glorified and exalted at God's right hand. God's plan was then executed and revealed by the Son, through the Spirit, to the apostles and prophets. John is looking at a picture of spiritual events going on behind the history that John himself had known.

8. For ages God's plan had been a mystery, hidden from all. Principalities and powers (spiritual beings) had not understood, but now were beginning to, Ephesians 3:10. Angels had desired to look into it (1 Peter 1:12), but it had been hidden from them also until the worthy one was present to make it all known. Prophets had been given glimpses, but also had not understood (1 Peter 1:10ff), not even their own words. Now Christ was revealing it all through His sacrifice and resurrection and through the work of the Holy Spirit in His apostles and prophets. In the vision, "bowls of incense" were the prayers of the saints, Psalm 141:2; Revelation 8:3-4. Though not particularly identified here, this writer believes the "harps" here are the same as the "harps of God" mentioned elsewhere, Revelation 15:2-3; 14:2-3. These "harps of God" are not harps of wood, harps of metal, harps of men, etc. They are "harps of God." Just as the incense of the vision represents the prayers of the saints, I believe that these harps represent the pure vocal strains of His people. Both would be the "sacrifice" that God desired, the "fruit of lips that give praise to His name," Hebrew 12:15. Especially read in the NASB, 14:2-3 and 15:2-3. It is noteworthy to me that although harps are mentioned, they are never mentioned as being played. Instead, every time they are mentioned...there is singing! In chapter 14, it is a voice that sounds like harpists playing; there is actually no playing going on. In chapter 15, it is the same as here. Each one has a harp, but there is no mention of playing. It is singing that goes on. The one who tries to justify the playing of piano, organ, or band instruments in worship today by referring to the instrument of God in the book of Revelation must fail miserably. The instrument of God is the human voice sounding out melodies from the heart.

John's Revelation

> be a kingdom and priests to our God; and they will reign upon the earth."
> 11. Then I looked, and I heard the voice of many angels around the throne and the living creatures and the elders; and the number of them was myriads of myriads, and thousands of thousands,

9. This "new song" is not as much new in *time* as it is new in *content*. The purchase of men with the blood of an innocent sacrifice is the focus of the song.

> Here very definitely the mediator's present rule or dominion over the universe is described as being a reward for His suffering and death. Both the particular and universal aspects of the atonement are beautifully combined. The Lamb did not purchase the salvation of every single individual. NO, he paid the price for His elect, that is, for men 'out of' every tribe and tongue, etc. Yet on the other hand, there is nothing narrow or natural about this redemption. It is worldwide in its scope and embraces every group: ethnic (tribe), linguistic (tongue), political (people), and social (nation). Together all the redeemed constitute a kingdom of priests (Revelation 1:6). By means of the incense of their prayers, the saints even now reign upon the earth.[11]

This is the influence for good that they have in their relationship with their Savior-King.

10. Christians reign with Christ now! Notice Christians are called "kings and priests," KJV, Revelation 1:6. We reign in life through righteousness, Romans 5:17. We reign with the apostles, 1 Corinthians 4:8. We reign by way of righteous judgment, 1 Corinthians 6:1-2. And we reign by enduring, 2 Timothy 2:12. By saints using wise discernment, living righteously, keeping in close fellowship with God by prayer, and serving their Lord at every opportunity, they pronounce judgment upon a sinful world and share in the reign with Christ.

11. The rest of the heavenly host (angels, not a few) now adds their praise to that being offered to the Lamb. The plan of the ages has come together in a great fulfillment. It is almost beyond thinking that this great explosion of praise, worship, and glory is directed at the Lamb because of what He desires to accomplish with you and me.

12. All honor and all glory belong to the one who did what no one else in all

> 12. saying with a loud voice, "Worthy is the Lamb that was slain to receive power and riches and wisdom and might and honor and glory and blessing."
> 13. And every created thing which is in heaven and on the earth and under the earth and on the sea, and all things in them, I heard saying, "To Him who sits on the throne, and to the Lamb, be blessing and honor and glory and dominion forever and ever."
> 14. And the four living creatures kept saying, "Amen." And the elders fell down and worshiped.

creation was able to do. This is summed up in the 7 particulars of power, riches, wisdom, might, honor, glory, and blessing. It cannot be coincidence that there are seven listed here. Complete glory and praise belongs to Christ.

13. After all the host of heaven, John must have been amazed to hear all of creation join in the praise of the Lamb that was slain. The picture that is presented to John (and the churches and to us) in these two chapters (4 and 5) is of God in His majesty on the throne. The Christ ascends to the throne because of His paying the redemption price. Because of His action in revealing and fulfilling the plan of God, the entire universe *should* (remember, this is a vision) offer up praise to the Lamb.

14. "Amen" or let it be, or so be it.

> In offering praise and paying homage befitting infinite deity to God on His throne, the quartet of living creatures sing the song of His absolute perfection: Holy, Almighty, Eternal. The chorus of elders praises Him in the song of creation, for by His will 'they were and were created.' An ensemble consisting of the quartet and chorus of elders join in a song of praise to the Lamb who is the Redeemer who purchased men unto God by His blood, proving Himself worthy to take and open the book. The myriad host of angels joins the heavenly worshippers with their 7-fold songs of praise to the Lamb. All creation then closes the series of songs with a stirring anthem of praise to God and to the Lamb. The sound dies away with the quartet's hearty Amen as a grand finale to the majestic scene.[12]

One must wonder at the strength of the apostle who could see such glorious majesty and hear the singing of this tremendous spiritual chorus that fills heaven and earth and still be able to record this for others. The sights and sounds of this vision numb the senses and take one's breath away.

John's Revelation

QUESTIONS ON CHAPTER 5

1. What is the scroll that is sealed up?

2. What is the significance of the seven seals?

3. Why is the scroll written inside and on the back?

4. Define "worthy" as it is used here.

5. Why was John weeping in this vision?

6. Who is the Lion from the tribe of Judah?

7. What did John see when he looked for the Lion of Judah?

8. Who is the Lamb that was slain, yet standing?

9. Explain "7 horns."

10. Explain "7 eyes."

11. What are the "7 spirits" and what is their task?

12. What are the bowls of incense?

13. What *might* the harps represent?

14. What was the price paid to purchase men?

15. Who *should* praise the Lamb and why?

16. Name five things about the work of Christ that the new song mentions.

> **Revelation 6**
>
> 1. Then I saw when the Lamb broke one of the seven seals, and I heard one of the four living creatures saying as with a voice of thunder, "Come."
> 2. I looked, and behold, a white horse, and he who sat on it had a bow; and a crown was given to him, and he went out conquering and to conquer.

THE REVELATION
chapter 6

INTRODUCTION:

In the physical world, what John is about to see happen would be impossible (like the "wheel within a wheel" of Ezekiel 1:16ff, that allowed the chariot throne to move in any direction). We must remember that this is a vision. Only here can we find one seal of seven removed and a portion of the book (scroll) revealed. Even then the writing on the scroll is revealed as a continuous picture to John. Confused? Keep in mind that most information is revealed and communicated by the use of words or language. This message (Revelation) is communicated by picture. Read the picture, not necessarily the words. It's been stated that this chapter is the beginning of the end of the book. The seven seals are opened and the seventh gives rise to the seven trumpets. The seventh trumpet gives us the seven bowls.

1. His cry is "come," whether to John or to the horsemen. The added "and see" (KJV) is rejected by nearly all biblical scholars. The "voice of thunder" implies a loud, clear voice that can be heard in every realm.

2. This horse and rider have been identified in a variety of ways from historical to hysterical. It seems to me that each interpretation is a result of one's overview of the message and one's willingness to make the book understandable and contemporary with the saints in the first century. Some of the more reasonable viewpoints are that this horseman represents...periods of time,[13] militarism or invasion[14] or the good effects of the church. Though each may have its arguments, I believe this horseman to be Christ. We will explain in the following. In Scripture, the horse (often associated with the war chariot) was used as a symbol of battle, majesty, strength, speed, terror, and conquest, Job 39:19-25; Jeremiah 4:13;

Habakkuk 1:8; Isaiah 31:1. The "bow" was a powerful weapon in that day used for hunting, conquest, and war. Though it was not a weapon used by the Romans, the Parthians, most feared enemies of the Romans, were proficient in the use of the bow. Because of their skill they were nearly the only enemy able to put up an effective resistance to the Roman army. The "crown" is the *stephanos* or victory crown, Revelation 14:14. Remember the color white and its relationship to purity and holiness? Because of this color the rider could not be Satan, the anti-Christ, or any type of speculated evil that some have put forth. With two exceptions, everywhere this word "conquer" is used in this book, it refers to Christ or to believers. The crown harmonizes nicely with 14:14 where Christ is the wearer. Also keep in mind the idea that the book is divided into seven parallel sections, each telling the same story with deeper significance as we progress. In Revelation 19:11, we have a parallel picture where we are told that the rider on the white horse is Christ. It hardly makes sense to have two riders on two white horses that represent different things when pictures are the means whereby the message is communicated. This would tend to confuse things. The differences in this rider and the one in 19:11 point to the fact that they are the SAME rider in different phases of the scheme. Here He is going forth to conquer. Later the rider has moved in position in the plan just like the Lamb moved in the throne setting, from being slain, yet living, to taking a place on the throne. Christ is pictured here as a Parthian cavalryman, dreaded and effective enemy of Rome, victorious and confident. Those Christians need not fear whatever followed Him.

3-4. Many have very easily put forth the idea of some kind of military power here with the red horse. This simply does not seem in context with Christ going forth "conquering and to conquer." He is the one at war here. Sometimes Matthew 24 is used as a commentary on these verses. This also would be strictly out of context considering the prophecy of Matthew 24 and the destruction of Jerusalem. We might reference Ezekiel 11:19; 33:11; 5:17; 14:21; and Zechariah 1:8ff. Here we find that there is a relationship between the horses, the riders, and doing the will of God. In Zechariah, the second, third, and fourth riders are all connected with the first. I believe that is also true here. The following horsemen are somehow related to the first one. Remember the symbolism of the Apocalypse is rooted in the Old Testament. If the rider on the white horse IS Christ going out in the message of the gospel, conquering and to conquer, then this must set the stage for understanding the other horses and riders. The rider on the red horse does not represent warfare except in a roundabout way. He represents warfare against God's people, i.e., persecution. Why is this so?

> 3. When He broke the second seal, I heard the second living creature saying, "Come."
> 4. And another, a red horse, went out; and to him who sat on it, it was granted to take peace from the earth, and that men would slay one another; and a great sword was given to him.

a) The red horse follows the white. Wherever Christ, His gospel, or His people go, persecution of some sort is sure to follow.

b) "Jesus told His disciples they would be persecuted, delivered up, and put to death for His sake and members of their own families would lead in such opposition (Matthew 10:21)."[15]

c) "He continued saying, 'think not that I am come to send peace on the earth: I come not to send peace, but a sword.'" (Matthew 10:34)[16] The word "sword" in Matthew 10:34 is *machaira*. The same word is used for the sword given to the rider on the red horse. The machaira was the short sword of the Roman infantry or the sacrificial knife. It was a butchering knife or a slaughtering sword for sacrifice or for the spiritual sacrifice of Christians upon a Roman blade figuratively, Genesis 22:6, 10.

d) "'That they should slay one another' indicates the slaughtering of men by their fellowmen. The word 'slay' (*sphatto*), is used here and also in reference to the Lamb slain in sacrifice (5:6) and to the souls underneath the altar that had been slain for the word of God and the testimony they held (6:4) confirms the position taken above."[17]

e) Let us keep in mind that Christ was giving this vision to believers who were being persecuted unto death (Jews, Nero, and Domitian?). The slaughter of believers was their immediate and foremost problem and concern.

The rider on the red horse DOES NOT refer to one specific person or persecutor. "He does not belong to one particular age. No century is without its rider on the red horse, the world is ever persecuting the church."[18]

5-6. Black is the symbol for grief, woe, mourning, and circumstances surrounding famine, Isaiah 50:3; Jeremiah 4:28; 14:2; 8:18-22. The "balance" (pair of scales, NASB) goes hand in hand with verse 6 where one eats his food by weight or by measure, Ezekiel 4:10, 16. This picture indicates a time of scarcity and the

> 5. When He broke the third seal, I heard the third living creature saying, "Come." I looked, and behold, a black horse; and he who sat on it had a pair of scales in his hand.
> 6. And I heard something like a voice in the center of the four living creatures saying, "A quart of wheat for a denarius, and three quarts of barley for a denarius; and do not damage the oil and the wine."

grief that would accompany it. Notice, however, that this is not a generic famine for everyone, but just upon certain products. The "measure" (quart, NASB) was literally a *choenix*, which was a dry measure almost equal to a quart. It is said that this would be enough for one day for one man of moderate appetite. The "denarius" (shilling, KJV) was the most important Roman coin circulated at this time and was equal to about 18-20 cents. This was apparently a day's wage for a common laborer at the time of Christ. These prices for food are high, but they are by no means famine prices. The implication seems to be that a man could earn enough to support himself, but how could he take care of a family at this rate? Only by buying the poor man's fare of barley rather than wheat. Notice that the oil and wine were not to be hurt. These were the more luxurious items that a poor man would not even consider buying. Once again then, the black horse does not represent an overall famine but a time of hardship for one class of people. I believe that it means economic hardship for those Christians. We have already studied how that one needed to be a member of a trade guild to work. If you did not worship that guild's deity, you suffered. Therefore, the Christian workman would not be able to work quite often. If you failed to worship the image of the emperor or offended the Jews, you would suffer, sometimes even unto death. Often there would be some sort of economic deprivation accompanying this. We can still see the same true today. If one is true to his convictions and will not miss worship to work or perhaps will not join a labor union that insists on violent means to accomplish their ends, he will be crowded out of his business, job, or profession. Many times a Christian will have to take a job with lower wages to stay true to the Master. Meanwhile, the oppressor has the abundance; no one can hurt his "oil or wine." The Christian is content with "barley" knowing that the true reward will come later if he perseveres.

7-8. The "pale" (KJV) or "ashen" (NASB) horse was a pale green color —the color of a person deathly sick. Notice that Hades follows death. Death cuts down and Hades gathers up. Hades is the "realm of the unseen," the place of disembodied spirits who await the resurrection day. Death and Hades are always mentioned in this book together. "Authority was given to them" means that not even death has a free hand, but that he works under a higher power, God. He is

John's Revelation

> 7. When the Lamb broke the fourth seal, I heard the voice of the fourth living creature saying, "Come."
> 8. I looked, and behold, an ashen horse; and he who sat on it had the name Death; and Hades was following with him. Authority was given to them over a fourth of the earth, to kill with sword and with famine and with pestilence and by the wild beasts of the earth.

given a broader field of labor than the black horse (saints vs. fourth of the earth). Nevertheless, he is still confined. Notice that he kills with...

a) "The sword." This sword is the *rhomphaia* or the great, two-edged, Thracian sword. It is the sword that the Lamb uses to make war, 1:16; 2:12, 16; 19:15-21. For the first time here is introduced the aspect of carnal warfare. This is military might represented. The Lord allows and uses the sword of nations to execute judgment on the earth.

b) "Famine." Famine is the companion of warfare and usually follows the ravages of war.

c) "Pestilence" (NASB) "Death" (KJV). These are those which die from any and all types of disease and plague. This is also the bosom companion of famine and war.

d) "Wild beasts of the earth." This would be all other types of death no matter how gruesome and terrible. These "wild beasts" may be cruel men at work.

These four make the passage correspond with Ezekiel 5:16-17; 14:21. The judgment symbolized by this rider is against the unregenerate people, but in such judgments Christians must necessarily suffer with the rest. Let us sum up the four seals and their significance.

a) The going forth of Christ in the gospel.

b) The persecution of saints as martyrs being slaughtered which followed the preaching of the truth, which brought the world and saints into conflict.

c) Discrimination in labor and business, which added economic hardship to the suffering of Christians.

> 9. When the Lamb broke the fifth seal, I saw underneath the altar the souls of those who had been slain because of the word of God, and because of the testimony which they had maintained;
> 10. and they cried out with a loud voice, saying, "How long, O Lord, holy and true, will You refrain from judging and avenging our blood on those who dwell on the earth?"
> 11. And there was given to each of them a white robe; and they were told that they should rest for a little while longer, until the number of their fellow ser-

d) The judgments upon society, instigated by God, which are the result of a pagan influence rejecting the divine message.

9. The altar here is from the Greek word *thusiazo*, which means to sacrifice.[19] These individuals were sacrificed or slain because of their reception and proclamation of the gospel (word of God). They had not gone back on it. They had kept the faith, even unto death.

10. Their cry is not for revenge but for a vindication of their death and the cause for which they had died, Genesis 4:10; Numbers 35:33; Job 16:18; Isaiah 26:21; Ezekiel 24:7; and especially Deuteronomy 32:43. It is ever right for God's people to cry out to him for the justice against their enemies that He has promised.

11. These saints were not in a final state of glory, but they were at rest. Their rest was to be a "little while." This "little while" (*chronon mikron*, Gk.) is the same "little while" we find in John 7:33 and 12:35. It is not a reference to waiting for eternity, but in fact means a "short time," then they would be avenged. This brings home to us once more that the focus of the fulfillment of the Revelation was to be in THAT DAY, not centuries later. The little time of their waiting seems to be parallel to the time of Satan in great wrath (12:12), "knowing that he hath but a short time." "Those that dwell on the earth" are the unregenerate. The white robes are the saints' reward. They are representative of their lives, unspotted and unblemished. They have been cleansed in the blood of the Lamb and signify forgiveness and mercy. See 7:14.

12. It is evident that the opening of this seal brings judgment into view. Most expositors believe this to be the final judgment at the Lord's return. We will show, however, that this is *not* the final judgment, but a judgment against whatever world power was persecuting the saints (obviously the Romans would be in view for those to whom this book was written). The Holy Spirit in presenting this vision

> vants and their brethren who were to be killed even as they had been, would be completed also.
> 12. I looked when He broke the sixth seal, and there was a great earthquake; and the sun became black as sackcloth made of hair, and the whole moon became like blood;
> 13. and the stars of the sky fell to the earth, as a fig tree casts its unripe figs when shaken by a great wind.
> 14. The sky was split apart like a scroll when it is rolled up, and every mountain and island were moved out of their places.

depends heavily upon Old Testament pictures and descriptions of final judgments brought against heathen nations that had sought the destruction of God's people. Isaiah spoke thusly concerning ancient Babylon, Isaiah 13:10, 13; 29:6. "I clothe the heavens with blackness, and I make sackcloth their covering," Isaiah 50:3; Jeremiah 4:23ff, 28. Joel also described a similar picture in describing a future judgment against Jerusalem: "The sun shall be turned into darkness, and the moon into blood," Joel 2:31. Jesus used these same figures in Matthew 24 to describe the destruction of Jerusalem by the Romans. Viewed in light of former judgments against specific world powers it would seem that judgment is being pronounced upon whomever is responsible for the suffering and slaughter of His saints (in answer to their cries, 6:10). The Roman Empire is in power, but we do not find that out until chapter 13.

13. In the writings of the Old Testament prophets, stars often represented rulers and leaders, Numbers 24:17; Isaiah 14:12; Daniel 8:10. However, this also might just enhance the picture of utter destruction and desolation, Matthew 24:29. The figs (*olunthos*, Gk.) are winter figs which grow but do not reach maturity. They fall off in the spring.[20]

14. As a scroll is rolled up at its end, so when a nation is finished, its heaven is rolled up or no longer visible. Notice the words of Isaiah concerning the heathen nations whose time had come in Isaiah 34:4. Mountains and islands are symbols of permanence and strength. It is a terrible day when these are moved or taken away. At the fall of Tyre, notice Ezekiel 26:15, 18; 27:35. All these things in the past were used as descriptive phrases to illustrate the fall and passing of a great national power when judged by Jehovah. I see no reason to change the usage here and try to make the Scriptures teach something else. This is the apocalyptic language, or the language of the prophets. It is intended to be figurative, not literal. It is intended to convey a horrible sense of terror at an impending judgment of God.

> 15. Then the kings of the earth and the great men and the commanders and the rich and the strong and every slave and free man hid themselves in the caves and among the rocks of the mountains;
> 16. and they *said to the mountains and to the rocks, "Fall on us and hide us from the presence of Him who sits on the throne, and from the wrath of the Lamb;
> 17. for the great day of their wrath has come, and who is able to stand?"

15. Men of all classes, degree, and social standing are judged alike. All are struck with terror, all seek refuge. Here is more evidence that this is not the final judgment because at that time the Lord will come "in a moment, in the twinkling of an eye," 1 Corinthians 15:52, see also 2 Peter 3:10. There will be no time to seek a hiding place then.

16. Furthermore, we find this idea of men seeking refuge and calling the mountains to fall on them in history along with the other ideas. Hosea spoke thusly when describing the destruction of Samaria by the Assyrians, Hosea 10:8. Isaiah used it to speak of Jerusalem's fate at the hand of the Babylonians (Isaiah 2:19) and Jesus said it would happen when the Romans came upon Jerusalem, Luke 23:30. It is clear that such language points to the judgment of a persecuting world power. Later in the Revelation it will be revealed that the Roman Empire suffered such a fate as predicted in Daniel 2. By divine judgment and providence God will vindicate His saints.

17. Nahum asked the same question (Nahum 1:6) about Jehovah's impending judgment against Nineveh. The answer was the same in both cases—none can stand before the Jehovah.[21]

John's Revelation
QUESTIONS ON CHAPTER 6

1. What is the purpose of "seals"?

2. What did the white horse signify?

3. How many white horses are mentioned in this book?

4. Who is riding the white horse NOT mentioned in this chapter?

5. What is the *stephanos*?

6. What did the red horse signify?

7. Why is it natural that the red horse should follow the white one?

8. What does the *machaira* imply?

9. What did the black horse signify?

10. What does "barley" indicate?

11. Not "hurting the oil and wine" would imply what?

12. What did the ashen (pale) horse signify?

13. What does the *rhomphaia* imply?

14. What is "Hades"?

15. Why were souls under the altar crying out?

16. Why were the martyrs slain?

17. How is the sun darkened and moon turned to blood?

18. What do stars, etc., often represent?

19. Who are "those on the earth"?

20. What is the key to understanding the figures and symbols in the Revelation?

John's Revelation

> **Revelation 7**
>
> 1. After this I saw four angels standing at the four corners of the earth, holding back the four winds of the earth, so that no wind would blow on the earth or on the sea or on any tree.

THE REVELATION
chapter 7

INTRODUCTION:

We have seen the heavenly throne presented in such worshipful majesty and power that we are assured this throne has power over all the heavens and the earth. We have seen seals opened and horsemen riding out over the earth. We have heard martyred souls crying out for an avenging of their sacrifice, and as a response to that cry we have seen a great judgment rendered on the persecutors. As judgment was brought forth, we saw these guilty ones cringing and crying out in fear of the Lamb, and the question was asked, "Who is able to stand?" We, along with John, await the opening of the seventh seal and the outcome of this drama, but instead we are presented with chapter 7, an interlude, and a pause in the vision. This is a calming pause. During this break we (with those early Christians) are reassured and comforted to have revealed to us the situation of the saints, whether on the earth or around the throne.

> "In these two scenes (in chapter seven, sic) God assures His saints that He watches after each one, keeping an accurate account. In ancient times He had assured His people by pointing to the host of heaven and declaring that He brings them out by number, calling each by name, and that for all their number not one was lacking (Isaiah 40:26). In the same way He assures His suffering saints that He is mindful of each one, whether living on earth or having died in the faith. Not one is lacking now."[22]

1. Obviously God, in the form of His angels, is holding back "those destructive forces which bring judgment upon mankind."[23] Verse 3 is where we are made to understand that this wind is a harmful force that is being restrained. The sixth seal is completed, and we understand this by the term "after this." "Four corners"

> 2. And I saw another angel ascending from the rising of the sun, having the seal of the living God; and he cried out with a loud voice to the four angels to whom it was granted to harm the earth and the sea,
> 3. saying, "Do not harm the earth or the sea or the trees until we have sealed the bond-servants of our God on their foreheads."
> 4. And I heard the number of those who were sealed, one hundred and forty-four thousand sealed from every tribe of the sons of Israel:

simply has reference to the common usage of this term, the farthest extent of the earth, Isaiah 11:12; 24:16; Matthew 24:31; Revelation 20:8. Evil or destruction is referred to in the Scriptures in the form of a wind, tempest, destroying wind, scattering wind, etc., Jeremiah 25:32; 49:36; 51:1; Daniel 7:2ff; Zechariah 6:5. One point for us to note is that though the wind may be a tempest or a zephyr, calm or strong, curse or blessing, it is still under the control of the Almighty One. Judgments are under His control. The use of the earth, sea, and trees here probably represents God's complete power over and use of His creation. It is certainly fitting that the invisible power of the wind should represent the invisible power of God.

2. The fact that the angel comes from the point of morning light may point to a message of joy and cheer. In 586 B.C.E. (Ezekiel 11:23; 43:2), Jehovah departed from His people going east. He returned from the same way. The seal was a sign of ownership, identification, or authority over (Genesis 41:42; Esther 3:10; 8:2; Daniel 6:17; Matthew 27:66; Song of Solomon 8:6; 2 Timothy 2:19), thus protective care.

3. This verse shows us the function of the winds, i.e., "to hurt." This resembles the picture that we find in Ezekiel 9:1-8. "On their foreheads" implies a visible place, conspicuous to all. Notice that those so marked or sealed are living on the earth. Though preserved from God's judgment, they are not necessarily protected from all harm. This same picture is presented in the vision of Ezekiel 9. In that vision, those who were sealed were saved alive. In historic fact, the righteous died right alongside the wicked (Ezekiel 21:3-4) when the invasion came. What does this mean? Only that being sealed is not indicative of physical preservation, but of spiritual safety. It is not a literal mark here but God's assurance that He has His eye on them. There is also a side issue that is worthy of note here. The winds of destruction are shown to be strictly under the power of God as they are held back until the saints are taken notice of. The efforts of nation invading

> 5. From the tribe of Judah, twelve thousand were sealed, from the tribe of Reuben twelve thousand, from the tribe of Gad twelve thousand,
> 6. from the tribe of Asher twelve thousand, from the tribe of Naphtali twelve thousand, from the tribe of Manasseh twelve thousand,
> 7. from the tribe of Simeon twelve thousand, from the tribe of Levi twelve thousand, from the tribe of Issachar twelve thousand,
> 8. from the tribe of Zebulun twelve thousand, from the tribe of Joseph twelve thousand, from the tribe of Benjamin, twelve thousand were sealed.

nation is not always as dependent upon the political wishes of men as we might think.

4. All scholarship of any note agrees that the number here is figurative. About the only ones who make it literal are Jehovah's Witnesses who have their own problems anyway with distinguishing between what is literal and what is figurative. Neither are their problems confined to the book of the Revelation. This number is a figurative one. This number, divisible by 10, 100, and 1,000 is representative of religious completeness and perhaps fixedness. The exact number of saints from each tribe is the evidence to us of the symbolic nature of this passage. It is hardly likely that such harmony is possible. Since the number is symbolic, we also understand the "sons of Israel" to be, not fleshly Israel, but spiritual. This group is the church, or all the saints, the redeemed on the earth that is living at any time in history.

5-8. As we have stated, this group is spiritual Israel. We might notice that Dan and Ephraim are omitted from the list while Manasseh and Joseph are included. Levi is also included, though he is omitted in some of the Old Testament lists, e.g., the three lists in Numbers 1 and 2. Levi received no inheritance and Joseph's inheritance went to his two sons Manasseh and Ephraim. Thus, there were actually 13 tribes (Joseph made 2), and their inheritance (Canaan) was divided 12 ways (Levi lived among all and did not receive a country). This peculiar inclusion of Levi and exclusion of two other tribes must cause us to wonder at this specific list. We can only speculate as to why Dan and Ephraim were omitted. A possible explanation is that through Jeroboam I, an evil king (1 Kings 11:26), Ephraim led Israel into idolatry, 1 Kings 12:25-33. Dan, for the most part, abandoned his inheritance early on in the taking of the land, and moved to the far north to Laish (later called Dan) where he settled and also practiced idolatry, Judges 18. These two tribes then are noted in Israel's history for their association with and promotion of idolatry.

> 9. After these things I looked, and behold, a great multitude which no one could count, from every nation and all tribes and peoples and tongues, standing before the throne and before the Lamb, clothed in white robes, and palm branches were in their hands;
> 10. and they cry out with a loud voice, saying, "Salvation to our God who sits on the throne, and to the Lamb."
> 11. And all the angels were standing around the throne and around the elders and the four living creatures; and they fell on their faces before the throne and worshiped God,
> 12. saying, "Amen, blessing and glory and wisdom and thanksgiving and honor and power and might, be to our God forever and ever. Amen."
> 13. Then one of the elders answered, saying to me, "These who are clothed in the white robes, who are they, and where have they come from?"
> 14. I said to him, "My lord, you know." And he said to me, "These are the ones who come out of the great tribulation, and they have washed their robes and made them white in the blood of the Lamb.

9-10. "After these things" implies that a *different* view or vision is presented to John's sight, in contrast with the vision of the 144,000. This is an uncountable multitude taken from among all nations and peoples of the earth to now stand before the throne. White robes should be easily understood by now as the righteous garb of God's people. The "palm branches...in their hands" were indicative of a festive occasion, Leviticus 23:26-32, 39-44, esp. verse 40; John 12:13. The verses that follow show that this is indeed such an occasion.

These then represent the saved of all ages in heaven, around the throne, while the 144,000 represent all the saved on earth at any time. They know their relationship to the Lamb.

11-12. All the angels worship here also. The angels have always been interested in the scheme of redemption, 1 Peter 1:12. They serve as "ministering spirits" for the sake of those who should inherit salvation, Hebrew 1:14. They had learned of the meaning behind it all through the church (Ephesians 3:10ff), and here in this picture of the end they fall down in adoration and worship. As in 5:12, *complete* honor and glory is implied by the sevenfold description of their worship in verse 12.

13. It seems appropriate that one who represents the redeemed should draw John's attention to the redeemed.

14. John's answer is a confession of humble ignorance and a questioning for more information. The utmost respect is used. "My lord" (*kurios*, Gk.) is equal to "sir" or "master." "The verb tense (used by the elder) here indicates a continuous coming, not a past or completed coming as indicated by the King James translation, 'they which came' out of the tribulation."[24] But what is this "great tribulation"? Some believe:

a) It is to take place at the end of the time period in which we now live;

b) It is the "tribulation" that would come upon the inhabitants of Jerusalem;

c) It is the afflictions that will come upon all Christians, John 16:33; Acts 14:22; 2 Timothy 3:12; and/or…

d) That it is the trouble which came upon the early church during the Roman period, beginning with Nero's persecution (A.D. 64) and continuing up until the edict of Constantine (A.D. 313), through which contemporaries of John were then passing.

Though the first is popular and common among many religious faiths today, it is completely without scriptural support; therefore, unworthy of our attention. The second is true in certain other passages, but there is nothing in this context to make us think of the destruction of Jerusalem. The third is also a valid argument and may be the correct one, but the fourth is the one which best harmonizes with this chapter and the book as a whole, I believe. Word of victory like this would lend great encouragement to and uplift the spirits of those saints who were enduring so much. This writer believes this was the main purpose behind this book and #4 falls into place admirably. The ones who were coming out of the great tribulation then were the ones who were living in *that* day of Roman persecution and were remaining faithful in spite of tremendous pressure to compromise. They were remaining pure while surrounded by pagan immorality. They were resisting economic hardship to be faithful to their calling and they were refusing to confess any as Lord, except Jesus, in spite of being under constant threat and in danger for their lives from the emperor-cult of that day. Their robes were still white.

> 15. "For this reason, they are before the throne of God; and they serve Him day and night in His temple; and He who sits on the throne will spread His tabernacle over them.
> 16. "They will hunger no longer, nor thirst anymore; nor will the sun beat down on them, nor any heat;
> 17. for the Lamb in the center of the throne will be their shepherd, and will guide them to springs of the water of life; and God will wipe every tear from their eyes."

15. "For this reason" or "therefore" refers to the fact that their robes (lives) are washed clean in the blood of Christ and they have a place before God's throne. "Serve Him day and night" implies continual service and worship. It seems that the Scriptures teach us that though not in his final state of glory, the Christian does indeed proceed into the "presence of the Lord" at his death, 1 Corinthians 5:6, 8; Philippians 1:23; Acts 7:59. After the judgment, the saints will be received into their final rest. "Tabernacle" is used here in the sense of shelter and protection.

16-17. Under divine protection with Jesus forever, without sorrow, without tears, in safety and security is the picture that we have put before us.

John's Revelation
QUESTIONS ON CHAPTER 7

1. What do the four angels signify in this vision?

2. Explain what a "seal" is.

3. Is there any significance in the direction of the rising sun?

4. Why would the number 144,000 itself be important in seeing this as a figurative number?

5. Why was the seal on their foreheads?

6. Who were the 144,000?

7. What O.T. passage closely resembles the "sealing" we read of here?

8. Can one be exempt from judgment and still suffer? Explain.

9. Why is the wind a good symbol for God's power?

10. What tribe is named that is usually not named? Which two are left out?

11. Who is the great multitude?

12. What is the great tribulation?

13. What would the seven-part worship of the angels indicate?

14. What do the ones "dressed in white" do?

15. What is the significance of having God's tabernacle spread over them?

John's Revelation

From Beneath the Altar

Revelation 8	the seventh seal, there was silence in heaven for about half an hour.
1. When the Lamb broke	

THE REVELATION
chapter 8
Section I, 3 (See page 12)

INTRODUCTION:

Chapters 8-11 is the third section in this letter. In this section we will be studying the trumpets of judgment. Refer to the OUTLINE OF THE APOCALYPSE in the INTRODUCTION. Remember, the book is divided into parallel sections, meaning that each section is covering the same material but with a deeper spiritual significance as we go into the book. The "trumpets" are not part of the "seals." They do not symbolize specific events in history such as nuclear war as declared by Lindsey in his *Late, Great Planet Earth*, but represent a series of happenings that can occur over and over throughout this age and at any time.

The first section dealt with the idea of Christ among the lampstands (churches) and looking toward a future reward. We can understand the first section covering the entire age of Christ's kingdom or Christian dispensation as it is so often referred to. The second section dealt with the seals or persecution of believers and looked forward to an avenging judgment to come. These warnings of judgment are not teaching an individual and personal punishment for wrongdoing, but rather a general punishing of a world that rejects God and is therefore overcome with sin. Certainly individual Christians will also fall under the influence of the warning actions, but rather than a warning of judgment to come, this letter would be a reassurance that God has not forgotten His children. These trumpet warnings represent to us the attitude and providential actions of God in behalf of His people in *all* centuries.

1. Some think that the seventh seal was not revealed; others think that the trumpets themselves constituted the seventh seal. It seems more reasonable that the angel with incense, we are about to read of, constitutes the vision of this seal.

> 2. And I saw the seven angels who stand before God, and seven trumpets were given to them.
> 3. Another angel came and stood at the altar, holding a golden censer; and much incense was given to him, so that he might add it to the prayers of all the saints on the golden altar which was before the throne.
> 4. And the smoke of the incense, with the prayers of the saints, went up before God out of the angel's hand.
> 5. Then the angel took the censer and filled it with the fire of the altar, and threw it to the earth; and there followed peals of thunder and sounds and flashes of lightning and an earthquake.

A half hour is not a long time, but it would seem so to one who was waiting. We might understand what the silence was about if we notice that the going forth of the Almighty in judgment in the Old Testament was often introduced by silence, Habakkuk 2:20; Zephaniah 1:7; Zechariah 2:13. "This silence makes the manifestations of the wrath of God all the more impressive."[25] It is the calm before the storm. The anxious wait with bated breath that makes the catastrophe to follow all the more magnificent.

2. "Seven" represents completeness. "There were 7 spirits yet there is one spirit; 7 churches yet there is one church; 7 horns, perfection of power; 7 eyes, perfection and fullness of insight; 7 seals, completeness and perfection of God's plan set forth in one book. Here are 7 angels and 7 trumpets, signifying unity, perfection, fullness, and completeness of whatever the angels were to do and the trumpets were to signify."[26]

3-4. "Another angel" implies another of the same rank. This dispels the theory that some have advanced that this angel is Jesus. Also note that Jesus is never referred to as an angel in Revelation. This altar is not the altar of 6:9, which the martyrs rested under. The altar of burnt offerings in the Old Testament would have been the type for that altar. The golden altar before the veil of the tabernacle and nearest to the mercy seat would be the type for this altar, Exodus 30:6; Hebrews 9:3-6. This altar is before the heavenly throne. The "golden censer" was a small dish or pan into which coals of fire from the altar were placed. Incense was then burned on these coals, Leviticus 10:1; 16:12. Although not necessarily so, the fact that "much incense was given to him" might picture for us the mediating power of the Christ or the intercession of the Spirit, both of whom are concerned with the prayers of the saints. Either one would also demonstrate to the Christian that one's prayers are not offered up alone, but in knowledge of and with the assistance of Deity.

> 6. And the seven angels who had the seven trumpets prepared themselves to sound them.
> 7. The first sounded, and there came hail and fire, mixed with blood, and they were thrown to the earth; and a third of the earth was burned up, and a third of the trees were burned up, and all the green grass was burned up.
> 8. The second angel sounded, and something like a great mountain burning with fire was thrown into the sea; and a third of the sea became blood,
> 9. and a third of the creatures which were in the sea and had life, died; and a third of the ships were destroyed.

5-6. Thus we have the answer of prayer extended to believers and coming back to the earth. It is a sure thing and to show that it is not just a whim of the angel, it is backed up with thunder, sounds, flashes of lightning, and an earthquake. These things remind us of the throne scene where we saw and heard them first and immediately bring to our mind the idea that this demonstration comes from God. So a judgment comes upon the unbelievers. At this point we leave the story of this dispensation revealed in the opening of the seals and begin to see the other side of this picture (answer to prayer) in the trumpets. In the Old Testament, trumpets were used to sound a warning for danger or impending judgment (Amos 3:6; Ezekiel 33:3ff; Hosea 5:8; Joel 2:1) or to call the people to a holy convocation, Joel 2:15. These trumpets illustrate a partial judgment or a warning call to the wicked.

7. As with the seals, we have a group of four and three. The first four affect the physical world and the last three affect the spiritual lives. Once again looking to the Old Testament, we find "hail and fire" used as God's weapons for battle, the destruction of His enemies, instruments of judgment against the rebellious, and against idolaters and liars, Job 38:22ff; Isaiah 30:30ff; Exodus 9; Isaiah 28:2, 17. The fact that it was "mingled with blood" might imply the blood of these being upon their own heads for their evil deeds, Genesis 9:6; Numbers 35:33; Isaiah 26:21; Joel 3:19; Psalm 79:10. Earth, trees, and grass being burned shows a great judgment upon that which evil doers worship instead of the truth, that is the natural world or carnal life. This destruction brought upon a third of the earth, trees, and grass implies a great judgment but *not* a total punishment, in other words, a warning. Total, personal judgment will be at the last day.

8-9. There are two ideas that are often used of viewing these calamities. One is that these things represent destruction brought upon societies and kingdoms—most obvious here, the kingdom of Rome. This is notable in light of the fact that

| 10. The third angel sounded, and a great star fell from heaven, burning like a torch, and it fell on a third of the rivers and on the springs of waters. | 11. The name of the star is called Wormwood; and a third of the waters became wormwood, and many men died from the waters, because they were made bitter. |

the kingdom of Babylon was also referred to as a "mountain" (Jeremiah 51:25, 42) along with other heathen powers, Isaiah 1:15; 64:1; Amos 4:1. The spiritual kingdom of God is likewise considered as a mountain in Isaiah 2:2-4; 11:9; Micah 4:2; and Hebrews 12:22. If this is so, then the sea (mass of humanity) is greatly affected (turned to blood) by the destruction of this kingdom.

The other popular thought here is that the earth and its life (first trumpet), the sea and its life (second trumpet), and the land waters and the men that drink of them (third trumpet), symbolize all aspects of this life in any age. These calamities represent all natural disasters that come upon man in any age. These are under the control of God and are meant to bring men to humility and repentance. They are especially aimed at worldly individuals who are in charge of furthering the cause of Satan and harming believers. I tend to lean toward the first idea, though a compromise would not be completely out of line. However, the last idea by itself would not actually blend with the picture of the seals and persecutions of saints.

The reason societies and kingdoms fall is their rebellion against God, and usually that rebellion causes some form of persecution of believers. The "... *something like* a great mountain burning with fire..." represents not a specific kingdom or empire but *any* kingdom or empire bound up in wickedness. This same figure was used of Babylon in Jeremiah 51:25, but as stated above would find its fulfillment for early Christians in the Roman Empire. By God's will these great powers, although appearing as mountains, will be destroyed (burned) and disappear in the sea (go back down into the sea of humanity from which they arose).

9. The sea is humanity, society, and it is affected greatly ("a third") when a great political power is destroyed. "Ships" here may be a reference to commerce and economic balance that is disrupted by such consequences.

10-11. "An interpretation of what John saw may be helped by looking at Isaiah's description of the king of Babylon's fall:

'How art thou fallen from heaven, O day-star (Lucifer, KJV), son of the morning! How art thou cut down to the ground, that didst lay low the nations.' Isaiah 14:12"[27]

In Matthew 24:29, wise men or leaders are referred to as stars. This picture comes from the Old Testament and is a sign of great judgment. "Wormwood" is a bitter wood mentioned several times in the Old Testament. It is usually used in connection with the consequences of idolatry, Deuteronomy 29:18; Jeremiah 9:1; 23:15; Amos 5:7; 6:12. Wormwood aptly symbolized sorrow and bitterness of life. The fall of this star brought great bitterness and calamity to the world. "When men prefer the bitter waters of idolatry to the fountain of the living water, they will receive these bitter waters with the fatal consequences that follow."[28]

The fact that the Scriptures speak of failing leaders as stars that fall is difficult to separate in these verses from the historic fact of the increasingly immoral and ungodly activity of the Roman leaders. Not only the Caesars themselves left their standards of nobility, but the statesmen and political leaders of the empire also "fell" from their place. It is likewise difficult to ignore the picture of this "fall" having a widespread influence as we see the star falling on the rivers and springs. This is surely similar to the influence Rome must have exercised over other nations and societies as she fell. As her leaders fell, so also Rome fell, and bitterness spreading like polluted water over all the empire would be the result of her influence.

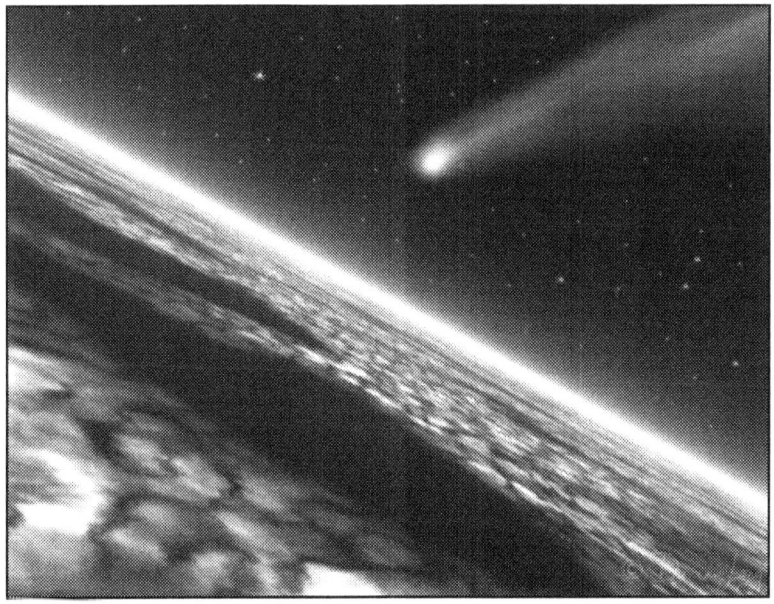

12. The fourth angel sounded, and a third of the sun and a third of the moon and a third of the stars were struck, so that a third of them would be darkened and the day would not shine for a third of it, and the night in the same way.	13. Then I looked, and I heard an eagle flying in midheaven, saying with a loud voice, "Woe, woe, woe to those who dwell on the earth, because of the remaining blasts of the trumpet of the three angels who are about to sound!"

12. Throughout the Old Testament, the darkening of the sun, moon, and stars was the announcement of impending doom, Isaiah 13:10; Joel 3:15; Amos 8:9; Jeremiah 4:23; 32:7ff; Matthew 24:29. A third being darkened once more implies a great judgment, but still a partial judgment to serve as a warning to the ungodly. "God's word is a lamp (Psalm 119:105), giving light and understanding (Psalm 119:130) which is the basis of all true wisdom (1 Corinthians 2:6-13) now summed up in Christ, Colossians 2:3." [29] This partial darkness seems to hint toward a lack of understanding and true wisdom. In the Old Testament, God took away wise and understanding men from Judah and Edom, Isaiah 29:14; Obadiah 8; Jeremiah 49:7. It should obviously not be thought of as unusual for nations and kingdoms to ignore wise leaders and thus lose good counsel in a downward slide of rejecting God. All the more reason is seen here for Christians to be involved as much as possible in the choice of leaders and judges that determine the course of a nation. Once again, this cannot and should not be applied to any specific historic event. Before total darkness engulfs any kingdom or society, minor judgments are handed down as a warning, a call to repentance. These four trumpets call for reformation, not destruction of mankind.

13. Though the KJV reads "angels," most authorities agree "eagle" (ASV) is the correct rendering here. "Midheaven" is where *all* can see and hear. The eagle was a strong, sharp-eyed, swift scavenger to these people, a bird of *prey* or *death.* Its appearance bodes ill ahead and this idea is backed up by its warning "woe, woe, woe." Certainly this would be an ominous symbol of what is to come. (Author's note: I am torn here between what seems to be the evidence of the text and harmony within the book. Though the scholars seem to think this is an "eagle" rather than an "angel," there is "another angel" in 14:6 also flying in "midheaven." The symbology of an eagle as an omen of death could fit well with the message, but the fact that there is "another *angel*" in 14:5, not "another *eagle,*" makes me lean toward the interpretation that this is an angel here also in spite of what the scholars say. We will leave the final decision with you the reader and trust you to get the message of the vision either way.)

John's Revelation

QUESTIONS ON CHAPTER 8

1. Why would there be a silence in the vision?

2. What is a "censer," and how was it used?

3. What might the incense accompanying the saints' prayers indicate?

4. Why was the censer of fire thrown down to the earth?

5. To whom were the 7 trumpets given?

6. What would a trumpet imply?

7. What was destroyed with the first trumpet blast?

8. What would only a third destroyed signify?

9. What was the mountain of verse 8?

10. What was the sea?

11. What might the destruction of the second trumpet blast imply?

12. What could the star of verse 10 symbolize?

13. What is "wormwood"?

14. What would bitter waters mean in a vision like this?

15. Why did the eagle fly in "midheaven"?

16. Darkness usually means what?

17. The eagle would be a symbol of what?

18. What is the principle lesson in this vision?

> **Revelation 9**
>
> 1. Then the fifth angel sounded, and I saw a star from heaven which had fallen to the earth; and the key of the bottomless pit was given to him.

THE REVELATION
chapter 9

INTRODUCTION:

Remember Propositions V and VI of the main introduction. We need not look for specific application in history of a great locust horde, or a mighty war, etc. These are visions and they represent principles of human and divine conduct, though certainly the primary and obvious fulfillment might especially be seen in the application to Rome. "Someone said that the seven letters instruct, the seven seals reveal, the seven trumpets warn, the seven personages act, and the seven bowls of wrath execute total judgment."[30]

In the first four trumpet blasts, John has seen warnings of impending judgments upon the earth, Rome, national leadership, and understanding.

1. Here John saw a star "which *had* fallen" (NASB), past tense. It is not "saw it fall" (KJV), as if he observed it presently. This "star" seems to be Satan. Jesus said in Luke 10:18, "I beheld Satan fallen as lightning from heaven." Our Lord was speaking of the devil's influence and power diminishing as the gospel was being preached by His disciples at that time. Notice also 12:7-12. The same picture will be presented in that place. What John seems to see here is one who at one time was a leader (i.e.,"star"). Without misusing the above passages and turning them into literal accounts, I do not believe it is too much of a stretch to view the devil as one of God's creation that had lost his former place of leadership and authority. "Key" is a symbol of power or authority. The authority to open the abyss (bottomless pit, NASB) "was given to him," meaning Satan only has as much power as God allows him to have. The abyss seems to be the dwelling place of demons, and therefore of every form of wickedness. It should not be looked upon in some cartoon fashion where Satan is the ruler. It is assured that He has no more wish to be there than anyone else. It is very possible that this picture is hell before the judgment, Revelation 20:1-3; Luke 8:31.

> 2. He opened the bottomless pit, and smoke went up out of the pit, like the smoke of a great furnace; and the sun and the air were darkened by the smoke of the pit.
> 3. Then out of the smoke came locusts upon the earth, and power was given them, as the scorpions of the earth have power.
> 4. They were told not to hurt the grass of the earth, nor any green thing, nor any tree, but only the men who do not have the seal of God on their foreheads.

2. This smoke, like the smoke of a great furnace that darkens the air and sun, has its beginning in the abyss, and is therefore an evil and wicked influence. It is the tool which Satan uses to blind the hearts of men and keep the light of wisdom and knowledge from them, 2 Corinthians 4:3-6. To walk (live) in this smoke is to live in an atmosphere of pollution caused by gross and complete wickedness. This is the moral decay and decadence that assisted in the downfall of Rome.

3. Locusts have always been a tool used by God to bring people to repentance, Exodus 10:4-20; Psalm 105:34-35; Deuteronomy 28:38; 1 Kings 8:35, 37; 2 Chronicles 7:13ff; Joel 1; 2. Scorpions have power to cause pain and fear, yet do not kill, verse 5. This same power was given to the locusts.

4. We see these are not ordinary locusts because they will not touch what ordinary locusts eat. They harm only the wicked, persecuting world. We are caused to think of what torment would affect only those who are not saints without affecting the Christians that live right there with them. This sting that accompanies the pollution from the abyss must be tied to sin. They did not harm the people of God (7:4) because Christians keep themselves pure from the torment that comes with moral decay. There is an interesting picture here of the pain and suffering that accompanies unrighteousness. Whether the burden is unhappiness, disease, heartache, guilt, etc., it is a peculiar burden that the impenitent must carry. This sting of sin can be seen daily in the burden of addictions, domestic violence, child abuse, alcoholism, divorce, and greed. Though Christians must sometimes bear up under a burden of physical suffering from ungodly men, the spiritual burdens above should be unknown to the child of God because of the avoidance of sin and the forgiveness offered in Christ. The sting of sin is reserved for the sinner. In as much as the Christian allows the pollution of the world to dim his vision, to that degree he will end up feeling the sting of sin.

5. We have seen that though God did not cause this harm to fall on man, he allowed it in order to bring them to repentance. We see His power manifested

John's Revelation

> 5. And they were not permitted to kill anyone, but to torment for five months; and their torment was like the torment of a scorpion when it stings a man.
> 6. And in those days men will seek death and will not find it; they will long to die, and death flees from them.
> 7. The appearance of the locusts was like horses prepared for battle; and on their heads appeared to be crowns like gold, and their faces were like the faces of men.
> 8. They had hair like the hair of women, and their teeth were like the teeth of lions.

here in the fact that He limits the time (5 months) this destructive force will be permitted to work on men's hearts. Those who refuse to learn from their mistakes and heed God's warnings to repent will endure greater suffering later. This "sting" is a warning to get men's attention.

6. Because of fear and pain and anguish of heart, men will seek release; yet the power of the locust is not sufficient to grant this wish, Job 3:20; Jeremiah 8:3; Ecclesiastes 4:2ff. Remember that these are people who have forsaken the way of righteousness and are tormented by their own wickedness. It is not unusual today to know individuals whose lives have been touched by the polluted air of the abyss who wish for death. Suicide is the third greatest killer among those who have their whole lives full of promise ahead of them—teenagers. This longing for death, depression, and hopelessness in our culture today can be directly tied to the throwing off of restraint and the deep inhalation of immorality.

7. It is best to try and examine the whole picture in verses 7 through 10 and get the complete image that John is being privileged to see. These locusts let loose from the pit are prepared like warhorses to rush into the fray and bring on destruction. Their faces are not the faces of horses but of men. This figure generally indicates intelligence in visionary pictures. These messengers of suffering are not acting stupidly. We are made to understand they are acting with intelligence, choice, and decision. It is not by accident that harm comes to the evildoer—it is by design. On their heads they wear a pseudo-crown of victory gold (*stephanos* - Gk.), because they expect to conquer. They exemplify the attitude of the purveyors of pornography, gambling, corruption, and evil judges. They meet and plan the downfall of men for their own profit, and they expect to win.

8. Their demonical appearance is highlighted by having hair like a woman but teeth like a lion. Perhaps it is possible to see the deceitfulness of unrighteousness here in the attractive feature of a woman's hair. This small attraction, however, is

> 9. They had breastplates like breastplates of iron; and the sound of their wings was like the sound of chariots, of many horses rushing to battle.
> 10. They have tails like scorpions, and stings; and in their tails is their power to hurt men for five months.
> 11. They have as king over them, the angel of the abyss; his name in Hebrew is Abaddon, and in the Greek he has the name Apollyon.

little comfort for the one who must face the teeth like a lion's. There is always a "catch" to the passing pleasures of sin. These beasts are ready to rend, tear, and terrify.

9. In their breastplates like iron we are shown invincibility. In the sound of their wings we are given at once a mind-picture of chariots and horses rushing to battle, and a sense of horror at their readiness to be busy in their task of destruction.

10. These have power, to be sure, but it is a limited power (see comments on verse 5) given to them by the Almighty. For "five months" and "hurt men," see comments on verse 5. This is a terrible and shocking picture that we see here and plainly it conveys strong messages. As with the entire book, however, we must be careful not to take the various parts of the vision too far. Instead we must try to step back and keep the "big picture" in view. This is all part of the imagery, which simply pictures the attractiveness, the deceitfulness, the harm, and the terribleness of sin.

11. The Hebrew word *abaddon* means destruction. The Greek word *apollyon* means destroyer. Is this "angel" Satan or is it the spirit of Satan which controls the wickedness and torment of the abyss? Scholars are divided, and it really doesn't matter. Whether Satan himself personally is in charge or whether he gives that charge to another, the effect is the same. For the purpose of simplification, we shall consider "the destroyer" as Satan. Truly that is what he is because he is a liar and a murderer from the beginning, and destruction is the result of following him, John 8:44. The horses having heads like lions indicate to us the fierceness of both horses and riders.

12. This warning is by John:

> We may ask what is signified by this first woe, with its smoke as a great furnace and the emergence of terrible locusts and their king. Numerous answers and explanations have been given to this question. It seems that we have before us a vivid picture of moral and spiritual

John's Revelation

> 12. The first woe is past; behold, two woes are still coming after these things.
> 13. Then the sixth angel sounded, and I heard a voice from the four horns of the golden altar which is before God,
> 14. one saying to the sixth angel who had the trumpet, "Release the four angels who are bound at the great river Euphrates."
> 15. And the four angels, who had been prepared for the hour and day and month and year, were released, so that they would kill a third of mankind.

decay, which brings torment to the souls of men. The torment does not kill, but it abides for a definite period. Sin is responsible for bringing this decay into the world, behind which is Satan with his diabolical purpose to destroy....This condition should serve as a trumpet warning to the world of unregenerate men to turn from Satan and sin to God—but how seldom do men heed the warning.[31]

The Second Woe (verses 13-21)

13. The golden altar is the one before the throne upon which the prayers of the saints were offered (8:3), not the altar of 6:9. We are not told the source of the voice, whether the voice is the prayers of the saints, the angel, or the altar itself.

14. These are not the angels of 7:1 who were restraining the 4 winds. These angels are restrained themselves. Neither are they necessarily bad angels. They were simply prepared for this purpose (verse 15) and are waiting to carry out the will of God.

15. Four is the world number; therefore, this judgment that is released is a worldwide judgment. It is against *all* wicked, unregenerate men. The Father has prepared these angels for this certain time (Acts 1:7) or rather any certain time. The judgments of warning are progressively more terrible. In this judgment we find a third of mankind is killed.

16. John was not able to count them, but he heard their number: 200,000,000. This surely is a figurative number implying such a vast force that it is uncountable and invincible. Recall that the angels of the churches represented their spiritual life, so also these 4 angels represent the mind and spirit of the great force. The angels are released and four great armies march forth. Like the churches are

> 16. The number of the armies of the horsemen was two hundred million; I heard the number of them.
> 17. And this is how I saw in the vision the horses and those who sat on them: the riders had breastplates the color of fire and of hyacinth and of brimstone; and the heads of the horses are like the heads of lions; and out of their mouths proceed fire and smoke and brimstone.
> 18. A third of mankind was killed by these three plagues, by the fire and the smoke and the brimstone which proceeded out of their mouths.
> 19. For the power of the horses is in their mouths and in their tails; for their tails are like serpents and have heads, and with them they do harm.

one church, so the four armies are one army. They represent a force able to do God's bidding at any time. It is not one certain army or nation here, but these four armies are all armies of the world. Therefore, all wars are being shown to us. Again in this book we are seeing that God is in control, even of the world's armies, and uses them for His purpose. It teaches us that these things also are a tool of God used for His judgment. To Christians in that day it more than likely represented the Parthians, a fierce cavalry of archers that kept Rome's eastern border in turmoil. The general meaning would be external invasion.

17. In the vision the riders and the horses are presented as one; however, this first description is probably the armor of the riders. It is the color of fire (red), hyacinth (smoky blue), and brimstone (yellow). This is striking since it aligns them with their horses out of whose mouths proceeded fires, smoke, and brimstone (a pale-yellowish color). In the Old Testament, brimstone was a sign of God's wrath upon the wicked and is so used here now.

18. In the Old Testament, many times plagues were symbols of divine visitation in judgment, here also. "A third" shows us the power and the terribleness with which this army has been endued. It is a great destruction, but not a total one.

19. "There have been many explanations of these heads and tails, but it seems wise to say simply that this great destroying cavalry-plague killed as it marched and left a terrible hurt in its aftermath."[32]

20-21. Obviously, the "rest of mankind" is the unregenerated world, the two-thirds who are not killed. Saints are not even considered in this vision. Though war and its destruction is used in every age to warn unrighteous men and to bring a partial judgment upon wicked societies, men still refuse to admit there are powers at work that are greater than themselves. They cast off the judgment as fate and

> 20. The rest of mankind, who were not killed by these plagues, did not repent of the works of their hands, so as not to worship demons, and the idols of gold and of silver and of brass and of stone and of wood, which can neither see nor hear nor walk; 21. and they did not repent of their murders nor of their sorceries nor of their immorality nor of their thefts.

ignore the warnings. They continue to engage in the worship of every stupid idol and refuse to repent. A society or nation that permits and encourages sin and evil doing must expect the trumpet judgment of war. Rome was no exception. Though not falling in a single battle, Gibbon records, in his *The Decline and Fall of the Roman Empire*, three great things that combined to bring about its destruction. They were natural disasters (volcanoes, earthquakes, famines, etc.), internal decay, and external invasion (from old and new enemies).

CONCLUSION:

As the first woe fell upon mankind, clouds of smoke from the abyss contaminated the moral and spiritual atmosphere of earth corrupting and debasing the minds of men. Out of this immoral atmosphere came locusts to torment (but not to kill) as decay and corruption set in upon mankind. In the second woe at the sounding of the sixth trumpet, destruction comes from without as the armies of the earth, symbolically portrayed as one huge army, march across the pages of history. Though inspired by the very spirit of Satan and of hell, these armies are used by God to accomplish His purpose. We are not to think of a physical army at a given point in history, but of God's death-dealing judgments as He uses the armies of time to execute His wrath; here one-third of mankind is killed as a result of God's judgment against idolatry and its fruit.[33]

Notice the words of Albertus Pieters:
> As for the great happenings of the trumpet series, I do not take much interest in locating them here or there in history, for it seems to me I know them. Have we not ourselves, twice, in 1914-1918 and again in 1939-1945 seen the bottomless pit opened, and the heavens darkened by swarms of evil things that issued from it? Has not the thunder of the 200,000,000 hellish horsemen shaken the earth in our own day, so that we can never forget it? So it seems to me, as I see the pageant unroll act after act; and finally I turn away with profound confidence in the plans of Him that sitteth on the throne, written in the unsealed orders that are in the hands of the Lamb.

QUESTIONS ON CHAPTER 9

1. Who is the star and what was given to him?

2. Explain the meaning of a "key."

3. What is the abyss in this vision?

4. What is the smoke and what does it do?

5. What were the locusts forbidden from hurting, and allowed to hurt?

6. What does the power of a scorpion signify?

7. What is the significance of the following?

    iron breastplates -

    crowns like gold -

    hair like women -

    teeth like lions -

8. What does the "face of men" indicate in John's visions?

John's Revelation

9. What did the tormented ones seek in this picture?

10. What meaning might this carry?

11. What does *abaddon* and *apollyon* mean?

12. What does the number four signify?

13. What might the four great armies represent?

14. Which historic army ever achieved this size and magnitude?

15. Why do you think there are so many representations of battle? (i.e., swords, chariots, horses, armor, etc.)

16. What happened to the rest of mankind who were not killed in the plagues of the 6th trumpet?

17. Do you think these two trumpets sound today? Explain.

Revelation 10	little book which was open. He placed his right foot on the sea and his left on the land;
1. I saw another strong angel coming down out of heaven, clothed with a cloud; and the rainbow was upon his head, and his face was like the sun, and his feet like pillars of fire;	3. and he cried out with a loud voice, as when a lion roars; and when he had cried out, the seven peals of thunder uttered their voices.
2. and he had in his hand a	4. When the seven peals

THE REVELATION
chapter 10

INTRODUCTION:

Between the opening of the sixth and seventh seals in chapter 7, there was a brief period of silence, for reassurance. So also between the sixth and seventh trumpet, at the conclusion of the second woe, there is a brief vision given to show that the saints are not forgotten as these judgments come upon the earth and the preaching of truth also continues in spite of these things.

1. "Another strong angel" puts him in the class of angels mentioned in 5:2 and 18:21. This is not Jesus because as we have pointed out, He is never referred to as an angel, but angels are His messengers or servants. We see, however, in the similarities in appearance to Jesus (1:16; 1:15; 1:7; 4:3) that this angel to us represents the holiness of God at work. There is definitely a connection between this angel and Deity that sends him.

2. The fact that he set one foot "on the sea" and one foot "on the land" tells us his mission is *all*-inclusive, that is, it goes out to the entire world. This "little book" is open; therefore, John can understand it. It is not to be confused with the book of chapter 5 that *only* the Lamb could open. It is also a "little" book, rather than one requiring 7 seals and written on both sides because of all that it contains.

3. "A great voice, as a lion roareth" also points to the idea that His message goes to all creation. In the Old Testament, God warned the wicked (Jeremiah

of thunder had spoken, I was about to write; and I heard a voice from heaven saying, "Seal up the things which the seven peals of thunder have spoken and do not write them."
5. Then the angel whom I saw standing on the sea and on the land lifted up his right hand to heaven,
6. and swore by Him who lives forever and ever, WHO CREATED HEAVEN AND THE THINGS IN IT, AND THE EARTH AND THE THINGS IN IT, AND THE SEA AND THE THINGS IN IT, that there will be delay no longer,
7. but in the days of the voice of the seventh angel, when he is about to sound, then the mystery of God is finished, as He preached to His servants the prophets.

25:30), called His children (Hosea 11:10), warned of judgment (Joel 3:16), and caused much fear (Amos 3:8) by using a roar of warning. In answer or response to His cry, the seven peals of thunder "uttered their voices."

4. In 1:11, 19, John was told to write what he *saw*, not what he heard. This should help us to see that even though the plan and power of God is revealed to a certain extent, still there are things that we do not and will not know until they are given to us. We cannot know the words of the thunder here for John was told to "seal" it up.

5. This is usually the action accompanying an oath, Genesis 14:22; Deuteronomy 32:40; Ezekiel 20:5ff; Daniel 12:7.

6. The angel swears by the omnipotence and eternity of God. There shall be no more delay "before the fulfillment of the divine purpose regarding the fortunes of the church on earth."[34] He is speaking to those Christians about the things that were going to soon take place.

7. He refers to what is about to happen. When the seventh trumpet sounds, then the mystery of God is finished "as He preached to His servants the prophets." The mystery is God's plan for redemption, the gospel, the establishment of His kingdom and power.

> This mystery was God's plan for human redemption, conceived in His mind, after the counsel of His will, summed up in Christ (Ephesians 1:9-11; 3:8-11). It was revealed by the Holy Spirit (Ephesians 3:1-5; 1 Corinthians 2:6-13; 1 Peter 1:12), made known to the Gentiles (Colossians 1:26ff; 2:2), and preached by the apostles to all men (Ephesians 6:19; Colossians 4:3; 1 Peter 1:12).[35]

> 8. Then the voice which I heard from heaven, I heard again speaking with me, and saying, "Go, take the book which is open in the hand of the angel who stands on the sea and on the land."
> 9. So I went to the angel, telling him to give me the little book. And he *said to me, "Take it and eat it; it will make your stomach bitter, but in your mouth it will be sweet as honey."
> 10. I took the little book out of the angel's hand and ate it, and in my mouth it was sweet as honey; and when I had eaten it, my stomach was made bitter.

8. Same voice that told him to "seal up" the words of the thunder. A supposition here is that this small book is the word of God concerning the rest of the visions revealed to us in chapters 11-22. John is told to get the book, eat the book, and then prophesy.

9. To understand what the book is here, we need to read Ezekiel 2:8-3:33; 14; Jeremiah 15:16ff; and Psalm 119:103. The scroll is the word of God. To our understanding at first it is sweet as honey, but there is a bitter side to it that comes after we ingest it into our being. Just like Ezekiel, John is given a message with two aspects—the reassuring aspect of not being forgotten by the God of providence and the aspect of wrath and judgment that causes so much suffering to those who reject God. Truly God's word is both sweet and bitter.

10. The results were as he was told. The reception of God's word is sweet, but there is always an inner bitterness or bitterness of spirit because of the condemnation of sinners and proclamation of God's intended judgment against wicked men and evil nations. This scroll is not the gospel because the scroll that was sealed in the hand of God on the throne was the plan of God, and that is the Good News. Again, this book is probably God's word concerning the rest of the visions that are revealed in chapters 11-22. This is how it ties in with verse 11. The knowledge of the revelation is sweet, but the facts are bitter when one considers the wrath of God and loss of immortal souls.

We might note that it is not just the reception of prophecy that is sweet and bitter; it is the reception of God's word in general. One who rejoices in the blessing of grace in our age must also face the trials, rejection, and persecution that will come with naming the name of Christ. To keep the hope of eternal reward one must be willing to suffer through difficulties and do right no matter what the world is doing around us. Serving the Lord Jesus will mean turning away from personal gain. Naming the Lord as one's elder brother may mean giving up one's physical family. Indeed, the gospel is both sweet and bitter and

11. And they *said to me, "You must prophesy again con-	cerning many peoples and nations and tongues and kings."

should be presented to a lost world in its completeness, always understanding that the sweet WILL outweigh the bitter in the end.

11. "Again" implies doing over what has already been done. There is going to be a deeper significance revealed to John as he speaks once again in the second half of the book of world-forces and righteousness in battle.

QUESTIONS ON CHAPTER 10

1. What might this "little book" represent?

2. What similarities are there between this angel and Jesus Christ?

3. The similarities in appearance between this angel and Christ imply what?

4. What may be indicated by his loud voice "as when a lion roars"?

5. Where were the feet of the mighty angel?

6. What is meant by the thunderous voices being "sealed up"?

7. How is the book both sweet and bitter?

8. When will the mystery of God be finished?

9. How did the little book taste?

10. What is the mystery of God?

11. What did it mean to "eat" the book?

12. What was John to do after he ate the book?

13. Is there something here for us today to consider deeply?

> **Revelation 11**
>
> 1. Then there was given me a measuring rod like a staff; and someone said, "Get up and measure the temple of God and the altar, and those who worship in it. 2. "Leave out the court which is outside the temple and do not measure it, for it has been given

THE REVELATION
chapter 11

INTRODUCTION:

This chapter seems to have given more writers more trouble in understanding than any of the others. I will not enter into all the different ideas that have been put forth concerning this vision. I will mention the one that I believe fits the scriptures and the pictures given here to tell us the story. I will also mention one other most popular idea because it has some merit, even though it seems to me not to fit the vision as closely as it should.

1. The "reed" or "measuring rod" (NASB) is the word of God. John 12:48 tells us the "word" will judge (measure) us on that last day. We must always "measure up" to what God requires. The "temple of God" is the church, God's dwelling place among men (1 Corinthians 3:16-17; 2 Corinthians 6:16; Ephesians 2:21) made of living stones, 1 Peter 2:5. The Greek word for temple here is *naos* or sanctuary, not *hieron* or temple. The temple here or sanctuary would be the Old Testament tabernacle with its one court and it is possible that this is what stands before John rather than the temple of Herod with all its courts and porches. This is understandable since the tabernacle was a shadow of the church. The altar is the golden altar where the prayers of saints are offered to God, 8:3. The worshippers in the temples are the 144,000 (7:4), the true Israel of God, the church on earth. All must measure up to the word of God. Note: Ezekiel 42:20; 22:26; 44:23; and Zechariah 2:5. We are caused to think that when something is "measured" by God, it is separated from the common or profane, thus is measured the temple, the altar, and the people. This blends well with the picture of God's church, separated from the world by His word.

> to the nations; and they will tread under foot the holy city for forty-two months.
>
> 3. "And I will grant authority to my two witnesses, and they will prophesy for twelve hundred and

2. Though the temple is measured, set apart, or protected, the "court that is outside the temple" is not so blessed. It is given to be trodden underfoot along with "the Holy City." There are two views that are both in harmony with Scriptures to explain the court outside the temple:

a) The measured temple is the inner or spiritual life of the church that is protected by God from harm. The outside court is the physical life of Christians which God has *not* promised to keep from being trampled underfoot and sacrificed. This view has some support in the next idea, that the Holy City is to be tread underfoot for 42 months.

b) The second popular idea is that the temple represents those who are faithful to God and separated from the world while the outer court is those who go back into the world and are unfaithful. It perhaps would include those who succumb to the doctrines of Balaam, Jezebel, the Nicolaitans, lukewarmness, and also those who had lost their first love. The problem with this idea is that it hands the lukewarm compromisers over to persecution while the faithful are protected. The facts say otherwise. It is the faithful who were persecuted while the compromisers often walked away scott-free.

I prefer the first idea. The Holy City is not Jerusalem as is thought by many, but instead is the church. In Revelation when the Holy City is spoken of, it is the "*new* Jerusalem" (21:2, 10), the city in which saints have a part (22:19), and the "beloved city," 20:9. In Revelation when "Jerusalem" is spoken of, it is the heavenly kingdom, 21:2, 10; 3:12. Thus, the Holy City is our spiritual Jerusalem, the church glorified in God's sight. The vision seems to say that though the faithful are numbered, measured, set apart, and protected by the Lord as well as their worship, nevertheless, the church is going to be abused, despised, and trampled. This would harmonize with other messages we have seen already in the book. Their spiritual life was protected and could not be harmed, but their physical lives were being handed over for a time.

Forty-two months and 1260 days are the same time. This is 3 1/2 years. It is half of seven (perfect, complete); therefore, this is a time of trouble, trial, and persecution. Not a literal 3 1/2 years, but a certain measured amount of time filled with trouble and persecution. We will go deeper into the times here in 13:5; Daniel 7:25; 12:7

> sixty days, clothed in sackcloth." 4. These are the two olive trees and the two lampstands that stand before the Lord of the earth. 5. And if anyone wants to harm them, fire flows out of their mouth and devours their enemies; so if anyone wants to harm them, he must be killed in this way. 6. These have the power to shut up the sky, so that rain will not fall during the days of their prophesying; and they have power over the waters to turn them into blood, and to strike the earth with every plague, as often as they desire.

3. This is the same period of time, a full time of trial and persecution. Sackcloth represents mourning because of the death and persecution the church had to face. Some believe these witnesses are the Old and New Testaments, which works out pretty well until we come to where they died and were resurrected. Just about everyone who takes this position goes with the idea of the resurrection being the reformation of the 16th century. I have trouble accepting the idea that the doctrines taught by the reformers like Luther, Calvin, Zwingli, and others were a resurrection of Bible truth. Though they were closer to the truth, the question comes down through history: Were they close enough? It seems more in harmony to say the witnesses are the apostles and prophets of the first century, those with the power of inspiration in teaching.

4. This picture comes from Zechariah 4. The lampstands hold up the light of God's word and the olive trees provide a continuous flow of oil for the lamps. In Zechariah 4, the picture of the lamps being fed oil continuously is a commendation of Joshua and Zerubbabel in their faithful leadership of God's people. The apostles and prophets were the foundation for the church on earth (Ephesians 2:20); thus, they held up the light, and it was from them that the word proceeded according to the guidance of the Holy Spirit.

5-6. These verses are in clear reference to the fire that consumed the enemies of Elijah (2 Kings 1:10-14), the power of Elijah to shut the heavens (1 Kings 17:1; 18:1-45), the power of Moses to turn water to blood (Exodus 7:20ff), and also the plagues. It is hard to avoid the similarities to God's servants in the Old Testament and the apostles and prophets serving God in the New Testament. These signs and wonders simply represent the miraculous powers of these men in the first century and the fact that as long as they had this job to do, no one was able to defeat them. Of course, most of this was in the recent past for these Christians in the last few years of the first century. What assurance could this vision be for them then? Only to remind them that when God had something to accomplish, nothing could stop His witnesses.

> 7. When they have finished their testimony, the beast that comes up out of the abyss will make war with them, and overcome them and kill them.
> 8. And their dead bodies will lie in the street of the great city which mystically is called Sodom and Egypt, where also their Lord was crucified.
> 9. Those from the peoples and tribes and tongues and nations will look at their dead bodies for three and a half days, and will not permit their dead bodies to be laid in a tomb.

7. There is a time, however, when the witnesses' job will be completed. At that time "the beast" will kill them. This is the first mention of "the beast." We will learn more of him later in chapter 13. Whether he is Satan or a puppet of Satan's, it matters not. He comes from the abyss, where the smoke and locusts proceeded from; therefore, he is as surely identified with evil as the strong angel with the divine rainbow was identified with Deity. He makes war against God's witnesses. Although the apostles and inspired teachers were driven from place to place, they were not overcome until their job was done. During the first century, the gospel was preached "in all creation under heaven" (Colossians 1:23), a magnificent accomplishment that we cannot seem to imitate even with the help of speedy transportation, instant communication, and electronic mass media. By the time the beast overcame the witnesses, their job was done.

8. Though the witnesses are dead, they are not forgotten. They are in open sight so they cannot be forgotten. "The great city" here is the world pictured as a city. It is called "Sodom" because of its immorality and "Egypt" because it holds people in bondage or captivity like the Israelites were held for 430 years. Whenever men serve sin they are in bondage to sin. They are slaves to whatever they present themselves, even if that is to sin, leading to death, Romans 6:16. This city is where Jesus was crucified because He was taken outside God's city, Jerusalem; therefore, He was completely under the world's power (physically, not spiritually).

9-10. This merry making continues for 3 1/2 days. Again, we see the number representing a time of trouble. This time the trouble seems to be on the other side, however. Though the world rejoices because it believes the conscience-burning power of the word is stopped, yet it is bothered and troubled. Making merry and giving gifts does not completely erase the witness that was given because their bodies are still there as a reminder in plain sight. They cannot be forgotten. This will always be the case with those who defy God's word. Even though their victory seems so sure, the dead bodies are plain to see; there is something unsettling that cannot be overcome. In this picture the evidence of their success

John's Revelation

> 10. And those who dwell on the earth will rejoice over them and celebrate; and they will send gifts to one another, because these two prophets tormented those who dwell on the earth.
> 11. But after the three and a half days, the breath of life from God came into them, and they stood on their feet; and great fear fell upon those who were watching them.
> 12. And they heard a loud voice from heaven saying to them, "Come up here." Then they went up into heaven in the cloud, and their enemies watched them.
> 13. And in that hour there was

(the dead bodies) are the very reminders of the words that tormented them. The only irony that is greater than this is the irony seen in the next few verses. That is the fact that their victory is not victory at all. By the power of resurrection, the witnesses continue to live. How hollow is the hope that expects to succeed by defeating Christ's purpose.

11-12. This nagging guilt and fear is more fully realized when after a certain time the witnesses receive life again, stand, and go up to heaven in a cloud at the command of a "loud voice from heaven" while their enemies watch. We have a picture of Jesus Christ's apostles and prophets (inspired teachers) persecuted and hounded yet not overcome until the gospel goes into all creation. At that time they are slaughtered and the power of the enemy rejoices at what he (they) considers a great victory. Yet their victory is hollow and empty because even at the moment of their greatest triumph, they have not really done anything—the witness is still with them. Almost immediately the cause that was preached, or the spirit of Christ arises once again and testimony continues (in Christians and the church) so that we see there really was no death, no end, no victory at all over the testimony and word of God. The early Christians, if they read this vision in faith, must surely have wept to see the power of God and how it would work in their culture. They simply could not be defeated!

13. All seven cities in the beginning of this book were quite familiar with the power of earthquakes, several of them having been destroyed and rebuilt because of the same. Earthquakes are also used in Scripture as a sign of God's power (Isaiah 9:5ff; Jeremiah 10:10; Job 9:4-6; Psalm 97:3ff; Isaiah 24:18ff) and judgment. The city here again is the world. A fourth part falling illustrates a partial judgment, and seven thousand being a full, complete number shows us the wisdom and knowledge, as well as the restraint of God behind this judgment. "The rest" giving glory to God does not imply conversion but simply recognition due to terror. The picture here is similar to national catastrophes such as September 11, when people cry out for God's blessing and recognize His work in some

> a great earthquake, and a tenth of the city fell; seven thousand people were killed in the earthquake, and the rest were terrified and gave glory to the God of heaven.
> 14. The second woe is past; behold, the third woe is coming quickly.
> 15. Then the seventh angel sounded; and there were loud voices in heaven, saying, "The kingdom of the world has become the kingdom of our Lord and of His Christ; and He will reign forever and ever."
> 16. And the twenty-four elders, who sit on their thrones before God, fell on their faces and worshiped God,
> 17. saying, "We give You thanks, O Lord God, the Almighty, who are and who were, because You have taken Your great power and have begun to reign.
> 18. "And the nations were enraged, and Your wrath came, and the time came for the dead to be judged, and the time to reward

shallow fashion, but fail to bring lasting change or repentance into their lives. They give glory in their terror, but it is not a life changing conversion. When the terror is over they go back to their evil ways.

14. This is an introduction to the third woe, a division in the chapter, and a change of scene.

> Your bond-servants the prophets and the saints and those who fear Your name, the small and the great, and to destroy those who destroy the earth."
> 19. And the temple of God which is in heaven was opened; and the ark of His covenant appeared in His temple, and there were flashes of lightning and sounds and peals of thunder and an earthquake and a great hailstorm.

15. Unlike the silence after the opening of the 7 seals, here we have loud voices and a song or chant of victory. Through Christ and His witnesses, this victory has been accomplished. Now Jesus is on His throne and ruling. He rules over His kingdom and He rules over the world as a whole. This kingdom has no end.

16. For 24 elders see comments on 4:4.

17-18. Thanks is given to God for beginning to reign (read Psalm 2 and Daniel 7) in the kingdom of prophecy. This kingdom's rule started in spite of the desires of worldly people. Jesus overcame everything they did to stop Him (death) and took His throne. This is the end of the third section, and it seems we have before us a view of the judgment day once again. This is in harmony with the idea that each of the 7 sections tells the story of the kingdom from beginning to eternity.

19. In the Old Testament, the glory of God's presence dwelt above the ark of the covenant in the Holy of Holies, Exodus 25:22; 2 Kings 19:15. This was evidence that God was with them and that He would keep His covenant with them. So it is that the ark is here exposed to all as a sign that God will remember His covenants and keep them, and it is further emphasized by great sounds and manifestations of power.

This is the end of the third section and the end of the first half (the struggle on earth, see INTRODUCTION, OUTLINE OF THE APOCALYPSE, p. 12). We have seen Christ take His throne as a Lamb that was slain, yet lived…as a leader of a great multitude…and now as King of Kings in heaven and over all the earth. We have seen Him active among His people. We have seen persecution come upon the saints, prayers and supplications offered, and the answer to those prayers in the form of partial judgments upon a wicked society and evil world. We have seen victory promised to those who will overcome, resist, and stand firm, even unto death.

We will now go even deeper into the spiritual background of this great struggle and find out what is behind these physical aspects that we can see.

QUESTIONS ON CHAPTER 11

1. What does it mean in verse 1 to measure something?

2. What are the temple and the courtyard?

3. What was John told to measure?

4. Who are the two witnesses?

5. What reminder of Elijah do we have in this chapter?

6. What reminder of Moses do we have in this chapter?

7. What does the picture of the lamps and olive trees signify?

8. What is the great city indicative of?

9. Why is the city called Sodom?

10. Why is the city called Egypt?

John's Revelation

11. When were they "allowed" to be killed?

12. What did the kingdom of the world become?

13. How long did witnesses prophesy?

14. Is this amount of time mentioned elsewhere?

15. What does this time figure mean?

16. What did the elders do at the sounding of the 7th trumpet?

17. What did the remnant do when 7,000 were slain?

18. What was seen in the temple of God?

From Beneath the Altar

Revelation 12	
1. A great sign appeared in heaven: a woman clothed with the sun, and the moon under her feet, and on her head a crown of twelve stars;	2. and she was with child; and she *cried out, being in labor and in pain to give birth.

THE REVELATION
chapter 12
Section II, 4 (see page 12)

INTRODUCTION:

Although chapter 12 is the beginning of new symbols and pageantry in the Revelation letter, the same problems and issues are dealt with, but from different aspects. Summers writes, 'The characters here are essentially the same; the conflict is the same but is presented under a different aspect; the outcome is the same as has been indicated in the beginning.' (REVELATION, A MESSAGE FROM PATMOS by Weldon E. Warnock, page 69.)

1. This sign or vision is seen from heaven's standpoint. This woman is not in heaven, she is in the vision. She is clothed in the total or complete light of God (sun, moon, stars). Since God's word is light, she has available to her the complete, revealed will of God. She is not the Jewish nation, the virgin Mary, nor the church in its New Testament sense. The woman is the "remnant" (daughter of Zion) or faithful few from the apostate Israelite nation. This true Israel also comes to include spiritual Israel or *all* of God's people *after* the man-child is born. Hebrews 11:40 illustrates how we (old and new covenant believers) are one group before God, shown here as the woman. Micah 4:10; 5:2ff and Isaiah 6:7ff bear this out. The crown of stars that she wears is the *stephanos* or victory crown.

2. The promise and hope of God had been in the womb of the faithful since Genesis 3:15. The remnant (woman) is in travail (pregnant, birth pangs), and will bring forth the Messiah and a nation would come from Him. The faithful few have cried out for a Redeemer down through the centuries. We also note that God's people have been involved with a spiritual struggle all down through history.

3. Then another sign appeared in heaven: and behold, a great red dragon having seven heads and ten horns, and on his heads *were* seven diadems.	a third of the stars of heaven and threw them to the earth. And the dragon stood before the woman who was about to give birth, so that when she gave birth he might devour her child.
4. And his tail *swept away	

3-4. Once again, the dragon is not in heaven, but is in the vision. In v. 9, he is identified as Satan. Seven is the complete or full number so "seven heads" represents fullness of intelligence or craft. Ten is the "power" number so "Ten horns" represent great power within his realm of operation. "Red" perhaps signifies violence, bloodshed, and the martyrdom of the saints. "Diadems" imply royalty crowns, not to be confused with the victory crown that Christ wears. These crowns indicate ruling power to some degree. Satan does indeed rule to a certain extent as he is allowed. Paul even referred to him as the god of this world and the prince of the power of the air. There are three main ideas as to his tail sweeping away a third of the stars:

- a) The verse emphasizes the power, might, and fury of the dragon as his tail sweeps away one third of the stars.

- b) The scene points to his time of rebellion against God when he led many angels to follow him and all were swept down, 2 Peter 2:4; Jude 6.

- c) The scene is parallel to Daniel 8:10 and stars represent the host of God, faithful men and leaders that Satan causes to fall.

With all three the great influence and power of the devil is stressed and this may be all that is intended. Number one seems to represent this idea best. The dragon has stood ready to devour the child and ruin God's plan from the very beginning. This brings to mind the account of Pharaoh and the Israelite oppression in Egypt (Exodus 1:15-19) as well as Herod in the New Testament and his slaughter of the babies. Satan thought to spoil the scheme of God by killing Abel, turning the world wicked, having it destroyed by a flood, leading the chosen nation Israel to sin and thus reject God, corrupt the seed of David on the throne of Israel, having Christ found by the wise men, reported to Herod and killed, and many other times throughout the Scripture and probably not a few that aren't recorded. The devil is devoted to his own cause if nothing else. He has always desired the destruction of the one who was to come, either directly (death on the cross) or indirectly (corruption of the seed).

John's Revelation

> 5. And she gave birth to a son, a male *child*, who is to rule all the nations with a rod of iron; and her child was caught up to God and to His throne.
> 6. Then the woman fled into the wilderness where she *had a place prepared by God, so that there she would be nourished for one thousand two hundred and sixty days.
> 7. And there was war in heaven, Michael and his angels waging war with the dragon. The dragon and his angels waged war,

5. In this verse is summed up the whole time from the birth of Christ to His ascension and glorification on His throne at the right hand of the Majesty. This obviously has reference to Psalm 2:6-9; Psalm 45:6; and Hebrews 1:8. The message to Christians was, if Satan could not harm Christ when He was at His weakest (in the flesh), what threat is he now? He couldn't touch Him while a babe, before he became a king. How could he hope to overcome Him on His throne?

6. The wilderness is where Moses fled, where Israel went, and where Elijah fled from Jezebel. Mary and Joseph fled into Egypt and Paul went to Arabia. The wilderness is where God's people are disciplined and protected. One thousand two hundred and sixty days = time, times, and half a time = 3 1/2 years. This is that number representing trouble and trial. This must be a certain period of trial, trouble, or uncertainty (half of 7, completeness, whole) for the faithful. Protected, but frightened perhaps? For a certain time God watched over the church, sheltered it, and nourished it.

7-8. The scene changes. Remember, this war is not in heaven. This is a vision of a war in heaven. If we admit that the first and last parts of this chapter are symbolic as all do, then we must also admit that this war is symbolic. Too many take this literally to show how Satan was cast out of heaven. This would be out of thought and context. The spiritual truth that we are shown here is that the dragon is no longer a furious, ferocious beast that sweeps the stars from the sky with his tail and threatens God's plan at every turning. He is a defeated foe, cast down to the earth and down from a high-handed control of men.

> Michael, whose name means, 'Who is like God?' stands as the dragon's opponent. He is named 3 times in the book of Daniel as 'one of the chief princes' (10:13), the 'prince of Israel' (10:21), and the 'great prince' (12:1) who stood for the people against their enemies, Persia and Greece. He is called the 'archangel' who contended with the devil over the body of Moses (Jude 9) and possibly the archangel of 1 Thessalonians 4:16.[36]

> 8. and they were not strong enough, and there was no longer a place found for them in heaven.
> 9. And the great dragon was thrown down, the serpent of old who is called the devil and Satan, who deceives the whole world; he was thrown down to the earth, and his angels were thrown down with him.
> 10. Then I heard a loud voice in heaven, saying, "Now the salvation, and the power, and the kingdom of our God and the authority of His Christ have come, for the accuser of our brethren has been thrown down, he who accuses them before our God day and night.

The picture of this vision is that after being defeated on earth in his plans to devour the man-child, Satan rushes to heaven after Him and is soundly whipped, not even by Jesus, but by one of His angels. Satan can't win, no way, no how!

9. The term serpent points to this one as being also the one in Eden, Genesis 3. The term devil (*diabolos*) means accuser or slanderer. It should only be used of Satan, not demons (as in KJV) because there is only one devil. The term Satan (*satanas*) means adversary, enemy, antagonist, etc. "There are three main views of this war:

   a) The vision represents the primeval war between Satan and God (out of context with the thoughts of the book).

   b) There was an actual war in which Satan attempted to invade heaven that he might defeat the man-child, but Satan was repulsed and cast down to earth.

   c) The vision symbolizes a spiritual warfare, which had been going on since the beginning, but reaches its climax in Christ's victory over Satan.

   The third position is more defensible by Scripture."[37] However, number two fits well if we can keep in mind that this is a vision, *not* recorded historical fact. We need to point out that in spite of its popularity with sensationalist preachers, the war is not what is being communicated. Instead the war is meant to communicate something itself.

10. Near the end of Jesus' stay on earth, He stated that Satan's time had come to be cast out (John 12:31) and explained how He could be the one to do it, John 14:30; 16:11. After His resurrection and victory over Satan, He stated that to Him was given "all authority," Matthew 28:18. Hebrews 2:14 also points out that by

John's Revelation

> 11. "And they overcame him because of the blood of the Lamb and because of the word of their testimony, and they did not love their life even when faced with death.
> 12. "For this reason, rejoice, O heavens and you who dwell in them. Woe to the earth and the sea, because the devil has come down to you, having great wrath, knowing that he has *only* a short time."
> 13. And when the dragon saw that he was thrown down to the earth, he persecuted the woman who gave birth to the male *child*.

His life and death, Jesus would bring Satan to naught. During His ministry, He talked of "binding the strong man," Luke 11:21ff; Matthew 12:29. Satan was bound and cast down by the truth that Jesus taught. He will remain bound so long as that same truth is taught, as we shall learn more of later in the book.

11. "They" refers back to "brethren" in verse 10. The brethren overcame Satan:

a) Because of the sacrifice of Christ. The victory that was Christ's is shared in by all those that call on His name in obedience.

b) Because they held fast to the faithful word. They would not forsake the testimony they had given due to their faith.

c) Because they had the martyr spirit. Whether they actually had to die or not, they were ready to sacrifice their lives for the cause.

This is also how we overcome Satan, if we are to do it at all. With the above three powerful forces in our life, Satan is helpless before us.

12. Although all those in heaven rejoice at the casting down of Satan, his anger is now going to be vented on the earth and sea (unregenerate world, society, etc.). The "short time" is a short time until the devil is bound and thrown into the abyss. This short time is equal to the "little time" of the martyrs (6:11), because when Satan is cast down, bound, then these martyrs would be raised up to sit on thrones with Christ. It is a limited time, a controlled time of persecution.

13. After the interruption of verses 7-12, the plight of the woman, God's faithful remnant, is resumed. We have seen Satan's defeat, Christ taking His promised authority, and the reasons for a Christian's overcoming power. Here we see Satan persecuting the church (woman) since the child was beyond his power, John 15:20.

> 14. But the two wings of the great eagle were given to the woman, so that she could fly into the wilderness to her place, where she *was nourished for a time and times and half a time, from the presence of the serpent.
> 15. And the serpent poured water like a river out of his mouth after the woman, so that he might cause her to be swept away with the flood.
> 16. But the earth helped the woman, and the earth opened its mouth and drank up the river which the dragon poured out of his mouth.

Hal Lindsey made the woman "Israel" and since the eagle is America's symbol, he has this passage implying an airlift of Israel by the U.S. 6th fleet in the Mediterranean...foolishness.

14. This vision seems to be a more detailed recounting of v. 6. The eagle is the natural enemy of the serpent. In the Old Testament, eagles' wings were a symbol of guidance, protection, safety, and strength, Exodus 19:4; Deuteronomy 32:11; Psalm 36:7; Isaiah 40:31. Time, times, and half a time = 1,260 days = 42 months = 3 1/2 years = half of 7. Seven is complete, whole, good, and safe; therefore, 3 1/2 would be a time of trouble, trial, uncertainty, persecution, etc. The serpent could not defeat the early church as it was nurtured and protected by God, but he gave it his best effort.

15. Floods are pictured as persecutions, troubles, and trials, Isaiah 8:4-8; 43:2; Psalm 144:7; Psalm 32:6. This flood is every evil thing Satan has ever used to try to harm the church or lead it astray: "delusions in the form of lies, false impressions of invincible power, false religious teaching, false philosophies, false charges and malicious reports intended to destroy the church."[38] Every evil thing that one might imagine (and a few more) pours out of the dragon's mouth in an effort to harm the faithful.

16. The influence of the word of God is such that there is some semblance of goodness even in the unregenerate world. Though not having the love or conviction to be in the church, the world still respects and helps those who are true believers at times, now and then. Therefore, here in this time we have the world defending the church to a certain extent. The time will come when not even this small bit of good will stop the evil flood that pours forth, but here Satan is defeated again through providential influence.

17. Satan has been defeated in his attack upon the man-child on earth, i.e., Jesus

> 17. So the dragon was enraged with the woman, and went off to make war with the rest of her children, who keep the commandments of God and hold to the testimony of Jesus.

in the flesh. He is defeated again as he seeks to destroy Him in heaven in this vision. He is defeated a third time as he turns his attention upon the church as a whole. He cannot win—that is the lesson of this chapter. The woman who is clothed in celestial light with the crown of victory on her brow is watched over and cared for. She may have struggles, uncertainties, and frightening times, but she is victorious, and the devil is the loser. "The rest of her offspring" are the saints individually. Jesus was just the "firstborn among many brethren," Romans 8:29. Not able to destroy the church as a whole, consisting of the faithful remnant and new believers, the devil went off to war with the saints individually. He even now attacks the individual. He will try to develop and use some allies in the vision to come, but that will do him no good either. He is a loser, and it was time for Christians to see that then, and it is time for Christians to start living that fact now!

QUESTIONS ON CHAPTER 12

1. What was the woman clothed in?

2. What would this mean?

3. Define the *stephanos*.

4. Why did the woman cry with pain?

5. Why was the dragon before the woman?

6. Who is the male child?

7. What is the difference between the "crown" of verse 1 and the "diadems" of verse 3?

8. Explain what 7 heads would signify.

    a. 10 horns -

    b. red color -

    c. sweeping tail -

9. What is this "wilderness" area?

10. What does the number 3 1/2 signify?

11. When did this war in heaven take place?

12. Where did Satan turn his wrath after failing with the man-child?

13. What are three terms given here for the dragon?

14. By what terms do we know Michael?

15. What forces are engaged in battle?

16. Because of what were they able to overcome the dragon?

17. When overcome, what did the dragon do?

18. Describe the rest of the woman's offspring.

19. What are two descriptions of the time the woman was in the wilderness?

> **Revelation 13**
>
> 1. And the dragon stood on the sand of the seashore. Then I saw a beast coming up out of the sea, having ten horns and seven heads, and on his horns *were* ten diadems, and on his heads *were* blasphemous names.

THE REVELATION
chapter 13

INTRODUCTION:

Daniel chapter 7 will be of some help in understanding this chapter. Please read that chapter first.

1. If you are reading in the KJV, please note: It is "He stood on the sand..." rather than "I stood on the sand...." Other translations point this out clearly. It is not so important where John stood, but the dragon gathered his helpers from the sea and earth; therefore, we see "He stood on the sand of the sea" between sea and earth. The sea is the whole of human society, including its tides and waves of war, violence, hatred, upheaval, nations rising and falling, etc. Revelation 17:15 would make this clear to us, as well as...

> Isaiah 17:12 - heathen nations like the sea.
> Isaiah 57:20ff; Jeremiah 49:23 - wicked are like the sea.
> Isaiah 60:5 - abundance of the sea like the wealth of nations.
> Jeremiah 51:13 - Babylon ruled over "many waters" i.e., many peoples.
> Jeremiah 51:42 - nations covered Babylon like sea and waves.
> Jeremiah 51:55ff - destroyer of Babylon described by roaring waves.
> Ezekiel 26:3 - many nations like the sea and waves against Tyre.
> Psalm 65:7 - tumult of peoples (nations) like roaring of the sea.

Daniel 7:17 states that the four beasts were four kingdoms that came out of the earth. Here, however, we are not seeing specific kingdoms, but a compilation of all those characteristics in one kingdom or beast. The idea of a beast presents a vision of brute force and ferocious power. As far as I can tell, the number ten represents completeness or power in a *certain realm* or given area. (Not to be

2. And the beast which I saw was like a leopard, and his feet were like *those* of a bear, and his mouth like the mouth of a lion.	And the dragon gave him his power and his throne and great authority.

confused with seven, which is perfection or completeness in *every realm.*) Ten horns would be a completeness or fullness of power (within his given realm) while seven heads would be a fullness of wisdom or intelligence, even beyond his own sphere. The dragon (12:3) had seven heads and ten horns with seven diadems on his heads. This beast has seven heads and ten horns with ten diadems on his horns. This close resemblance could very well show us that he possesses the characteristics of Satan. His wisdom and intelligence is directed against God while his power is given to him through the authority of one greater. Prominently placed, for all to see, upon his heads were the names that identified his total disrespect and disregard for God.

The theme of this vision actually began in 12:17 when the dragon, enraged, went off to make war with the offspring of the woman. What we will see here was how that was accomplished. This explanation of spiritual things would have been important for those early Christians to see. It is also a valuable tool for building our faith and helping us to remain strong during events that seem to pass our understanding.

2. Notice in Daniel 7:3-12 the lion, leopard, and the bear. There is also a fourth beast. Daniel 7:17 tells us that they are kings or kingdoms (it makes no difference because one represents the other). In verse 12, "their dominion was taken away, yet their lives were prolonged." Each kingdom fell before the next (Babylonian to Medo-Persian to Macedonian to Roman), yet the spirit of that conquering power lived on in the next kingdom. I believe the fourth beast in Daniel 7 is the same beast in Revelation 13 who came up out of the sea. He is a combination of all the kingdoms before him. He was to the early Christians, persecuting Rome. He is to us today, a principle. He represents to us today *any* kingdom, government, or ruling power that Satan manipulates as his helper.

> As God had given the Lamb His power, throne and authority by which to carry out His purpose, so Satan gives the beast his power, throne, and authority by which to wage his war. The divine rule has its diabolical counterpart in the dragon and misdirected political power which serves as the dragon's vice regent.[39]

> 3. *I saw* one of his heads as if it had been slain, and his fatal wound was healed. And the whole earth was amazed *and followed* after the beast;

3. There are several main views that could explain the head with the wound that was healed. They are...

   a) The slain head represents Nero who was slain. This would fit nicely *if* the beast were, in fact, Rome. The healing of the fatal wound could perhaps be when Domitian came to power (A.D. 81-96). He is referred to frequently by commentators as a reincarnation of the persecuting spirit of Nero.

   b) The fatal wound to the head is the wound given to Satan by the resurrection, ascension, and glorification of Jesus Christ.

   c) The fatal wound represents a lessening of Satan's power when he was cast out of heaven by Michael and his angel army, 12:7-12.

The problem with a) is that it limits the beast to a specific earthly power. This idea *may* be right *if* we are correct about the date of the book's writing and *if* we are correct about the focus of the message (i.e., Rome's persecution, not the Jews or anybody else). Most of the scholars who subscribe to Nero being the slain head also make Domitian the "fatal wound" healed. Though this is a popular viewpoint, I'm not sure that history factually supports Domitian's persecution as being anywhere near comparable to Nero's. More accurate reports are that Domitian directed most of his bloody activities toward family members and those he thought threatened his power on the throne rather than toward the Christians. One evidence of this would be the fact that John was exiled rather than just being executed as we would expect from one with such a bloody reputation.

The problem with b) and c) is that this beast *is not* Satan, but only represents him, being given his authority. Thus it does not necessarily follow that since the beast is wounded, Satan is hurt. There is also this to consider...Did Satan ever completely recover from b) and c), i.e., Christ's wounding him or his loss of place in heaven? I think not! c) is also part of the *vision* of John. We do not know that this literally took place and can therefore be referred to in a figurative way in another vision. a) seems to be the "lesser of 3 evils" so to speak.

The difficulty really seems to lie in explaining the fatal wound that heals. It would seem to represent at first consideration the slaying of Nero. If the beast

4. they worshiped the dragon because he gave his authority to the beast; and they worshiped the beast, saying, "Who is like the beast, and who is able to wage war with him?"	5. There was given to him a mouth speaking arrogant words and blasphemies, and authority to act for forty-two months was given to him.

were Rome, specifically the government of Rome, then this wound unto death would have been some kind of great shock to the empire. In a wider view of the empire, however, it could just as easily represent *all* the slain emperors of that day (3 or 4 in a decade) or even the civil wars and rebellions that were coming with greater frequency all across the Roman world of that day. There's really nothing to limit our thinking just to Nero. Any or all of the above could be likened to a death blow to this great world power which they not only survived but healed, creating respect and even awe in the world at large that this "beast" could live through such a problem. It is much the same today when a great leader of a powerful nation is killed. We are always amazed when the nation picks itself up and continues its course. It would seem wise not to focus on any one situation. Rome fighting against God can be representative to us of any power fighting against God.

Because of the beast regaining his full strength and power, the world in general is amazed, respects, and follows after the beast.

4. In worshipping authority, one worships where that authority comes from. In worshipping the authority and power of the beast, the people are, in fact, worshipping the dragon because that is where his power proceeded from. Praise, which should be only for God, is given up to the beast. We can see all this in the emperor worship of Rome. We can also see a great deal of confidence placed wrongly in the Roman Empire. "Who can make war with him?" indeed. God can and did make war with this world power that persecuted His people and that power was defeated. Misplaced patriotism and confidence in the war-making technologies of men is a danger that many are falling prey to today. These principles are timeless. We should learn the lesson from history that when God determines a nation to fall, it will fall!

5. Not only was worship wrongfully directed to the beast, but also he took it upon himself to make claims that were blasphemies and lies. He accepted and perhaps commanded the worship to continue. Read Daniel 7:8, 20. Notice, however, that this "mouth speaking arrogant words" was "given to him." Not even this beast takes power to himself but is "given" authority. No one acts unless God allows it. He only has authority for "forty-two" months. This length of time

6. And he opened his mouth in blasphemies against God, to blaspheme His name and His tabernacle, *that is*, those who dwell in heaven. 7. It was also given to him	to make war with the saints and to overcome them, and authority over every tribe and people and tongue and nation was given to him.

has been previously introduced and commented on. The Holy City is trampled 42 months (11:2), the witnesses prophesied 1,260 days (11:3), the woman was protected in the wilderness 1,260 days (12:6), and she would be nourished for time, times, and half a time, 12:14. These are all the same length of time. They all happen simultaneously, and they are all *not* to be taken literally. They are equal...3 1/2 years. Three and a half, being half of seven, represents a certain measured time of trouble and trial. This time seems to be the time the church would be persecuted and harassed. This time is mentioned (3 1/2) so that the Christians would know that there *would* be an end to this persecution. It would not continue forever.

6. Not only does he wear blasphemous names on his head, but also this beast opens his mouth against God, His holy name, and His church...even those who dwell in heaven.

7. From this verse and verse five we see four things given to the beast...

    a) a mouth, speaking arrogant words and blasphemies,
    b) authority, to continue forty-two months,
    c) authority, to make war with and overcome the saints,
    d) authority, over every tribe, people, tongue, and nation.

Read once again Daniel 7:8, 20ff.

God allows this momentary victory. Remember, the beast has authority for only 42 months, or rather a certain measured time (however long or short it may be). This seems to imply the "little horn" in Daniel 7 is the persecuting element of Rome. This would continue for a time until judgment was rendered on behalf of the saints when the time came for them to possess the kingdom. This is what happened. As related in Daniel two, in some way the kingdom of God broke down the kingdom of Rome. This was a judgment planned and executed by God. The beast coming to an end is related in Daniel 7:9-12.

8-9. There are two types of people...saved and lost. Those who follow God and

John's Revelation

> 8. All who dwell on the earth will worship him, *everyone* whose name has not been written from the foundation of the world in the book of life of the Lamb who has been slain.
> 9. If anyone has an ear, let him hear.
> 10. If anyone *is destined* for captivity, to captivity he goes; if anyone kills with the sword, with the sword he must be killed. Here is the perseverance and the faith of the saints.

those who don't. Everyone who is not of the called, the chosen, will end up worshipping Satan, i.e., serving him in some way. These people did it through the beast or empire and it was accomplished through emperor worship. It is unclear here whether John has reference to the Lamb slain from the foundation of the world or names written in the book since the foundation of the world. Both points would be true through Ephesians 1:4-11. The warning to hear, if able, applies to the information about the Lamb being slain and having one's name written in the book of life, as well as to what he is about to say.

10. There seems to be two main ways to look at this verse.

    a) The world who kills the saints with the sword and leads them into captivity will themselves be killed and taken into captivity.

    b) A warning to the saints. If they use the sword or other means of force to resist the beast, *they* will perish with it or be lead into captivity. This warning would apply to both groups.

Because of what we've been reading about the beast being Rome and Rome representing government's power used by Satan along with the authority being given to the beast to overcome the saints for forty-two months, I believe the second explanation would be the best. The Lord is telling His saints not to resist this force with force for their own master had said, "All they that take the sword shall perish with the sword."

> In revealing the beast and his great power, John had shown the beast's ability to overcome the death stroke (verse 3), his power to make war against the saints and to overcome them (verse 7), and the worship that would be given to him by the world (verse 8). How shall the saints react to this power and opposition? They were not to resist the civil powers (Romans 13:2; 1 Peter 2:13), but were to fight against the powers of evil with spiritual weapons (2 Corinthians 10:3-5; Ephesians 6:10-18). Nor were they to fear them that could destroy the body, but who had no

> 11. Then I saw another beast coming up out of the earth; and he had two horns like a lamb and he spoke as a dragon.
> 12. He exercises all the authority of the first beast in his presence. And he makes the earth and those who dwell in it to worship the first beast, whose fatal wound was healed.

power beyond that; they were to fear him whose power extended beyond the body to include the soul (Luke 12:4ff); for their victory would be in their faith (1 John 5:4). This leads to the conclusion that John was writing of the saints; if they would follow the world's method of warfare by resisting with the sword, they would suffer the world's consequence of such methods. Therefore, they are to accept captivity of the sword; in doing so they clearly demonstrate the patience of the saints and their faith in God to give the victory in His own way.[40]

11. This beast comes from the earth; therefore, it is possible that he is full of the river that the dragon sent after the woman (12:16), i.e., lies, hypocrisies, false charges, deceits, etc. This is just a thought. Being from the earth clearly shows those Christians and us that this beast is not divine. It does not come down from heaven. He has the horns of a lamb (gentle looking and inoffensive), but when he speaks he reveals his true nature for his voice is like the voice of a dragon. Later references to this beast as the "false prophet" (16:13; 19:20; 20:10) identify this docile-looking, but black-hearted beast as being connected with religion that deceives. Notice 2 Corinthians 11:15. To the people of John's day perhaps this beast would mean emperor worship.

> David Smith says concerning this second beast that it was an image of the priesthood which administered the impious cult of the emperor, a blasphemous counterpart of the Lamb which was slain, our Great High Priest. John and his readers knew what the imperial cult meant since it was better organized and enforced in Asia Minor than in any other part of the Roman Empire. It was composed of deputies whose duty was to build images of Domitian, altars at the images, and legislate in any way they considered best to enforce the state religion.[41]

The above should be borne out in the verses that follow. We should not confine the principle to emperor worship, however, because the idea of false and deceiving religions lives and prospers on down to the present time.

12. He is inferior to the first beast as is evidenced by the fact that he does all that he does "in his sight" or in his presence. This also shows there is a connection

> 13. He performs great signs, so that he even makes fire come down out of heaven to the earth in the presence of men.
> 14. And he deceives those who dwell on the earth because of the signs which it was given him to perform in the presence of the beast, telling those who dwell on the earth to make an image to the beast who *had the wound of the sword and has come to life.
> 15. And it was given to him to give breath to the image of the beast, so that the image of the beast would even speak and cause as many as do not worship the image of the beast to be killed.

between the two. He uses all his power to get the people to worship the first beast. Emperor worship or the Caesar Cult was used as a form of politics to get allegiance to the empire. False religion has always tried to deceive man into thinking he was pleasing God while he worships at the feet of material things, power, wealth, and prestige.

13. These are not true signs but false wonders. Everywhere the truth of God is manifest, there also Satan attempts to deceive. Everywhere true signs are manifested in this book, there are also the false signs of Satan. In 11:5, the true witnesses had power over the fire while here the dragon's helper lays claim to the same power. Pharaoh's magicians were poor imitators of the true power given to Moses and Aaron. Still they keep trying and deceiving those who will not trust God first and foremost. This continues down to the present day and 2 Thessalonians 2:9 indicates that Satan's coming will always be this way. Men need to learn to believe in God rather than in what they think they might see.

14. The preceding comments are confirmed when we see that the people were deceived because of these signs. Notice Matthew 24:24; 2 Thessalonians 2:9ff; and 2 Timothy 3:13. The difference between true miracles and false wonders is shown in Acts 8:5-13. The greatest honor that can be given is worship. As stated in v. 12, this beast uses his power to deceive people into worshipping the first beast. This amounts to idolatry, because to worship Rome, the emperor, or any carnal thing is to worship material gain, self, wealth, etc. These things are the image of the first beast. In addition, early Christians might have seen in this "image" the busts and statues of Caesar that were prominently displayed and given homage in most parts of Asia Minor.

15. It was given to the second beast to make the image live and act (breath = spirit = life). How could the religion of Rome make the image of the government of Rome live and act? We have stated that the image of Rome is prestige, wealth,

> 16. And he causes all, the small and the great, and the rich and the poor, and the free men and the slaves, to be given a mark on their right hand or on their forehead,

selfishness, etc. By the condemnation of all those who do not worship Caesar as well as all these things, the image speaks, lives, and acts. The Christian was put in the position of acknowledging Caesar or Jesus as Lord. One meant instant death and eternal life and the other meant living on a few more years and reaping eternal death.

16. Like false miracles as opposed to true miracles, here we have a seal of Satan as opposed to those sealed to God. The saints are sealed by His name and the name of God (7:3; 9:4; 14:1), victors in the struggle are promised His name on their foreheads, 3:12; 22:4. Here the beast causes *all* to be sealed to him by a mark or engraving on their forehead or on their right hand. Since God's mark or seal was not a physical mark but a spiritual recognition of devotion to Him, it is most reasonable to say that this mark also is not a brand, stamp, or other physical mark of the Roman kingdom, but is a stamp of anti-Christ or "paganism impressed upon the character and conduct of idolaters."[42]

Keeping this idea in mind, i.e., the seal/mark of Satan is the equivalent

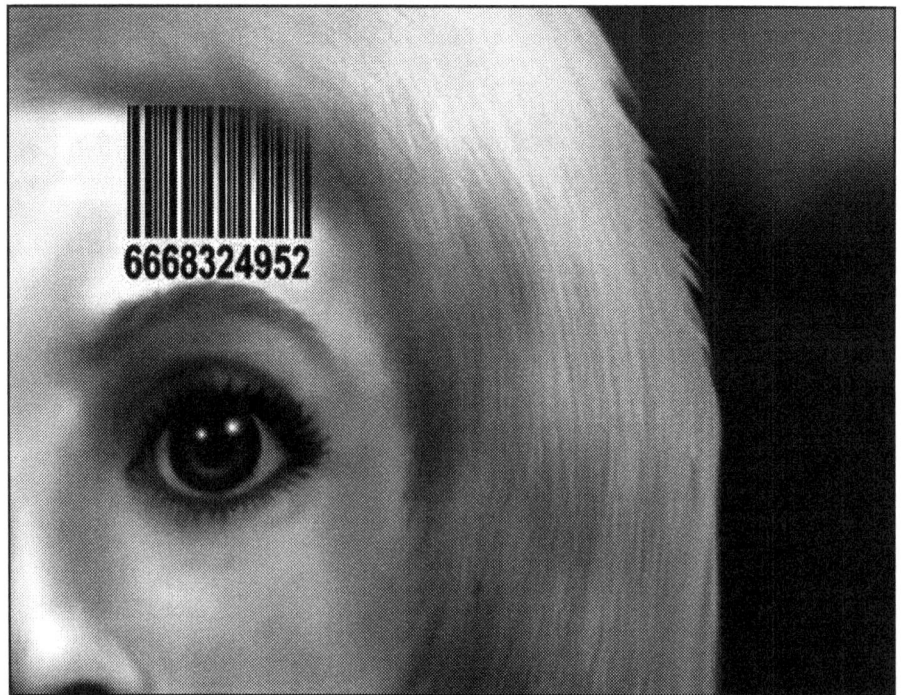

> 17. and *he provides* that no one will be able to buy or to sell, except the one who has the mark, *either* the name of the beast or the number of his name.
> 18. Here is wisdom. Let him who has understanding calculate the number of the beast, for the number is that of a man; and his number is six hundred and sixty-six.

opposite of the seal of God, will help one to resist all the modern day prophecies and interpretations of this mark as a brand, bar-code, stamp to be read under florescent lights, etc., etc. If the seal of God is a figurative, identifying, spiritual thing, then so must this seal/mark of Satan. These marks identify the servant with his master, either God or Satan. They are marks of character, understanding, obedience, commitment, etc.—not physical, visible marks. It is interesting to note here that the marks may be place on the forehead. From that vantage, the wearer might not be able to see his mark, but everyone else certainly can. A reminder to the Christian would be that others are always able to see the mark of Christ in your life even though one may, at times, feel it is not visible.

17. Just as the seal of God is His name, the mark of the beast is connected with his name also. No one would be able to purchase or make a living unless they had that mark. This ties in with chapter 6:6 where the rider on the black horse represented hunger and poverty because the world would turn against the saints. It would become difficult even to live unless one was willing to compromise with the world and accept the mark of idolatry and worship Satan through his workers. Of course the world always stands ready to get along with and fellowship the one who accepts that lifestyle.

18. There are more ideas than one would care to think about as to what this number means. However, it does mean something and because the ideas are varied does not mean they are all wrong (or right for that matter). "Here is wisdom" is the admonition. The one who has understanding is told to "calculate the number of the beast;" therefore, it *can be understood*. We may not understand because we lack knowledge, but it is possible for someone to know.

The idea that many have of transposing letters and numbers in the Hebrew or in the Greek seems to me to miss the idea of the rest of the book. The early Christians would not have done this. It is not in this kind of code to be decoded. It is a vision that has a meaning in itself. We should seek that meaning. This number has been worked with and played with until it at one time has meant every great figure in history from Nero to Hitler.

When John says, "the number is that of a man" he omits the definite article; therefore, the number is *not* that of one certain man, but of man in general. Numbers have meant something all the way through the book so far, not specifically, but symbolically. Ten represents fullness or power in a certain sphere, seven represents perfection or completeness in every sphere. Three and a half, being half of 7, represents trouble and tribulation. Seven is tied to perfection or deity, so six, which falls below the sacred 7, can never be 7 or reach perfection. It symbolizes the imperfect, that which is human and destined to fail. It is said that to the Jews the number six was an omen or symbol of dread and doom, so when it was tripled, 666, it was just being emphasized. It represented the completeness of doom and failure.

If this is so, then we see true wisdom in recognizing Rome or any power antagonistic to God and His Christ as being carnal, of man, and doomed to failure. We should not give into it because every effort to stand against God by men must end in utter and complete failure, just like the men who are involved. This idea would also be in harmony with the rest of the book and other scriptures. It was a powerful message for those persecuted Christians to understand, and it likewise is powerful for us. No matter how powerful the authority may seem to us or how dangerous the threat, all government is of men and will perish as men.

Please keep in mind also that a name in the Scriptures is not just a label. A name identifies the character or the nature of the one named. In Luke 1:35, when the holy offspring was given a name, the angel was not telling Mary what to call the child. He was telling what the child <u>was</u>, His nature or character. What is the point? The name of the beast stands for his nature. The name is best described by a numerical value. The number is 666 and the name is MAN. Christians should have no fear, because this brutal force wielding pseudo-miracles is not divine —it is of man. And again, it is not going to last forever; it is doomed to failure.

John's Revelation

QUESTIONS ON CHAPTER 13

1. What does the "sea" signify?

2. The sea beast had attributes of a leopard, bear, and lion. What did this imply?

3. Why was the whole world amazed at the sea beast?

4. Who gave power to the beast out of the sea?

5. Who would worship the sea beast?

6. Who did the sea beast make war with?

7. What is the time period of "42 months"?

8. What are some other terms for this same time period?

9. What was the Lord's instruction about "the sword"?

10. What does this mean?

11. Explain "horns like a lamb" and "speaking like a dragon."

12. What was the "mission" of the earth beast?

13. How did he accomplish his task?

14. What is the "mark" of the beast?

15. What did the earth beast look like?

16. Where did the earth beast exercise authority?

17. Who could buy and sell?

18. Explain the "number of a man."

19. What (possibly) is the beast from the sea?

20. What (possibly) is the beast from the earth?

> **Revelation 14**
>
> 1. Then I looked, and behold, the Lamb *was* standing on Mount Zion, and with Him one hundred and forty-four thousand, having His name and the name of His Father written on their foreheads.

REVELATION
chapter 14

INTRODUCTION:

It is worthy to notice here that the prophetic word does not take the saints into persecution and tribulation and leave them there. We have seen the church oppressed and seemingly overcome by the dragon and his two helpers, government or force, and (false) religion. What happens now? The vision that John sees in this chapter turns to a different viewpoint. We will see the security of believers, the call to repentance, and the judgment to come.

1. Jesus is standing on Mt. Zion with 144,000 gathered round Him. I see no reason to differentiate between this group and the group in 7:4 who were sealed. This shows us that the seal of God is His name and the name of the Lamb. See comments on 7:4. This 144,000 was not a literal number, but represents all the redeemed upon the earth at any time. This helps us understand what Mt. Zion is. It is not heaven. In the Old Testament, Zion was the mountain that Jerusalem was built upon, most specifically the peak where the temple was located. Thus, very quickly the name of the mountain came to stand for the name of the city itself, Jerusalem. Because of its use, it came to represent Jehovah's dwelling place among His people, Psalm 48:3, 13. The people looked to Zion as where their help would come from, Psalm 20:2. So far as the Messiah was concerned in prophecy, Jerusalem is where He would take the throne of David with power (Psalm 2:6; Micah 4:1-2, 7) and rule and send forth the law of God. When the "day of Jehovah" came, then these would be safely found in Zion, Joel 2:32. The ransomed ones that came to Zion would come with singing, gladness, and joy, Isaiah 5:10. The New Testament writer of Hebrews (12:22) calls the church Mt. Zion. There are many more passages to show the evolution of the term "Zion" or "Mt. Zion," but these should suffice to show that Mt. Zion represents the peace, security, and safety of those who are sealed to God or members of the body of

> 2. And I heard a voice from heaven, like the sound of many waters and like the sound of loud thunder, and the voice which I heard *was* like *the sound* of harpists playing on their harps.
> 3. And they *sang a new song before the throne and before the four living creatures and the elders; and no one could learn the song except the one hundred and forty-four thousand who had been purchased from the earth.
> 4. These are the ones who have not been defiled with women, for they have kept themselves chaste. These *are* the ones who follow the Lamb wherever He

Christ. Those that gather round the Lamb have this security even in the midst of all that the dragon can do. This spiritual safety can be had here on earth (not in heaven) and is found in the church where God's people can be found following the Lamb.

2. John, while he beheld the saints around the Lamb, hears a voice from heaven that sounds majestic (like many waters), loud in volume (like loud thunder), and melodious or beautiful to hear (like harpists playing their harps).

3. Some believe that the voice from heaven was singing while the saints were "learning." Because of the pronoun "they," I tend to believe it is the redeemed singing the victory song, and the idea of learning the song means knowing it. No one can know the victory (not even the heavenly host) except the saints. It is a song that comes with experience. "Purchased from the earth" is the same as redeemed from the world or "bought with a price."

4. The passage speaks of spiritual virginity or purity here. Any form of idolatry or false religion is known as spiritual adultery or fornication, 2 Corinthians 11:2. These redeemed are followers of Christ (Matthew 16:24) who go wherever the Lord leads. These are purchased or redeemed or paid for with the blood of Jesus (1 Peter 1:18-19) and are called first fruits. The term "first fruits" has reference to the harvest. The first fruits are generally thought of as the best and that which is dedicated to God. The idea of first fruits also includes the idea of faith because giving up the "first fruits" to God implies that there is more to come. Note 1 Corinthians 16:15 where the household of Stephanas was described as the first fruits of Asia. There were more converts to come, but these were the first. 1 Corinthians 15:20, 23 puts Christ in the same boat where there is going to be a resurrection to glory for many, but Jesus was the first. James 1:18 speaks of the converted Jews (James 1:1) being the first fruits because many would be converted, but they were the first. Because of all this, I'm led to believe that this 144,000 who represent the church on earth at any time are called first fruits

> goes. These have been purchased from among men as first fruits to God and to the Lamb.
> 5.   And no lie was found in their mouth; they are blameless.
> 6.   And I saw another angel flying in midheaven, having an eternal gospel to preach to those who live on the earth, and to every nation and tribe and tongue and people;
> 7.   and he said with a loud voice, "Fear God, and give Him glory, because the hour of His judgment has come; worship Him who made the heaven and the earth and sea and springs of waters."

because they most specifically represent first century Christians undergoing persecution from the dragon. They were the first, but in ages to come there would be many more Christians.

5. They had neither admitted to nor taught anything that was untrue (no lie). So far as their profession or teaching, they were blameless. This term "blameless" usually means that no charge could be laid at their feet. Most specifically, in the context of the last chapter, it would be seen that these had not called Caesar "Lord"—in the context of earlier chapters they had not named Zeus as "Savior"— and in general they had not weakened to the pressures of idolatry and confessed any pagan gods. This would have been the spiritual "adultery" and "lie" that is described.

6. The term "mid-heaven" (*mesouranema*, 8:13; 14:6; 19:17) means *the very highest point in the heavens*. This angel or "messenger" is here because from this point *all* who live on the earth can hear his message. This "eternal good tidings" is the "eternal gospel" and is so translated in newer versions. This angel seems to represent God's teachers, preachers, apostles, and prophets as well as explaining the extent to which the gospel went into the earth.

7. Notice the message of the angel—"Fear God," "give Him glory," "worship Him." This is the point of all the lessons, sermons, and messages that have ever been delivered. Notice also the description of God here. He is the God of creation. Whether all aspects of creation listed here are figurative, representing parts of the vision (man, societies, kingdoms, etc.) or whether here they are literal (representing all of the created world) makes no difference. One of the first things man does in forsaking God is to ignore Him as creator, Romans 1:20-25. The message of the angel then is a message that goes to the heart of idolatry, false religion, and all manner of unrighteousness. The message is an *announcement* of judgment. The one who created all things certainly has the authority to judge what He has created.

> 8. And another angel, a second one, followed, saying, "Fallen, fallen is Babylon the great, she who has made all the nations drink of the wine of the passion of her immorality."
> 9. Then another angel, a third one, followed them, saying with a loud voice, "If anyone worships the beast and his image, and receives a mark on his forehead or on his hand,
> 10. he also will drink of the wine of the wrath of God, which is mixed in full strength in the cup of His anger; and he will be tormented with fire and brimstone in the presence of the holy angels and in the presence of the Lamb.

8. The second angel comes and speaks of Babylon who refused to heed the warnings of the first angel. When he says she has fallen, it sounds as though it has already come to pass. This is because when God decrees something, it is as good as done. Fifty years before ancient Babylon fell to the Medes, God said through His prophet, "Babylon is suddenly fallen and destroyed: wail for her," Jeremiah 51:8. We will have more to say about Babylon later, but suffice to say here that she is representative of the carnal mind of mankind, i.e., it is lust and seduction personified. Rome exemplified this spirit, yet it goes farther than just Rome. The "wine of the passion of her immorality" refers once again to the spiritual fornication. All the nations that look to the carnal mind for wisdom and guidance have been guilty of forsaking God. All who have taken part in her false worship or "made love" to Rome for her commercial and political advantages have drunk of her "wine."

9-10. The third angel delivers his message, a warning against any type of idolatry. Most especially to those of John's day this applied to the cult of emperor worship. The "mark" is the mark of 13:17. The one who worships the beast and his image (or follows false religion, idolatry) is the one who will drink (full strength) of the wrath of God, unmixed with mercy, mixed in anger. Mercy, grace, and pardon are offered with the gospel of peace. Those that refuse the gospel will be refused mercy. This suffering the wrath of God will be in eternal torment. The illusion here between verses 8 & 10 is too obvious to miss. Like a drunkard who is so intent on drinking that he neither cares nor notices what he drinks, so are the people and nations that follow Rome's lead. They are so intent on drinking Rome's "wine" that they do not realize they will end up drinking God's "wine."

11. This shows the serious consequences for accepting Caesar as Lord instead of Jesus. Also the acceptance of any other would bring a similar fate. It is an

> 11. "And the smoke of their torment goes up forever and ever; they have no rest day and night, those who worship the beast and his image, and whoever receives the mark of his name."
> 12. Here is the perseverance of the saints who keep the commandments of God and their faith in Jesus.
> 13. And I heard a voice from heaven, saying, "Write, `Blessed are the dead who die in the Lord from now on!' " "Yes," says the Spirit, "so that they may rest from their labors, for their deeds follow with them."

eternal punishment. "They have no rest day and night" stands opposed to those who serve around the throne "day and night," 7:15. It also presents an interesting commentary on the statements of some to the effect that those who are unrighteous will be unconscious or simply cease to exist. Understanding that this is a vision, there is still the idea that this is in harmony with Jesus' teaching that torment will be lasting.

12. In 13:10, almost the same phrase was found to mean: hold on and be steadfast, do not resist (perseverance, patience), because those that persecute you will meet their reward. Here the idea is the same. In light of what is promised for those who forsake the gospel...hold on! This is endurance. We note here that it is not just faith in Christ Jesus that is kept, but also the commandments of God. Both actions and attitude are important.

13. In contrast to verses 10-11, we see the result of a strong faith. Those who resist the idolatry and carnal attitude of Rome and the world will be happy, fortunate, or blessed. Their labor and work and toil and suffering will be left behind, but their deeds "in the Lord" follow them into judgment, commending them to God's grace. In contrast to the torment from which there will be no rest, here rest is the reward.

There continues in this picture the contrast between good and evil that we have seen throughout the entire book. Those that die in the Lord are "blessed" (happy, commended), as opposed to those who serve the beast and die under judgment in sin, guilt, and fear. The former "rest from their labors" while the latter have "no rest day and night" in their torment, verse 11. The first group is told that "their deeds follow after them" while the second group leaves all their earthly, carnal pursuits, and pleasures behind; they are left with nothing.

> 14. Then I looked, and behold, a white cloud, and sitting on the cloud *was* one like a son of man, having a golden crown on His head and a sharp sickle in His hand.
> 15. And another angel came out of the temple, crying out with a loud voice to Him who sat on the cloud, "Put in your sickle and reap, for the hour to reap has come, because the harvest of the earth is ripe."
> 16. Then He who sat on the cloud swung His sickle over the earth, and the earth was reaped.
> 17. And another angel came out of the temple which is in heaven, and he also had a sharp sickle.
> 18. Then another angel, the one who has power over fire, came out from the altar; and he called with a loud voice to him who had the sharp sickle, saying, "Put in your sharp sickle and gather the clusters from the vine of the earth, because her grapes are ripe."

14. Chapter 14 is the end of the fourth section, and it is in harmony with the book that scenes of judgment are under consideration at this point. John looks and sees the Christ, sitting on a white cloud, wearing the (*stephanos*) victory crown (6:1), and carrying a sharp sickle. We begin to see judgment because a sickle is an instrument of the harvest.

15. Jesus receives the instructions to reap because the hour is come and the harvest is ripe. "Ripe" (NASB) in the original is "dry." In the Septuagint, the term is used in Joel 1:17. The implication is that this is a harvest of grain. The Bible often speaks of the righteous being gathered into the barn while the wicked are destroyed. See Matthew 3:12; 3:30. This appears to be the point of this vision. This is the first part of the harvest, the reaping of the righteous.

16. This is the first harvest. Note 1 Thessalonians 4:15-17. The dead in Christ shall rise first and

> | | |
> |---|---|
> | 19. So the angel swung his sickle to the earth and gathered *the clusters from* the vine of the earth, and threw them into the great wine press of the wrath of God. | 20. And the wine press was trodden outside the city, and blood came out from the wine press, up to the horses' bridles, for a distance of two hundred miles. |

then those that are alive will meet the Lord in the air and thus always be with the Lord. Though this vision presents a picture of two harvests—one for the righteous and a second for the wicked—we can still understand that it is one and the same judgment.

17-18. In 2 Thessalonians 1:7, we are told that mighty angels will be with the Lord on the last day. It is possible that here is revealed their function. While the Lord takes those that are His, His angels reap those who are unconverted. This seems to be the idea of this vision anyway, since one of the angels taking part is "the one who has power over fire." This is God's final answer to the prayers of the saints. Like Christ is a vine and those that follow Him are the branches who bear precious fruit, so is now presented a picture of those who are earthly-minded and have given in to the dragon. They are the fruit of the earth. God never hastens the day when men might be destroyed, but always waits until their cup of iniquity is full or their "fruit is ripe," Joel 3:13; Isaiah 63:1-6.

19-20. The wine press in the vision shows us the completeness and power of the Lord's judgment. The wicked are cast into the press and trodden down or completely subjugated until their blood runs as deep as a horses bridle for 200 miles. In spite of what the literalists try to teach about this book, I agree with the observation made by one commentator...there is not enough blood in the world to make a river flow this deep for this far. This obviously is a figurative picture, and we must seek the principle behind it rather than teach a literal winepress of judgment.

We have seen from the first five verses that in spite of the dragon's persecution, the redeemed are spiritually safe because they have come to the Lamb on Mt. Zion. The gospel has been preached in all creation (first angel). Those that reject it and follow after carnal lust as exemplified in Rome are going to be brought low (second angel). If anyone rejects it and gives into the dragon's helpers, such as the false religion of Rome or any other type of spiritual idolatry, they will suffer from God's wrath. God's judgment is assured. Those that are redeemed are blessed and happy, and those who refuse will suffer in the most terrible way that one could imagine. STAND FIRM!

QUESTIONS ON CHAPTER 14

1. Who are the 144,000?

2. Where/what is Mt. Zion here?

3. Where does Mt. Zion get its name?

4. What are "first fruits"?

5. What characteristics identified the 144,000?

6. What 3 things are used to describe the voice that John heard?

7. What is the "new song"?

8. Who were the only ones who could sing it? Why?

9. What is significant about "midheaven"?

10. To whom was the everlasting gospel to be preached?

John's Revelation

11. How is God identified in this chapter?

12. What is the "wine" of Babylon?

13. What kind of "wine" does God have?

14. Who was to drink of "the wine of the wrath of God"?

15. What does a "sickle" signify?

16. What do the "grain" and the "grapes" represent?

17. What does the "winepress" running with blood signify?

18. Who drank of the "wine of the passion of her immorality"?

19. Describe the punishment of those who worship the beast and his image.

20. What is the condition of those who "die in the Lord"? Why is this so?

From Beneath the Altar

THE REVELATION
chapter 15
Section II, 5 (see page 12)

INTRODUCTION:

These next two chapters are the fifth section in our study of seven parallel sections.

"I am fully convinced that the 'seven seals' and the 'seven trumpets' and the 'seven bowls of wrath' do not relate to different times, nor different events in time, but rather cover from the beginning of time until the end of time...."[43] Thinking along this line, we have seen the entire scheme of redemption sealed up and opened by the Lamb. We have seen the gospel preached in every corner of the earth and we have seen the earth reject it, going so far as to bring sore trials and persecution upon the few who accept Christ, many times even death. In the trumpets, we have seen a warning to repentance and a partial judgment upon a third of society in order to bring this repentance about. We have also seen a rejection of this warning. Now we are going to see in this section the wrath of God revealed. These bowls of wrath are going to represent God's judgment on a wicked society. However, to reassure and comfort the saints we are first of all shown a vision of the redeemed in heaven.

Remember: the trumpets warn and the bowls pour out the wrath of God. The trumpets are a partial judgment, to get the attention of those involved, while the bowls are the final judgment on society. Notice the similarity.

"TRUMPETS"	"BOWLS"
1. wrath upon the earth	1. wrath upon the earth
2. wrath upon the sea	2. wrath upon the sea
3. wrath upon the rivers and fountains of water	3. wrath upon the rivers and fountains of water
4. wrath revealed in heavenly bodies	4. wrath revealed in heavenly bodies (sun)
5. suffering in the kingdom of darkness	5. suffering in the kingdom of darkness
6. war against wickedness beginning at Euphrates River	6. war against wickedness beginning at Euphrates River
7. great voice from heaven, lightning, thunders, earthquakes, and great hail	7. great voice from heaven, lightning, thunders, earthquakes, and great hail

> **Revelation 15**
>
> 1. Then I saw another sign in heaven, great and marvelous, seven angels who had seven plagues, *which are* the last, because in them the wrath of God is finished.
>
> 2. And I saw something like a sea of glass mixed with fire, and those who had been victorious over the beast and his image and the number of his name, standing on the sea of glass, holding harps of God.
>
> 3. And they *sang the song

1. This is the third "sign in heaven" John has seen. The first two were the radiant woman (12:1) and the dragon, 12:3. Once again we have the number seven indicating a completeness or finality of judgment. These plagues are "the last," because although there had been plagues before, in these "the wrath of God is finished." "Finished" comes from *teleo* (Gk.) which means to "find its consummation, or reach perfection." The end of what has been promised is drawing near.

2. Perhaps this is the same "sea of glass" we found in chapter four at the throne scene. If there is any relationship between the laver of cleansing in the tabernacle and the sea before the throne implying a cleansing or sanctification, then it is possible this picture presents to us the saints cleansed, holy and sanctified, standing upon or trusting in the power of the Lamb to redeem. The fact that it is mingled with fire may refer either to the fire of judgment coming upon the world or to the fiery trial the saints had been told they would have to endure, Zechariah 13:9; 1 Corinthians 3:12-15; 1 Peter 1:7; etc. I still believe these "harps of God" (5:8; 14:2) in the vision represent the voices of the saints raised in melodies coming from the heart in worship to God. We must notice again, as in every place they are mentioned, that they are named as having "harps of God," but no playing is mentioned. Instead we hear singing, the true soul music of God. The victorious ones are not just the martyrs, but this group includes all those who have refused to worship the beast or his image.

3. The "song of Moses" is the song of deliverance that Moses and the children of Israel sang when delivered out of the hands of the Egyptians at the Red Sea, Exodus 15. The song of the Lamb then would be the thanksgiving for deliverance from the world and the bondage of sin and death. This simply tells us that saints of all ages will be gathered before the throne together. This praise is a mixture of praises from the Psalms, prophets, and the writings of Moses.

   a) "great and marvelous are thy works," Psalm 40:5; 92:5

> of Moses, the bond-servant of God, and the song of the Lamb, saying, "Great and marvelous are Your works, O Lord God, the Almighty; Righteous and true are Your ways, King of the nations!
> 4. "Who will not fear, O Lord, and glorify Your name? For You alone are holy; For ALL THE NATIONS WILL COME AND WORSHIP BEFORE YOU, FOR YOUR RIGHTEOUS ACTS HAVE BEEN REVEALED."
> 5. After these things I looked, and the temple of the tabernacle of testimony in heaven was opened,
> 6. and the seven angels who had the seven plagues came out of the temple, clothed in linen, clean *and* bright, and girded around their chests with golden sashes.

    b) "Lord God, the Almighty, righteous and true are thy ways." Psalms 145:17
    c) "thou King of the nations (ages)," Jeremiah 10:7
        "The phrase 'of the saints' (KJV) is rejected by all modern scholars since it has little textual support...."[44]

4. a) "who will not fear," Jeremiah 10:7; Psalm 86:9
       (fear here means reverence or respect)
   b) "all nations will come and worship," Psalm 86:9
   c) "for thy righteous acts have been revealed," Psalm 98:2

5. "Temple" here is from *naos* (Gk.), the "Holy of Holies" in heaven, not Solomon's nor Herod's temple. Previously (11:9), John saw the ark of the covenant when the temple was opened. This is what held the law or commandments in the Old Testament. Now he sees the temple opened again, and this time angels proceed out to render judgment on those who reject His Law. Get this picture. They are proceeding from the Holy of Holies, the place where the ark would have been, where the word of God on stone tablets have been preserved. They proceed from the presence of God.

6. These angels, as we see by their dress if nothing else, are obviously from God. It is difficult to avoid the similarities between this vision and a top-level government meeting of some kind. These angels proceed out of the temple as if they had been in council with Jehovah. The decision has been made and so now they go forth to accomplish their tasks.

> 7. Then one of the four living creatures gave to the seven angels seven golden bowls full of the wrath of God, who lives forever and ever.
> 8. And the temple was filled with smoke from the glory of God and from His power; and no one was able to enter the temple until the seven plagues of the seven angels were finished.

7. The angels "had 7 plagues" (verses 1, 6), but here they are given the "bowls of God's wrath" by the cherubim, 4:8. Imagine 7 angels with the spiritual power of divine plagues being given bowls of God's wrath to mix with those plagues and pour out on the earth. It is high time to be afraid.

8. The smoke is God's glory in action, Exodus 19:18; Isaiah 4:5; Exodus 40:34; 1 Kings 8:10. When the place is full of smoke, no one is able to enter or change the determinate mind of God. His mind is made and He is unapproachable. When judgment is rendered, then all will be clear and easy to see. Until that time, no one can interfere with this decision being carried out.

John's Revelation
QUESTIONS ON CHAPTER 15

1. What does the number 7 signify?

2. What is the "sea of glass" reminiscent of?

3. What might explain the fire mixed with the sea?

4. What were those standing on the sea victorious over?

5. What (possibly) might the "harps of God" represent?

6. What are the "Song of Moses" and the "Song of the Lamb"?

7. Where in the Scriptures is this "song" found?

8. How were the 7 angels dressed?

9. What might we understand from their clothing?

10. What are "the four living creatures"?

11. What is represented in the "smoke" from God?

12. Where did the seven angels get the "bowls of wrath"?

13. What did the seven bowls contain?

14. Where were the seven angels (besides heaven)?

15. How long was no one able to enter the temple?

> **Revelation 16**
>
> 1. Then I heard a loud voice from the temple, saying to the seven angels, "Go and pour out on the earth the seven bowls of the wrath of God."
>
> 2. So the first *angel* went and poured out his bowl on the earth; and it became a loathsome and malignant sore on the people who had the mark of the beast and who worshiped his image.

THE REVELATION
chapter 16

INTRODUCTION:

Commentators and scholars such as Pieters, Lenski, Milligan, and Hailey candidly admit that they do not understand all the symbols and realities behind these visions of the bowls. Therefore, it would ill behoove me to be dogmatic on any ideas that I have gleaned from these men. Whatever aspect of reality that each bowl represents, let us remember that the whole picture is one of the wrath of God being poured out upon an unregenerate world, finally and terribly. The "big picture" seems to be the one that the Lord is most interested in getting across.

1. John once again hears the great voice; however, it is out of the temple this time, therefore from divinity. The command is to all seven angels. Since the wrath of God is poured out "into the earth," the seven bowls affect the world of impenitent men.

2. All those who participated in and followed after the Roman system of false religion (emperor worship) as well as any other false religion, which is what the Roman system means to us, receive the wrath of God here described as a loathsome (evil, troublesome, destructive), malignant (painful, virulent) sore (abscess, ulcer, foul and angry sore). There is plainly a picture here of men diseased with a sickness. Those who refuse to seek spiritual health and healing in Jesus Christ, who refuse His bread of life, milk of the word, and water of life will suffer the consequences of sin. Like a malignant cancer, unrighteousness will be evident to others as well as self, and God here is making it as evident in one's flesh as it is in one's life.

3. The second *angel* poured out his bowl into the sea, and it became blood like *that* of a dead man; and every living thing in the sea died. 4. Then the third *angel* poured out his bowl into the rivers and the springs of waters; and they became blood.	5. And I heard the angel of the waters saying, "Righteous are You, who are and who were, O Holy One, because You judged these things; 6. for they poured out the blood of saints and prophets, and You have given them blood to drink. They deserve it."

3. In 13:1 and 8:8, the "sea" was worldly society. Worldly society as a whole is dead in sin. When the final judgment of God is given, then there is no hope and no repentance (every living thing in the sea died), and it will be clearly observed to be dead. As a "dead man's blood" would be rotten and putrefied, unable to carry or give life of any kind, so society will be exposed and condemned for having the same qualities. This prophetic language is the same as that used by the prophets to forecast the downfall of national powers. Notice Zephaniah 1:2-4 or Jeremiah 4:23. None of this literally happened. It is the prophecy of horror against a great power.

4. Those who seek these waters turned bitter (8:11) must suffer the same fate as the above. This could have been avoided if they had sought after the river of life instead. These fountains and rivers (inland waters) would be all the things that go together to make up societies or any society as a whole, just as various streams and rivers go together to make up the sea. Perhaps these are families, clans, tribes, etc. Hal Lindsey, the literalist, prophesies a big run on Coca-Cola when all the fresh drinking water is turned to blood...this is more foolishness. This is a vision which has as its start a diseased earth with a bloody sea and putrid liquid running into it where there is nowhere to turn for cleansing or refreshment.

5-6. Just as we have seen an angel with power over fire given unto him (14:18), now we have an angel with power over the waters. Each angel (messenger) has control over some element in order to further God's purpose. The first one had power to bring judgment (fire) upon man while this one must work somehow among men. This angel pronounces God righteous because He judges. He also explains why the wrath of God is manifest. It is because they poured out the blood of the innocent that they are given blood to drink. Because they were thirsty for blood, they are given more than they wanted. In other words, "they deserve it" (NASB). This may be all that the imagery of this vision is meant to communicate.

> 7. And I heard the altar saying, "Yes, O Lord God, the Almighty, true and righteous are Your judgments."
> 8. The fourth *angel* poured out his bowl upon the sun, and it was given to it to scorch men with fire.
> 9. Men were scorched with fierce heat; and they blasphemed the name of God who has the power over these plagues, and they did not repent so as to give Him glory.
> 10. Then the fifth *angel* poured out his bowl on the throne of the beast, and his kingdom became darkened; and they gnawed their tongues because of pain,
> 11. and they blasphemed the God of heaven because of their pains and their sores; and they did not repent of their deeds.

7. The angel declared God righteous while here the altar declares the judgments of God are also righteous. This is because they proceed from a righteous judge. It is a powerful "amen."

8-9. That which is intended to warm, comfort, and bring life is now used by God to scorch, burn, and bring pain and suffering. Today we might say that they refused the light of the Son, so they are given the light of the sun, more than they wished. Unlike the plagues of darkness God has used in the past, once again He gives them more than they want. Instead of repentance, these are so hardened they fill the cup of their own iniquity with blasphemy. This seeming call for repentance leads one to believe that perhaps the writer is being presented with more than just a vision of the wrath of God being revealed finally upon the ungodly. See note at the end of the chapter.

editor's note...Where we have seen God's wrath turned upon men and society in general in the symbols of the earth, sea, rivers, and sun, now we shall see the same revealed against spiritual wickedness, i.e., the beast and his agents.

10-11. God now manifests His wrath directly upon the throne of the beast and his kingdom. All those under the dominion of the beast suffer under the loss of understanding and wisdom (light). Isaiah 3:4 and Ecclesiastes 10:16 confirm the serious consequences upon a kingdom when its leaders are like children because they lack wisdom. The leaders in Rome are said to have exemplified this type of stupidity often. These ones are left without guidance as well as having the pain of the first plague added to them. These also are so hardened in heart that even now they refuse to repent.

> 12. The sixth *angel* poured out his bowl on the great river, the Euphrates; and its water was dried up, so that the way would be prepared for the kings from the east.
>
> 13. And I saw *coming* out of the mouth of the dragon and out of the mouth of the beast and out of the mouth of the false prophet, three unclean spirits like frogs;

12. The River Euphrates was the northern border for the kingdom of Israel. It was perhaps looked upon as some protection from enemies. However, as it was in chapter 9, here also is where the enemies proceed from. Both Assyria and Babylon came from this direction when they marched against God's people in the Old Testament. There are two generally accepted ideas as to who the "kings of the east" (sun rising) might be. They are:

a) the forces of God coming out of the rising sun in judgment.

b) the forces of evil coming forth to meet God after having been restrained.

Though the picture painted in a) is very attractive, the River Euphrates and what it represented, as well as the following explanatory verses, make me choose b) as being more correct. Like the Red Sea parted and the Israelites crossed over on dry land, so now the river dries up and the approaching kings use it for a road.

In his book *The Late Great Planet Earth*, Hal Lindsey declares the "kings of the east" to be "the yellow peril," a great oriental army from Asia. Red China, with intercontinental ballistic missiles and a "human wave" of 200 million soldiers, will fulfill this passage. We include his interpretation here for your information and entertainment, but I decline to spend much effort dealing with such unfounded, inventive speculation.

13. The word "coming" has been added. John did not see "spirits like frogs" *coming* out of their mouths, but he saw these spirits at work already and tells us where they came from, i.e., out of the mouths of the dragon, beast, and false prophet. The false prophet is the second beast (13:11), or the beast out of the earth representing false religion (most especially emperor worship in Rome). I note that these unclean spirits are understood as coming from the "mouths" of the dragon, beast, and false prophet. This might indicate that the medium through which the 3 originators worked their deceit is first and foremost…words. Just like God works through the saving power of His word (Romans 1:16), so also Satan and his ministers work their deceit through the word. People wishing to

> 14. for they are spirits of demons, performing signs, which go out to the kings of the whole world, to gather them together for the war of the great day of God, the Almighty.
> 15. ("Behold, I am coming like a thief. Blessed is the one who stays awake and keeps his clothes, so that he will not walk about naked and men will not see his shame.")
> 16. And they gathered them together to the place which in Hebrew is called Har-Magedon.

make wise choices between righteousness and unrighteousness must always weigh a man's words carefully.

14. Contrary to the KJV, these are "spirits of demons" not "devils," because there is only one devil. The point of these frogs/spirits/deceitful words is to muster the forces of all those who stand opposed to Jehovah. The "whole world" would be the unregenerate world. Whether their signs are real or deceiving we are not told; and it really does not matter, for whoever thinks that they can stand against God is already deceived.

15. Inserted here is a parenthetical statement to be on guard against the deceiving power of this influence. This deception of world leaders to an anti-God stance is something that has been going on since one man started ruling another. It will probably continue until this world is no more. This is why in the midst of it all, Jesus steps in and says His coming will be unannounced (like a thief); so His brethren should remain awake (undeceived) and keep their garments (not allow their blood-washed, white robes to be taken).

16. We continue the thought from verse 14 here. The "day of God" from verse 14 is a day of judgment upon the unrighteous. This mustering of forces is looking toward that great day, and the gathering is at Har-magedon (KJV, Armageddon). This term literally means "mount at Megiddo." Thus we have seen a preparation for battle that will take place on the day of God's great judgment. The location of the battle would be at Armageddon or the Mount of Megiddo. This is an interesting choice of settings.

"The Bible speaks geographically of Megiddo and its three heights (Joshua 17:11), Megiddo and its towns (Judges 1:27), the waters of Megiddo (Judges 5:19), and the valley of Megiddo (2 Chronicles 35:22; Zechariah 12:11), *but makes no mention of a Mount of Megiddo.*"[45] [emphasis mine, cpm]

Megiddo guarded the northern entrance to Israel. It was the place of many

> 17. Then the seventh *angel* poured out his bowl upon the air, and a loud voice came out of the temple from the throne, saying, "It is done."
> 18. And there were flashes of lightning and sounds and peals of thunder; and there was a great earthquake, such as there had not been since man came to be upon the earth, so great an earthquake *was it, and* so mighty.

decisive and historic victories such as Deborah and Barak against Jabin and Sisera (Judges 4, 5), Gideon and his 300 men against the Midianites (Judges 7:1), King Josiah against Pharaoh Neco (2 Kings 23:29ff; 2 Chronicles 35:22), which gave the Babylonians victory over the Assyrians and world power. Here also Saul was slain on the eastern extremity of the plain (1 Samuel 31:1-6) and Ahaziah, king of Judah, was slain (2 Kings 9:27). From all this and wanting to keep in harmony with interpreting the book according to Scripture, not wild supposition, it would seem that Megiddo is the place of decisive victory *for the Lord*. No matter who is doing the fighting, Megiddo is the place of God's judgment upon the enemies of His people and false leaders of the same. Anyone from Deborah to Pharaoh could be victorious at Megiddo if he was doing the will of God.

Therefore, Armageddon or the Mt. of Megiddo here is not a literal place on this earth where a last great battle is going to be fought, and those who look to a great battle of Armageddon someday are sadly mistaken in their expectation. It is, and always has been, a scene of God's judgment and decisive victory for His people. I believe this was accomplished in the defeat of Rome and paganism (19:19-20) and is also accomplished at any time Satan's forces are overthrown in a decisive victory for God's people. God fights at Megiddo anytime He fights because He ALWAYS wins!

17. Pouring the bowl upon the air indicates a pouring out of God's wrath upon Satan so that there is nowhere (in his realm) to hide. Notice Ephesians 2:2 where Satan is referred to as "the prince of the power of the air" (NASB). "It is done" means this series of plagues is completed, finished. It is pronounced by Deity since it comes from the temple and the throne.

18. As the nation of Israel saw when they gathered at Mt. Sinai before the Lord, as in the throne scene (4:5), the seals (8:5), and the trumpets (11:19), so here we see flashes of lightning, peals of thunder, sounds, and great earthquakes. There seems to be an increasing intensity with each manifestation probably tied to the intensity of the scene itself.

> 19. The great city was split into three parts, and the cities of the nations fell. Babylon the great was remembered before God, to give her the cup of the wine of His fierce wrath.
> 20. And every island fled away, and the mountains were not found.
> 21. And huge hailstones, about one hundred pounds each, *came down from heaven upon men; and men blasphemed God because of the plague of the hail, because its plague *was extremely severe.

19. "Babylon the great" and "the great city" are one and the same. There seems to be a picture of an earthquake so great (verse 18) it splits the city into three parts. In Ezekiel 5:1-5, we have the same idea of being split into three applied to Jerusalem who had become sinful and rebellious. The idea is utter destruction. Once again, remembering whom the book is written to, I cannot help but believe this Babylon the great is Rome. As Rome fell, so also the "cities of the nations" that followed her fell. In 14:10, God promised that anyone who worshipped the beast and his image and received a mark, that is, that followed after Rome and her religion, would also drink of the wrath of God, mixed full strength in the cup of His anger. Here it is remembered and accomplished.

20. In this mighty fall of power, there would be no place of refuge—neither in the mountains nor in the far off islands of the sea.

21. This last part of the seventh bowl seems most terrible of all. Hail, the weight of a talent, is rained upon men. A talent could be anywhere between 60 to 100 pounds, but is probably closer to 90-96 pounds (NASB, about one hundred pounds each). Whichever it is, it would be heavy enough to bring instant death. These that were not killed still refused to repent, but instead blasphemed God.

CONCLUSION TO SECTION 5

We have seen the first four bowls poured out on an unregenerate world. The fifth is poured upon the throne of the beast or Rome. The sixth opens the way for spiritual forces of darkness to wage war against righteousness. The seventh is poured out upon the realm of Satan as a whole. Notice in verses 9, 11, and 21 John tells us that no repentance came forth from the wrath of God revealed on these people. Since on the last day the time for repentance will be over, I must think that as terrible and final as this vision seems, this is not a scene of the *final* wrath of God, but is His final wrath upon an ungodly society, namely Rome. This would be in the spirit and intent of the book. It would be the answer to the cries of those under the altar and the prayers of the saints. It also would represent to us His vengeance upon those who persecute His children.

Some of the elements of the bowls have yet to be developed, but they are all covered in the record of the bowls. The city fell under the seventh, but the fall will be described in chapters 17 and 18. The battle of Armageddon is previewed here, but will be developed in chapter 19. The devil has been defeated 'in the air' but his defeat will be developed in chapter 20.[46]

QUESTIONS ON CHAPTER 16

1. Where did John hear the loud voice from? What does this signify?

2. What did the first bowl of wrath become when poured out?

3. What might this signify?

4. Who was it poured out on?

5. Where was the 2nd bowl poured out?

6. What has this place represented in past passages?

7. What was the result of the outpouring?

8. Where was the 3rd bowl poured out?

9. Why is this what they deserve?

John's Revelation

10. Where was the 4th bowl poured out? What was the result?

11. Did it bring men to repentance? How do you know?

12. Where was the 5th bowl poured out?

13. What was the effect, specifically and generally?

14. Darkness often indicates what?

15. Where was the 6th bowl poured out? Why?

16. Where did the unclean spirits come from? What would this signify?

17. What was their task?

18. Where is the gathering place of the kings of the earth?

19. What is significant about this place?

20. Where was the 7th bowl poured out and what did this mean?

21. Who was given the cup of God's wine/wrath?

From Beneath the Altar

Revelation 17

1. Then one of the seven angels who had the seven bowls came and spoke with me, saying, "Come here, I will show you the judgment of the great harlot who sits on many waters,
2. with whom the kings of the earth committed *acts of* immorality, and those who dwell on the earth were made drunk with the wine of her immorality."

THE REVELATION
chapter 17
Section II, 6 (see page 13)

INTRODUCTION:

In this, the sixth section of the Revelation, we are presented with and receive explanation for the two women or cities. The first woman is the Holy City, the new Jerusalem or the church. The second woman is Rome. She represents to us today political oppression, false religion, worldly lusts and desires. The fall of this second city is important enough to devote the following chapters to it.

1. The word judgment (*krima*, Gk.) here means "judicial verdict, the condemnation and punishment of the harlot."[47] As the "sea" in 8:8 was society in general, so here "many waters" are "peoples, and multitudes, and nations, and tongues," according to verse 15. John was going to see the verdict rendered and condemnation come upon this one who was over many nations and people. There are many ideas put forth as to who this "great harlot" is, but to me it seems fairly clear that it is Rome. That is who this book is about, and Rome's condemnation is what would seem right and encouraging for those Christians undergoing persecution.

2. World leaders committed fornication by playing up to Rome and sacrificing any standards, morals, etc. that would hinder them from accomplishing their own desires. The leaders are not the only ones guilty, however, because "they that dwell in the earth" also were carried away in the material rewards and pleasures of "making love" to Rome, so that they go so far as to worship her. Some of the rewards they would receive would be protection, government assistance in disaster relief (earthquakes), possession of property, a free economy (taxes taken into account), etc.

> 3. And he carried me away in the Spirit into a wilderness; and I saw a woman sitting on a scarlet beast, full of blasphemous names, having seven heads and ten horns.
> 4. The woman was clothed in purple and scarlet, and adorned with gold and precious stones and pearls, having in her hand a gold cup full of abominations and of the unclean things of her immorality,
> 5. and on her forehead a name *was* written, a mystery, "BABYLON THE GREAT, THE

3. Some have suggested a similarity between this "scarlet colored beast" and the beast of chapter 13. It might be worth our while to notice...

<u>chapter 13</u>

a) out of the sea
b) 7 heads, 10 horns
c) name of the blasphemy
d) warred with the saints
e) wounded to death, healed
f) all world wondered

<u>chapter 17</u>

a) out of the abyss
b) 7 heads, 10 horns
c) names of blasphemy
d) make war with the Lamb
e) was, is not, is about to come
f) earth shall wonder

If it is the same beast, then here is the political empire of Rome upon which sits all the abominations, fornications, etc. of Rome (the harlot). The seven heads are seven mountains (verse 9) and they are seven kings, verse 10. The ten horns are ten kings, verse 12. Remember the nature of a name once again in Scripture. It is not simply a label, but to God a name was a description of character. We will discuss these later. Rome carries its sinful manner of life like a pack animal carries a burden.

4. Scarlet is the color of luxury, royalty (Matthew 27:28), or sin (Isaiah 1:18). Purple also could be luxury and royalty. These colors together, along with gold, precious stones, and pearls would present a magnificent picture of splendor and glory. This harlot then would be impressive and attractive so as to lure attention and cover her true self. A golden cup would complete the picture of a regal queen and one would expect the best and sweetest of wines,

John's Revelation

> MOTHER OF HARLOTS AND OF THE ABOMINATIONS OF THE EARTH."
> 6. And I saw the woman drunk with the blood of the saints, and with the blood of the witnesses of Jesus. When I saw her, I wondered greatly.
> 7. And the angel said to me, "Why do you wonder? I will tell you the mystery of the woman and of the beast that carries her, which has the seven heads and the ten horns.
> 8. "The beast that you saw was, and is not, and is about to come up out of the abyss and go to destruction. And those who dwell on the earth, whose name has not been written in the book of life from the foundation of the world, will wonder when they see

yet here we see it is full of abominations and unclean things. The cup is like her, and in both we can see the deceitfulness of sin working.

5. Her name is a mystery, not because it cannot be known, but because she has tried to keep it secret and it is now revealed. Her true self is revealed by her name on her forehead. Once again then we see that a name is used for identification—not just identifying the person, but identifying the character of the person. She is BABYLON in that she is magnificent in appearance like the ancient city. She is the MOTHER OF HARLOTS AND THE ABOMINATIONS OF THE EARTH because she brought these things forth. She led other governments to imitate her and encouraged them in doing so. We are given the impression that every evil thing comes from her. So far as those Christians were concerned, this would be correct. Most all evil that came upon them came from Rome.

6. She is overcome with all the martyrs and sacrifices she has caused. She is drunk on blood. These singular victories have caused her to think herself as mighty and invincible, as she actually represents all that is low and shameful. Like the drunk that she is, she will soon stagger and fall. She has exalted herself on the tears, heartaches, and suffering of good people. She is a prostitute covered with innocent blood. Good men will always "wonder" or marvel greatly that others can be so deceived. To believe that the pleasure of sin is lasting, that persecuting God's people will conquer them, or that gold and scarlet equals true nobility, these are the deceits of Satan that Rome (and many today) buy into.

7. The angel notices John's wonder at a harlot drunken on innocent blood and arrayed in splendor in the wilderness. The beast and the woman are one, indivisible " for lust rides upon, controls, and governs any ravenous, persecuting and self-seeking political beast. At the same time, the beast supports such a harlot."[48]

> the beast, that he was and is not and will come.
> 9. "Here is the mind which has wisdom. The seven heads are seven mountains on which the woman sits,
> 10. and they are seven kings; five have fallen, one is, the other has not yet come; and when he comes, he must remain a little while.
> 11. "The beast which was and is not, is himself also an eighth and is *one* of the seven, and he goes to destruction.

8. Perdition (*apoleia*, Gk.) means destruction, utter ruin, or loss of well-being. It is *possible* that the "was, and is not, and is about to come up..." refers to the fact that the Roman government *was* a terrible thing until Nero was slain, and so at this writing it *is not*. Many look upon Domitian as being almost a reincarnation of Nero and under his reign Christians suffered terribly so that it *is about to come*. I have my doubts about Domitian, but the only other suggestion that I have is that this should be taken in a more general view. The beast *was* in that it had been persecuting saints. It *is not* in the sense that as this book was being written, persecution had slacked up. And it *is about to come up*..., i.e., persecution is going to begin again, whether it was Domitian or another emperor. This view would fit better with the facts of Domitian rather than the traditions and it would go along with the idea of warning the saints not to slack up in their alertness.

We can see the message without necessarily identifying the players, as the Christians of that day would have been better able to do. The unregenerate world that followed Rome wondered as they saw Rome turn its hatred on God's people time and time again. One point upon which there is no dispute, however, is that the beast is going to destruction. The message of this verse is the message of the book—perseverance and hope for God's people because ruin awaits their persecutors.

9-11. There have been many ideas put forth on these passages; but rather than spend time with those ideas, many of which seem silly and fruitless, I believe there is a more logical explanation. Rather than try and count empires and Caesars and try to make them fit into some kind of numerology formula, let us be consistent and use the same system that we have been using thus far in the book. The number seven repeatedly means completeness and the number 10 is the number representing power. The seven mountains lead us directly to the idea that this is Rome, since that city was often referred to as being built on seven hills. The seven kings here are the complete rulers of Rome, i.e., all of them. The fact that five are gone, one is and one is yet to come, shows us that we are near the end of the total rule of Rome IN THIS VISION. The fact that the beast

> 12. "The ten horns which you saw are ten kings who have not yet received a kingdom, but they receive authority as kings with the beast for one hour.
> 13. "These have one purpose, and they give their power and authority to the beast.
> 14. "These will wage war against the Lamb, and the Lamb will overcome them, because He is Lord of lords and King of kings, and those who are with Him *are the* called and chosen and faithful."
> 15. And he *said to me, "The waters which you saw where the harlot sits, are peoples and multitudes and nations and tongues.

himself is the eighth (out of seven mind you) shows us that the ungodly leaders, political Rome, and Satan are all intertwined together. When the leaders are taken down, then they go into perdition or destruction. They draw their power from the abyss or Satan, and as all anti-God powers, are torn down after a little while. This then is not intended as some secret code for the Caesars to be identified. It was intended as a timeline for the empire to show the Christians that the end was near.

12. Remember the number ten represents power, a fullness of it. The beast has ten horns; therefore, this is the power of the beast. It could be a reference to the nations or provinces ruled by Rome who gave their support to Rome. It could also be a reference to the territories ruled by kings under Roman control like Herod in Judea. This makes more sense than the idea that it is the kings who are going to be gathered against the Lamb. They do have authority themselves but it is only *with the beast*. It also might go along with Daniel's vision of toes on the great image in Nebuchadnezzar's dream. And their authority is short-lived, lasting only an "hour," i.e., a short, measured time.

13-14. As those in Christ are of one mind, so it is that those in Satan also are of one mind, and they throw their support behind the beast so that he (they) fights against the Lamb. This was accomplished by the nations joining Rome in its fight against the Christians. However, as this entire book points out, the Lamb and His followers will overcome whether it seems so or not. The reason they will overcome is plainly stated. They will overcome "because He is Lord of Lords and King of Kings." He has *all* power and *all* authority. It is foolish for any man or group of men to believe they can stand against Him. This reveals some of the power in the deceitfulness of Satan's words. That he can consistently down through the ages convince man to stand against his Creator and God, flying in the face of all authority, is tribute to his guile and temptation.

> 16. "And the ten horns which you saw, and the beast, these will hate the harlot and will make her desolate and naked, and will eat her flesh and will burn her up with fire.
> 17. "For God has put it in their hearts to execute His purpose by having a common purpose, and by giving their kingdom to the beast, until the words of God will be fulfilled.
> 18. "The woman whom you saw is the great city, which reigns over the kings of the earth."

15. Here and in verse 1 we are told the harlot sits on the waters; yet in verse 3 John saw the woman sitting on a beast. These verses show us that though the woman and the beast represent different ideas, they are one, entwined. They are political Rome and the lust and desire of Rome. These people (waters) are the nations and races that Rome ruled over.

16. Though the ten kings support the harlot at first, at the end they hate her. This is because they were involved in these evil activities for selfish reasons, just like individuals who are lured into immorality to gratify their own lusts and then hate themselves and the other for the deceit and their own foolishness. Though governed by lusts, political powers run by evil desires hate the desires and their own weaknesses. Because of this they will ultimately turn on that which formerly they loved.

17. Showing once again that God is in control, we see that God uses their evil hearts and desires to unite them for His purposes and then destroy them for their wicked rebellion. It is never God's intention to judge or condemn without cause. It is always His will for men to repent. He will allow men to fill up the cup of their own iniquity, by their own choice, thereby deserving the judgment that comes upon them.

18. There should be no doubt after this verse that the harlot is Rome, "the great city that reigns over the kings of the earth." "The great city" represents the three methods of Satan's fight against the church

   1) political power or brute force,
   2) false religion or deceit, and
   3) the lusts and desires of the world.

"The great city" represents to us the world and all that is evil in the world that fights against the church as well as any power of society turned against the Lord and His works.

John's Revelation

QUESTIONS ON CHAPTER 17

1. What was the angel going to show John?

2. What was the relationship of the harlot to the kings of the earth?

3. What does this relationship mean to us?

4. What does the woman sit on in this chapter? (3 times)

5. What do the 10 horns signify?

6. What is the meaning of "purple and scarlet"?

7. How did her appearance contrast with her wine?

8. Upon what was she "drunk"?

9. Who is this harlot?

10. What did the angel say the 7 heads were?

11. How could the beast be described as "was, is not, and will come"?

12. Why would the Lamb be able to overcome the beast and 10 kings?

13. What do "the waters" signify?

14. What would be the end result of the allegiance between the kings and the beast?

15. Why?

16. Who would assist the Lamb in His battle?

John's Revelation

Revelation 18

1. After these things I saw another angel coming down from heaven, having great authority, and the earth was illumined with his glory.

2. And he cried out with a mighty voice, saying, "Fallen, fallen is Babylon the great! She has become a dwelling place of demons and a prison of every unclean spirit, and a prison of every unclean and hateful bird.

THE REVELATION
chapter 18

1. "After these things" refers to that which follows the vision in chapter 17, not a period of years, months, etc. The importance of what this angel has to say is shown by the fact that he has great authority and the earth is illuminated by his glory. In his authority we also see that he comes from the presence of deity since all authority of any kind ultimately proceeds from God. His illumination says the same thing in that we are reminded of the face of Moses that shined so bright after communion with God that he had to put a veil on to hide it.

2. In chapter 17, we saw a harlot in the wilderness. In 17:18, this woman is described as the "great city, which reigns over the kings of the earth." In 18:2, we find that the "great city" is now called Babylon. See also 18:10, 16, and 18-19. This vision should be understood in the same way chapter 13 was. There we had a sea beast, an earth beast, and an image of the first. To the first century Christians, these would be understood as Rome, the religion of Rome (emperor worship), and the worldliness that was the image of Rome worshipped by men. We, however, can see that the principles go farther than that. To us the various beasts represent government power or brute force, *any* false and deceiving religion, and once again the carnality that most people worship and follow after. So it is here. The woman is the great city Babylon of chapter 18. To those of that time she would be Rome (refer to 17:18), but to us Rome represents the world in all its sensuality, immorality, worldliness, etc. The fall of this power is so sure

> 3. "For all the nations have drunk of the wine of the passion of her immorality, and the kings of the earth have committed *acts of* immorality with her, and the merchants of the earth have become rich by the wealth of her sensuality."
> 4. I heard another voice from heaven, saying, "Come out of her, my people, so that you will not participate in her sins and receive of her plagues;

that the angel speaks of it as already accomplished, in the past tense. This is the same way God spoke to Isaiah (Isaiah 21:9) 150 years before the fall of ancient Babylon. It was such a sure thing that it was spoken of as already being done (past tense), although it was really yet to come. See 18:8 where it is still in the future.

In contrast with her majesty, power, luxury, sensuality, etc., is the fate of her after her destruction. Every foul and wicked thing is her inhabitant. A "hold" (KJV) is a "prison" (NASB), or someplace where something is kept. Rather than something good and righteous, this also tells us the end result of worldliness and sin. Her end result is to be a haunt of unclean scavengers, diseased eaters of carrion. We see the same picture here of this figurative "Babylon" as Isaiah was presented of the actual Babylon. Isaiah 13:19-22.

3. "Wantonness" (KJV) is sensuality or lust characterized by an abundance of material wealth. This verse is the explanation of the "why" behind verse 2, her destruction. The "fornication" (KJV) or "immorality" (NASB) spoken of here is not sexual but political and moral. This is brought out in the mention of the merchants. Those who wield power in the world, kings and merchants, had abandoned conviction, conscience, and righteousness to woo Rome and the riches and power she possessed. This continues today as individuals forsake goodness and mercy to woo this world and its riches.

4. A voice of warning, representing God, calls His people out of the temptation of the harlot. To them this would be Rome, but the principle comes to us in the shape of the world in general. This same call comes more directly to us through other apostles. Note: 2 Corinthians 6:14-18 and Ephesians 5:11. "Be ye separate" is always the call of God to His people. To participate in the sins of those around us is to draw the same deserved punishment that will come upon them. How many Christians down through the ages have consoled themselves with their

> 5. for her sins have piled up as high as heaven, and God has remembered her iniquities.
> 6. "Pay her back even as she has paid, and give back *to her* double according to her deeds; in the cup which she has mixed, mix twice as much for her.

sonship and deceived themselves into thinking that they would somehow avoid punishment for committing the same sins as the world engaged in. How sad.

"To receive not her plagues, would be to escape the wrath of God that shall come upon her and her children. This is why the true child of God cannot, yea dare not, fellowship error."[49]

5. God allows wickedness to continue until a certain point is reached. It then can be allowed to continue no longer. Note: 2 Chronicles 28:9; Jeremiah 51:9; Ezra 9:6. This has been referred to as the "leavening principle." When there is not enough righteous leaven remaining in a nation, people, or city, then God brings judgment. It is the principle seen in the Old Testament when the Lord would have spared Sodom for 10 righteous souls that could not be found. In the time of Abraham, he was told that he could not possess the promised land because the cup of Amorite iniquity was not yet full. Four hundred and thirty years later, however, that land was taken from them and given to Israel. The northern 10 tribes of Israel were allowed to pursue their God-rejecting way until they reached the point of sacrificing their own children. At that point God had enough and sent them into Assyrian captivity. The Southern tribes of Judah lasted another 150 years or so; but when they reached that same point of perversion, they also were laid under the punishment of Babylonian captivity. God will give time for repentance because He is a merciful God, but it appears that when the "point of no return" is reached, then judgment is swift and harsh.

This passage also intimates that sin will not be forgotten. Again, we see this principle revealed in the Old Testament when God repeatedly forgives His people Israel but remembers their sins against them when they finally commit themselves to the path of error and idolatry.

6-7. If we sow one seed, we reap an entire ear of grain; sow the wind and reap the whirlwind; sow a hundredfold and we reap a thousand fold. It is a deceit that says one can sow wild oats and then pray for crop failure. Sin's pleasure only lasts a season, then judgment is rendered. Those that glorify themselves are the ones who set themselves against God and these are the very ones God sets himself against. She exalts herself by saying and believing:

7. "To the degree that she glorified herself and lived sensuously, to the same degree give her torment and mourning; for she says in her heart, 'I SIT *as* A QUEEN AND I AM NOT A WIDOW, and will never see mourning.'
8. "For this reason in one day her plagues will come, pestilence and mourning and famine, and she will be burned up with fire; for the Lord God who judges her is strong.
9. "And the kings of the earth, who committed *acts of* immorality and lived sensuously with her, will weep and lament over her when they see the smoke of her burning,

a) I am a queen, b) and am not a widow, c) and will never see mourning.

She is in actuality a "whore" (KJV) not a queen. She is not a widow simply because she will have no husband, she is a "harlot" (NASB). She boasts about not seeing the very thing God says she shall see. Concerning self-glory, read 2 Samuel 22:28; Proverbs 11:2; Proverbs 16:18, 29:23. Notice the boasting of Tyre and ancient Babylon (Ezekiel 28:2 and Isaiah 47:7ff).

8. Because of the above attitude, every terrible thing will come up against her as a judgment of God. And it will happen in "one day" or very, very quickly. "Pestilence" (NASB) is disease. "Mourning" would imply death. "Famine" would indicate suffering, being inclusive of the other two with the addition of suffering without the benefit of death. The point is to show how low she will be brought from where she thinks she sits now. The one who saw herself as a queen beyond the reach of ordinary mortal sorrows will become the modern day bag lady, literally buried under sorrow, grief, and disgrace.

9-10. The great ones of the earth will weep at her destruction, not because they care for her, but because they will lose all they could gain from her. They actually weep for themselves and their own losses and this is shown by the fact that they keep their distance. A lot of tears, lots of talk, but they kept their distance because they feared her torment. These "kings of the earth" are the national, political leaders who got into bed with Rome for the power she offered and thus shared in the activities that brought about her destruction. They have good reason to

> 10. standing at a distance because of the fear of her torment, saying, 'Woe, woe, the great city, Babylon, the strong city! For in one hour your judgment has come.'
> 11. "And the merchants of the earth weep and mourn over her, because no one buys their cargoes any more--
> 12. cargoes of gold and silver and precious stones and pearls and fine linen and purple and silk and scarlet, and every *kind of* citron wood and every article of ivory and every article *made* from very costly wood and bronze and iron and marble,
> 13. and cinnamon and spice and incense and perfume and frankincense and wine and olive oil and fine flour and wheat and cattle and sheep, and *cargoes* of horses and chariots and slaves and human lives.

fear her torment seeing as how they were involved in the same activities. Thus is seen the fellowship and friendship of sin.

11-13. The same idea as verses 9-10, but instead of those who court her for power, these woo her for wealth. Notice verse 11. They weep not for the harlot (Rome) but for the fact that their trade is ruined. Imagine the picture that John is presented with. All the imports and exported goods of this great international power are marched before his eyes. One article that stands out in the list is the one mentioned last in verse 13. Rome has not only traded in slaves but in human lives. There is a distinction between the two. Slave trade, though repugnant to us today, would have been an acceptable business in that day. These "human lives" must be something different than slaves, however. We are given no indication of what they were. Their trade in human life might have been the execution of Christians, political shenanigans that abused the populace, or corruption in the criminal justice system that would allow the innocent to be harmed by evildoers instead of protected by their government. History says the moral climate of Rome was deteriorating rapidly and this is testified to by the high rate of divorce as well as the homosexuality and pedophilia of her Caesars. Maybe their trade in human life included all or any combination of these. One thing to see, however, is that this trade was listed before John right alongside of trade in cattle, sheep, and horses. This meager value placed upon human life, to equate it with animal life, must surely be a contributing factor to her destruction, and we would do well to resist this same attitude in our society today. The same attitude is seen today that dishonors marriage, encourages homosexuality and pedophilia, and treats the unborn, sick, and elderly as animals to be put to sleep by abortion and euthanasia. It is seen in cloning human beings for surgical replacement parts and a multitude of other inhuman scientific efforts.

> 14. "The fruit you long for has gone from you, and all things that were luxurious and splendid have passed away from you and *men* will no longer find them.
> 15. "The merchants of these things, who became rich from her, will stand at a distance because of the fear of her torment, weeping and mourning,
> 16. saying, 'Woe, woe, the great city, she who was clothed in fine linen and purple and scarlet, and adorned with gold and precious stones and pearls;
> 17. for in one hour such great wealth has been laid waste!' And every shipmaster and every passenger and sailor, and as many as make their living by the sea, stood at a distance,

14-17a. Note that all these things mentioned are luxuries, as is pointed out in verse 14. All the splendid things of this world cannot help her. These represent the same temptations of worldliness that we must contend with today. Those who weep and mourn now are those who have been pulling the strings for so long. They were "rich" because of her and now all they see is "waste." They, like the political leaders, stand at a distance, disassociating themselves from Rome because they fear her torment. They also contributed to her downfall and shared in her evil activities. They fear a similar sharing in her pain. Here is an eternal lesson in picture form of all those who follow selfish indulgence instead of being guided by God. They will suffer the consequences of their activities while their "friends," the ones who used them for their own profit, distance themselves from the situation. No amount of distancing will work, however, and their judgment also is waiting.

17b-19. These also either ran the merchant's (above) ships or made their living from them. These also profited from the vice and wickedness of the great harlot. We could point out parallels in the great and wealthy men who manufacture liquor and beer of every kind and those who claim to be innocent, who only drive the trucks to deliver it. We could name the vice of prostitution, pornography, sex shops, internet activities, and the like, and how the individual who joins in this is supporting organized crime, drugs, murder, and every foul and wicked thing on a national and international level. All down the line weep because they have lost their wealth when the woman is judged by God. They all seem surprised that this judgment happened so quickly, i.e., "in one hour." Isn't it easy to place great confidence in the seeming stability and strength of ungodly activities. The Christian should not be deceived, however. Everything can be brought down quickly! We must also notice that all step back and do their mourning at a distance because they fear the same torments. Can it be that all down the line that associated with and profited from the worldliness and immorality knew in

> 18. and were crying out as they saw the smoke of her burning, saying, 'What *city* is like the great city?'
> 19. "And they threw dust on their heads and were crying out, weeping and mourning, saying, 'Woe, woe, the great city, in which all who had ships at sea became rich by her wealth, for in one hour she has been laid waste!'
> 20. "Rejoice over her, O heaven, and you saints and apostles and prophets, because God has pronounced judgment for you against her."
> 21. Then a strong angel took up a stone like a great millstone and threw it into the sea, saying, "So will Babylon, the great city, be thrown down with violence, and will not be found any longer.
> 22. "And the sound of harpists and musicians and flute-players and trumpeters will not be heard in you any longer; and no craftsman of any craft will be found in you any longer; and the sound of a mill will not be heard in you any longer;

their hearts that they were guilty by their association with such. We might pass the blame for our involvement in sin while we enjoy its passing pleasures, but the truth is that in our heart of hearts we often know that we are as guilty as the rest by our participation. Come out and be separate is the call of the Lord.

20. This is a relief to the saints, however, and an answer to prayer. The saints share the attitude of their God toward sin. They rejoice in the promises of God as they see them come true. Judgment is for the saints, against evil, and from God.

21. Consider a millstone large enough to be pulled by oxen. Consider the power it would take to lift it and the violence it would cause when thrown into water. Thus is the power of the Lord over Babylon the great. Also consider the idea that once it disappears beneath the waves, it is gone quickly and it is gone for good—not a trace remains to be seen.

22-23. The same idea here as in verse 2. It is noteworthy to see that there were beautiful and good things in Rome, just as there is good in almost every evil thing to some degree. Music, work, understanding (light), and the home…these are some of the most valuable aspect of life that God has given us under the sun. But nothing will make up for unthankful hearts that walk in greed, selfishness, and immorality. There is no more good and beautiful things to be found there. She is desolate. Once the facade is taken away we see it was all deceit anyway. There will be no more entertainment and pleasantry, no more craftsmen or laborers, no

> 23. and the light of a lamp will not shine in you any longer; and the voice of the bridegroom and bride will not be heard in you any longer; for your merchants were the great men of the earth, because all the nations were deceived by your sorcery.
> 24. "And in her was found the blood of prophets and of saints and of all who have been slain on the earth."

more homes or families or children. Sin, immorality, selfishness, cruelty, deceit, materialism, idol worship, hunger for power, ingratitude and injustice—these are all diseases that will eat away at a society until it is so sick and perverted it cannot be allowed to stand.

24. Once she can deceive no longer, we see the blood of God's righteous that has been spilled here. Purple robes will not cover these bloodstains. All her corruption is brought to view. Every wrong done to God's people will ever be remembered and brought to light sooner or later. That is what judgment is all about, whether it is judgment on a city, a nation, or finally on this world in which we live.

QUESTIONS ON CHAPTER 18

1. From where did the "great angel" get his authority?

2. How do you know?

3. What had happened to Babylon?

4. What was the relationship of "the nations" with Babylon?

5. What did this mean?

6. What was the relationship of "kings" with her?

7. What was the "merchants" relationship with her?

8. Who was told to get out of Babylon?

9. Why?

10. To what degree would Babylon be repaid for her activities?

11. In what 3 ways did she think of herself?

12. What 2 time periods are used to describe her fall?

13. What does this mean?

14. Why would the kings mourn and weep over her?

15. Why would they stand at a distance?

16. Why would the merchants mourn?

17. What one commodity in the list of luxury goods stands apart?

18. Who are the people of verse 17?

19. What is the opposite attitude of mourning expressed in this text, and who is to have it?

20. When all of that which is attractive and beautiful was taken away from Rome, what was left exposed?

John's Revelation

Revelation 19	2. BECAUSE HIS JUDGMENTS ARE TRUE AND RIGHTEOUS; for He has judged the great harlot who was corrupting the earth with her immorality, and HE HAS AVENGED THE BLOOD OF HIS BOND-SERVANTS ON HER."
1. After these things I heard something like a loud voice of a great multitude in heaven, saying, "Hallelujah! Salvation and glory and power belong to our God;	

THE REVELATION
chapter 19

INTRODUCTION:

Verses 1-10 of this chapter should be included as an ending to the last chapter in form, subject, and thought. This is the answer to the command of 18:20 where heaven was told to rejoice. They are rejoicing because God's justice is being seen in this judgment of wrath.

1. After seeing how the world will lament the falling of Babylon and why she deserves her terrible judgment, John hears a loud voice like a multitude. They are praising and giving glory to God. The term "Hallelujah" means in Hebrew "praise ye Jehovah." Could this be the great multitude of chapter 7? It would work contextually, but we cannot be dogmatic because in the NASB John does not say that he actually hears a great multitude, but "as it were" a multitude.

2. The reason for the praise is because His judgments are true and righteous and they have avenged the blood of His bondservants. Implication is made once again that she deserves all the judgments of God that have been handed down. The very fact that He has judged the harlot shows that His judgment is true. His judgments are "true" because they are penetrating and accurate. Being able to discern the motives and secrets of men, God's judgments will always be correct beyond any point of question. His judgments are "righteous" because they are undeniably right. In God is no darkness at all! His judgment is the difference between black and white, right and wrong. When God determines something as wrong, it is absolutely so. Likewise, when He declares one as righteous, no one can impugn or deny it.

> 3. And a second time they said, "Hallelujah! HER SMOKE RISES UP FOREVER AND EVER."
> 4. And the twenty-four elders and the four living creatures fell down and worshiped God who sits on the throne saying, "Amen. Hallelujah!"
> 5. And a voice came from the throne, saying, "Give praise to our God, all you His bond-servants, you who fear Him, the small and the great."
> 6. Then I heard *something* like the voice of a great multitude and like the sound of many waters and like the sound of mighty peals of thunder, saying, "Hallelujah! For the Lord our God, the Almighty, reigns.

3.   With a second shout they end the praise as they began it. What an emphasis! The fact that the smoke of torment goes up "forever and ever" shows that there shall be no end to this torment. See also Jude 7; Isaiah 34:8ff; 66:24.

4.   A second (24 elders) and a third (4 creatures) group add their amen (so be it) to the glory given. It is about all one can do. We see here all heaven agreeing with the sentiments of the song. We also see agreement with the judgment of destruction. The judgments of God are surely deserved and this is obvious to all in heaven who observe it.

5.   Once again, a voice proceeds from the presence of God, that is, from His throne. It gives instruction to all the saints (bondservants), (servants, KJV). When the Revelation refers to servants, I believe they are workers upon the earth because there is a clear message that when one leaves this life in a faithful state, he leaves his work behind and enters into his rest. Therefore, these bondservants represent the church on earth. Praise is due to God as well as fear (reverence), because He has proven once more that His word is firm and that He will care for His kingdom. The command to praise God (give thanks?) would have been appreciated in that day as they saw God's love exhibited. However, this command to praise comes down to us today in the form of this book. In knowing what God does, has done, and can do, we also should appreciate and praise Him in gratitude.

6.   The saints on earth add their voices to the elders and creatures and the resulting sound is again "as it were" a great multitude, as the sound of many waters, and as the sound of thunder. It is a tremendous voice of deafening, all-encompassing praise for the Lord who reigns. The term Almighty "denotes sovereignty over all creation."[50] We note that the Christ applied this title to Himself in 1:8 bringing home the fact of His equality with the Father, not to be denied or diminished.

> 7. "Let us rejoice and be glad and give the glory to Him, for the marriage of the Lamb has come and His bride has made herself ready."
> 8. It was given to her to clothe herself in fine linen, bright *and* clean; for the fine linen is the righteous acts of the saints.
> 9. Then he *said to me, "Write, 'Blessed are those who are invited to the marriage supper of the Lamb.'" And he *said to me, "These are true words of God."

7. This is the third woman that has been introduced (radiant woman - chapter 12, harlot - chapter 17). She is the bride of the Lamb. We must think of this relationship between Jesus and His bride in the same way that early Christians would have. At that time an engagement or betrothal was looked upon and referred to as already being married. Remember, for example, Mary and Joseph. Mary was taken care of as a wife, and Joseph considered putting her away, even before they were actually married. It was the custom that a marriage feast would begin the actual marriage. Thus the church is referred to as a virgin *and* a bride (2 Corinthians 11:2; Ephesians 5:23-32) at the same time, and thus the comment here in verse 7 that the bride has "made herself ready." She is preparing for the marriage feast that is to come.

8. "Fine linen, bright and clean" should be understood in the same way as "holy and without blemish," Ephesians 5:27. This clothing for the bride is explained as the "righteous acts of the saints." This lesson is brought out in other places in the New Testament. Just like a bride now would not wear a wedding gown that is soiled and spotted, so the bride of Christ, or the church, will be presented to Christ clean and white. All spot or soil will be cleaned out of the church. The spots would be sin and saints who engage in the ways of this world.

9. "He" here could be the voice from the throne (verse 5) in the form of some person according to verse 10. Or it could be the angel from the previous chapter. This is the fourth beatitude we have seen to be written. The one who is invited to the feast, i.e., the faithful member of the kingdom or Christian, is blessed, fortunate, or happy. "As the seer had introduced the fall of Babylon in 14:8, but reserved the description of the fall to chapter 18, so here the Lord speaks of the feast as if it is taking place, but reserves the revealing of the actual occasion until chapter 21."[51] It is then pointed out that these words can be relied upon because they are "true words of God."

10. John is probably overwhelmed at the scenes he has beheld and so tries to pay homage to whoever this is. He is corrected with the admonition to worship God,

> 10. Then I fell at his feet to worship him. But he *said to me, "Do not do that; I am a fellow servant of yours and your brethren who hold the testimony of Jesus; worship God. For the testimony of Jesus is the spirit of prophecy."
> 11. And I saw heaven opened, and behold, a white horse, and He who sat on it *is* called Faithful and True, and in righteousness He judges and wages war.

not a fellow servant of God. It is interesting to view other created beings in this light of humility, whether angels, cherubim, or something else. All have their own place of service. The testimony of Jesus is the spirit, or life of all prophecy. Most directly this would define the *"prophecy"* of this book. In testifying the words of Jesus, one would be "speaking from God" (the definition of prophecy). John's assurance of future events is also included in the definition of prophecy.

11. We change scenes now to view a warrior-king on a white charger. The last time we saw a rider on a white horse, He was going forth "conquering and to conquer." Here He is judging and waging war. Do not be mistaken. Once again this is not the final day of judgment, but the day of judgment against those who have hindered His kingdom. On that last great day, He will not be judging and waging war. He will be judging and giving reward. Notice that He is called "faithful and true" and He judges and wages war in righteousness.

The appellation of "faithful and true" would mean a great deal to early Christians who were literally laying their lives on the line for Jesus Christ. The picture of Him waging war on their behalf and standing true to His promises to them would have gone a long way toward encouraging them and helping them to be steadfast. He judges and wages war "in righteousness," i.e., not for selfish or political reasons, but according to the standard of truth. His motives are always pure and dedicated to God's ways.

> 12. His eyes *are* a flame of fire, and on His head *are* many diadems; and He has a name written *on Him* which no one knows except Himself.
> 13. *He is* clothed with a robe dipped in blood, and His name is called The Word of God.
> 14. And the armies which are in heaven, clothed in fine linen, white *and* clean, were following Him on white horses.
> 15. From His mouth comes a sharp sword, so that with it He

12. The description of the Lord's eyes is the same as in 1:14. Satan wore seven diadems or crowns of royalty while the sea beast wore ten, but Jesus wears "many" or "a great number." This might show the power or extent of His rule. Since one's name stands for one's self or character, therefore all that one is, it seems likely that Jesus is the only one who can truly know and understand who Jesus is. Paul wrote in 1 Timothy 3:16 that the mystery of godliness was great, that is, the one who revealed in the flesh, vindicated in the Spirit, and taken up in glory. If this mystery was "great" for the apostle, I'm not sure that we're going to be able to explain it here. Simply put, there is no explanation for this phrase since only Jesus can truly know the object of this sentence, i.e., His name or self.

13. As the Word of God, Jesus is the ultimate revelation of God's will and the active force of God's purpose. The fact that as the Father speaks the Son acts illustrates for us the idea that the Word is made flesh. This is a phrase peculiar to John and his writings. Rather than a robe "dipped in blood," a robe "sprinkled with blood" is more probably right. Note Isaiah 63:1-6. This blood is not the blood of the Christ who died on the cross, neither the blood of His followers. This blood belongs to the enemies of Jesus. This would serve to show His wrath. This is a picture of warfare, of righteous indignation, and protection of His servants. It is a picture of vengeance or repayment for loved ones and brethren caused to suffer and die. It is a picture of courage and victory and inspiration to those who follow the great commander.

14. Because of the white garments (3:5; 6:11; 7:9, 14; 19:8) and white horses, this army, or armies, seems to be made up of victorious saints. The war we speak of is the war mentioned, but not yet described in 16:14-16. John is seeing these victorious and righteous hosts pass in review, as it were.

15. There are two main ideas concerning the sword from His mouth. We see in it either the power of the word (gospel) or we see a sword of judgment. Either idea has merit. In the "rod of iron" we see the power of a king, an unbreakable strength, able to crush His enemies. Note Psalm 2. In the picture of the winepress,

> may strike down the nations, and He will rule them with a rod of iron; and He treads the wine press of the fierce wrath of God, the Almighty.
> 16. And on His robe and on His thigh He has a name written, "KING OF KINGS, AND LORD OF LORDS."
> 17. Then I saw an angel standing in the sun, and he cried out with a loud voice, saying to all the birds which fly in midheaven, "Come, assemble for the great supper of God,
> 18. so that you may eat the flesh of kings and the flesh of commanders and the flesh of mighty men and the flesh of horses and of those who sit on them and the flesh of all men, both free men and slaves, and small and great."
> 19. And I saw the beast and the kings of the earth and their armies assembled to make war against Him who sat on the horse and against His army.

recall 14:19-20. This is a picture of vengeance and judgment carried out by the Son in the name of the Father.

16. "The Lord has a name known only to Himself, and is known to the saints as 'faithful and true' and the 'word of God;' but to all, friends or enemy, He is known as 'King of Kings, and Lord of Lords.'"[52] There is an interesting note here for those folks today who adamantly stand opposed to Christians getting tattoos. This form of decoration doesn't seem to have been unknown to the apostle as he sees the Lord with his name written on His thigh.

17-18. Standing in the sun implies being in broad daylight and able to be seen by all. Perhaps even an intimation of glory is seen here. This scene of invitation to all the eaters of dead flesh is a picture of the complete and utter destruction of the ungodly. No class of man is safe: commander, mighty men, riders on horses, slave or free. All are consumed by the wrath of God, leaving only carrion for the vultures.

19-20. According to 16:13, they are gathered together at Har-magedon, the Mountain of Megiddo, to make war against the Lamb. Watch this passage closely, however. Note that THERE IS NO BATTLE! There is no battle described because the warfare between Satan and the Lamb and the followers of each has already been broken down and given to us on a more daily level in descriptions of the persecutions and admonitions to be strong. There is no battle because sin and sinners can never stand against the poser of the Lamb of God. The battle is all in the mind of the evil ones. It is an imaginary wish that can never take place.

> 20. And the beast was seized, and with him the false prophet who performed the signs in his presence, by which he deceived those who had received the mark of the beast and those who worshiped his image; these two were thrown alive into the lake of fire which burns with brimstone.
> 21. And the rest were killed with the sword which came from the mouth of Him who sat on the horse, and all the birds were filled with their flesh.

The devil can never actually stand against our God. It is laughable to think so. In fact, the entire history of mankind presents itself as a huge comedy routine when we can look behind the scene to see how little power Satan actually has to affect the plan of God. The tragedy is that so many men fall prey to this idea that they can somehow, somewhere, sometime… come out victorious by joining forces with the dragon. Here the end result is described, going even a bit farther in the next chapter. The idea of being "cast alive" into the lake does not mean these two beasts were individuals, but that they were still alive and fighting when they were brought to their complete and final end. Rome, its persecuting power, and its religion went down kicking.

21. Those that followed these beasts were also killed, but were not cast into the lake of fire. That will be their fate upon the last day. We leave them simply with their life taken away, which is exactly what happened when Rome and its paganism was destroyed.

John's Revelation

QUESTIONS ON CHAPTER 19

1. Define Hallelujah.

2. Who is this great multitude?

3. Why are God's judgments true and righteous?

4. What does smoke rising forever imply?

5. What was the contribution of the elders and cherubim to the song?

6. What does "Almighty" mean?

7. Who is the bride of the Lamb?

8. How would the bride "make herself ready"?

9. What is the fine, bright linen she clothes herself with?

10. What would stain these marriage garments?

11. Who are the "blessed" ones in this chapter?

12. Why was John's worship rebuked here?

13. What did he see when heaven opened?

John's Revelation

14. What does a diadem signify?

15. What might his eyes as a flame of fire indicate?

16. Whose blood is upon his robe?

17. Explain the sharp sword from his mouth.

18. What is the rod of iron for?

19. All will know Jesus by what name?

20. Why were the birds of heaven called?

21. What happened to the beast and the false prophet?

22. What happened to their army?

From Beneath the Altar

> **Revelation 20**
>
> 1. Then I saw an angel coming down from heaven, holding the key of the abyss and a great chain in his hand.
> 2. And he laid hold of the dragon, the serpent of old, who is the devil and Satan, and bound him for a thousand years;

THE REVELATION
Section II, 7 (see page 13)
chapter 20

INTRODUCTION

We are beginning the seventh or last section of this letter to make our study complete. This chapter is noted among all others as having the distinction of the "millennium" (thousand year period) mentioned in it. From this mention comes a host of false doctrines and theories. We believe this chapter is not so concerned with the thousand year reign as it is with the fate of Satan and the saints. However, we will spend some time with this idea since so many do believe and teach it.

1. "Angel coming down from heaven" is a consistent picture that we have seen to show us from whence the power precedes to control the great deceiver. "The key" symbolizes power or authority and the "great chain" is that which is used to bind Satan. We are NOT being taught here that Satan is bound with a literal chain just as we are NOT taught in the next verse that he is literally cast into the abyss. This is a vision. Whenever we forget this, we are close to straying from the context and missing the message. We must look for the message in the vision, not take the vision itself as true.

2. The devil's four names are given again here. He is strong and ferocious as a dragon. He is cunning and full of deceit as a serpent. As the devil, he is an accuser and slanderer of God and man. And as Satan he is the adversary and opponent. This "thousand years" should not be taken literally. It makes no sense to apply symbolic meanings to numbers all the way through the book, such as 4, 7, 3 1/2, 10, 666, 144,000, etc., and then jump up in this passage and declare that this thousand years is a *literal* one thousand years. In Psalm 50:10, is it literal when God says that the cattle on a thousand hills are His? If so, then what about the cattle on hill number one thousand and one? Don't they belong to Him also? Obviously this number simply represents a large, complete number...but not a specific one. Again, in Psalm 105:8, is it literal when we find that God will

3. and he threw him into the abyss, and shut *it* and sealed *it* over him, so that he would not deceive the nations any longer,	until the thousand years were completed; after these things he must be released for a short time.

remember His word for a thousand generations? If so, then does He forget His word with generation number one thousand and one? Once again we repeat, the number represents a large, complete number...but not a literal one. The devil was going to be bound for a great number of years until whatever God is doing is completed, but not necessarily one thousand years exactly. This writer believes that Satan began to be bound as Jesus and His apostles taught the coming of the kingdom and need for repentance. We see again this illustration in Luke 10:18. Jesus was seeing Satan lose power at the news of the coming King and the preaching of the gospel. It started there in the first century, it is continuing now, and will continue until the last person that will be saved is saved. We will comment further on this as we continue.

3.   The point in binding Satan and casting him into the abyss was so that "he should not deceive the nations any longer." Therefore, we submit that this vision is a figurative binding. Satan is not helpless for he "prowls about like a roaring lion, seeking someone to devour," 1 Peter 5:8. But his activities *are* hindered or restrained. This most often is the meaning of the term "bound" in the New Testament. Satan is "as a dog, chained to a wire between two trees. He can operate only within the limited distance between the trees, and to the length of the chain from side to side."[53]   The point in this is to say that to get into the dog's power you must willfully go into the area he has authority over. He is not loose to attack you at any and all times. So it is with Satan. To get into his power you must willfully go near to him and the things of this life he controls. He cannot set his teeth in you if you stay away from him and resist him when he approaches you. He is bound so that he cannot reach you if you will resist him. The binding stopped his deceit. He *cannot* deceive you today unless you allow it. 2 Corinthians 2:11 tells us that his "schemes" are not something that we cannot know about. He is bound until the thousand years are completed, that is, during the time that Christ reigns (verse 4), however long or short it may be. After that time he will be released for a short time. Do not confuse this "short time" with the "little while" or "short time" already discussed. That was the time of Roman persecution, the first couple hundred years of the church's existence. This "short time" will be at the end of time, *after* the thousand year reign of Jesus Christ. This writer has believed for a long while in the idea that when there is not enough "salt" to provide a "leavening influence" on the "loaf," God brings a destroying judgment upon it. This principle was illustrated with

> 4. Then I saw thrones, and they sat on them, and judgment was given to them. And I *saw* the souls of those who had been beheaded because of their testimony of Jesus and because of the word of God, and those who had not worshiped the beast or his image, and had not received the mark on their forehead and on their hand; and they came to life and reigned with Christ for a thousand years.

Sodom and Gomorrah. When there were not enough righteous people to save it, it was destroyed. So it also was with the Amorites (Genesis 15:16), with Israel, with Jerusalem, with the Jewish nation, etc. So also it must be with this world. When there are not enough Christians to save it any longer, that is, when the last one has been saved, God will destroy it.

Let's tie it all together now. Jesus said He saw Satan *like a star falling from heaven* in Luke 10:18 when He sent His seventy out to proclaim His coming and to work miracles in His name. Satan began to be restrained at the good news of repentance and the coming kingdom. When Jesus died it was Satan "bruising his heel," but when He was resurrected He bruised Satan's head, Genesis 3:15. That power to bind, restrain, or bruise Satan's head is in the gospel, Romans 1:16. As long as that gospel is proclaimed, Satan's power is hindered, he is bound. After the last person is saved (a time that only God can know) and the gospel has no more effect on this world, then Satan will be loosed. He will be loosed because there will be no proclaiming of the word to bind him. He will be rampant for a little while. Then since there are no saved to continue this earth for, God will destroy it finally.

4. The "they" sitting on the thrones must refer to the following. They are made up of two groups...

  a) those that had been beheaded because of the testimony,
  b) and those who had not worshipped the beast or his image.

These seem to be 1) those who had given their lives for the gospel, and 2) those who had not given their lives but were of the same spirit, being willing to suffer for the sake of the gospel, but never being called upon to do so. These groups might also be...1) those who had given their lives for the gospel, and 2) those still alive on the earth. This last idea seems worthy of note. For the phrase "came to life," see the next verse. The judgment given is the judgment cried for in 6:10. Perhaps it is also a reference to 1 Corinthians 6:2-3 where we are told that saints will judge the world as well as angels.

> 5. The rest of the dead did not come to life until the thousand years were completed. This is the first resurrection.
> 6. Blessed and holy is the one who has a part in the first resurrection; over these the second death has no power, but they will be priests of God and of Christ and will reign with Him for a thousand years.

5. These that "came to life" (verse 4) and reigned with Christ seem to be saints, both living and dead. The "first resurrection" when they came to life was baptism (Romans 6:4-11, NOTE: Christians are alive to God in Christ Jesus because they have put off the body of sin and death in baptism). "The rest of the dead" are those who are spiritually dead in their sins. Because they are not resurrected from the watery grave of baptism, they will not come to life or come to know God until Christ's reign is over and they face Him on the judgment day.

6. This verse is my reason for what is said on verse 5. According to verse 14 the second death is the lake of fire. The ones who will not be affected by the second death are Christians. It is through obedience in baptism (thus the first resurrection) that we put off the old man of sin who would condemn us to that fiery lake. Note especially Romans 6:4-5. We are raised (resurrected) from a watery grave in baptism as Christ was raised from His tomb. We see a "likeness" of Christ's death, burial, and resurrection in New Testament baptism, and we are allowed to participate in such through this obedient act. Notice also in 1 Peter 2:9, Peter calls Christians in general a "royal priesthood." The idea of a royal priesthood is one of priest-kings (thus we reign with Him, or at the very least we share His royalty by sharing His priesthood). John also refers to Christians (Revelation 1:6) as a kingdom of priests. Paul says (Romans 5:17) that we are kings when he states that those who receive God's grace "reign in life through... Jesus Christ."

Note once again that the reign is taking place *now*. Jesus is a "priest-king," i.e., He reigns at the same time He is a priest. If He is a priest now, then He must also be a king now. If He is a king reigning now, then so are Christians because they reign with Him during this time period (thousand years). Children of God should not be looking for and praying for a kingdom to come because it is already here. The kingdom began in John's day (Mark 9:1; Colossians 1:13) and continues even now as the church, Matthew 16:18-19. The figurative "thousand years" began at that time in history when our Lord became a King, inheriting His throne, and this time period during which Christ rules and Satan is bound continues until judgment day.

John's Revelation

> 7. When the thousand years are completed, Satan will be released from his prison,
> 8. and will come out to deceive the nations which are in the four corners of the earth, Gog and Magog, to gather them together for the war; the number of them is like the sand of the seashore.

7. For an explanation of the "loosing of Satan," see comments on verse 3. When the spirit of conviction and loyal devotion that upholds the word of God is gone or no longer distinguishes God's people, Satan will be freed.

In one sense it has always been this way. Evil triumphs when good men do nothing. Whenever the influence of righteousness is absent or unused, Satan's influence grows out of all proportion. Men even come to believe the devil's way is the only way simply because they are not exposed to a higher and nobler ideal. Thus comes the encouragement for the people of God to always strive to be that "light" or "salty flavor" that reveals a better way to the sons of men. What John was presented with here is simply the end result of "bad" proceeding to "worse."

8. Understanding this verse is dependent upon understanding who "Gog and Magog" is. Rather than assigning these terms to modern day nations and governments unknown to the saints that this letter was written to, it would seem to make better sense to continue letting the Bible explain itself. I repeat, "Gog" here is *not* Russia as is presented by a large group of pre-millennialists, including Lindsey. Nor is it any other present day power. In order to figure out what *God* meant by using this figure, look to Ezekiel 38-39.

> "Gog, of the land of Magog was the prince of the countries to the north (38:2ff), the east, west, and south (38:5). He would command a great horde with which he would invade and cover the land of Israel (38:6-9). His eye would be upon the spoil of the land to take it for himself (38:10-13). He would continue even into the "latter days"—the Messianic period (38:16)—but he would be utterly destroyed, buried in defeat, as the birds would gorge on the carcasses of his forces (chapter 39). God said that He had spoken of Gog's coming, but no prophet ever named Gog or Magog. Yet the prophet foretold over and over of the heathen enemies who would come against Israel and who would be defeated and destroyed by his hand. Therefore, we conclude that Gog, of the land of Magog, symbolized all the heathen enemies of God's people from the time of the prophets to the Roman Empire, all who sought to thwart His purpose and to destroy His king."[54]

> 9. And they came up on the broad plain of the earth and surrounded the camp of the saints and the beloved city, and fire came down from heaven and devoured them.
> 10. And the devil who deceived them was thrown into the lake of fire and brimstone, where the beast and the false prophet are also; and they will be tormented day and night forever and ever.
> 11. Then I saw a great white throne and Him who sat upon it, from whose presence earth and heaven fled away, and no place was found for them.

Here in Revelation Gog and Magog represent all those who are against God and anti-Christ in their attitudes. Some think this is Armageddon of chapter 16; others think this is a different battle. I feel it is different. This seems to be a presentation of the outnumbering of the saints at the end of the world by the servants of Satan, not the battle between good and evil that focused in the first century and continues through the centuries. But it really does not matter. Both battles imply the same thing—a gathering to try and stand against God. It cannot succeed. It did not when Rome tried it and it will not at the end of time.

9. Wherever, whenever, and in whatever form this battle takes place, it consists of Satan against Christ and is seen in the world against the church. Satan will always lose. The clear picture here is one in which the saints are surrounded, outmaneuvered, and outnumbered. There is no way they can win and they are mere moments from being overwhelmed. Yet what has taken place all through history takes place here. God stands by his people and rescues them. The devil's hordes never really stood a chance. What is the message? Take heart Christian. No matter if it appears you are outnumbered and cannot win. God and His people always win in the end. They cannot lose.

10. The devil is finally and completely cast down here. He shares the same fate as his former followers, comrades, and tools. Notice: the torment will go on "forever and ever." Contrary to popular mythology, hell is not the devil's habitation or his throne. He is not deity and he will most certainly suffer torment here with those who join him in resisting the will of Jehovah. This is why the demons pleaded to be cast into a herd of swine on the shore of the Gadarenes rather than be tormented before their time. They do not look forward to it anymore than men do.

11. We have seen several judgments of wrath and righteousness and warning. Here though we finally see the great and last judgment. The great white throne indicates the degree of purity involved. Whether it is the Father or the Son who

> 12. And I saw the dead, the great and the small, standing before the throne, and books were opened; and another book was opened, which is *the book* of life; and the dead were judged from the things which were written in the books, according to their deeds.
> 13. And the sea gave up the dead which were in it, and death and Hades gave up the dead which were in them; and they were judged, every one *of them* according to their deeds.
> 14. Then death and Hades were thrown into the lake of fire. This is the second death, the lake of fire.

judges, it makes no matter for they are one in purpose, John 5:22, 27; Matthew 25:31ff; Acts 17:31; Romans 2:16; 14:10; 2 Corinthians 5:10. We can often read of the fact that this earth is going to be taken away (Hebrews 1:11ff; Psalm 102:25-27; 2 Peter 3:10) and here John sees it take place at the end of our time. "No place found for them" indicates that they are totally gone, out of existence.

12. Jesus said there would be a general resurrection, John 5:28ff; Acts 24:15. These "books" seem to record the character and deeds of the individual. This is not to say that God keeps literal books, but that these represent that there is a record of our deeds, whether in the mind of God or elsewhere, and it is not forgotten. This vision of judgment surely gets the message across. In this vision the wicked alone are not judged, but all must give an account (2 Corinthians 5:10; Romans 4:12) and receive a reward, whether eternal punishment or eternal life, Matthew 25:46. The "books" contrast with the "book," notably a singular volume that we surmise contains the name of God's living ones.

13. Not only from tombs and graves do men return to God, but from whatever place they are. It is possible that this has reference to the sea of humanity once again. It is likewise possible that this simply represents all those dead whose bodies were lost to the grave. Death is what claims the body. Hades is what claims the soul. Resurrection implies a reuniting of soul and body. Each one will be judged according to works, not intentions, hopes, wishes, beliefs, or any other such thing, Ecclesiastes 13:14; Hebrews 4:13.

14. Death is the last enemy to be destroyed (1 Corinthians 15:26), and here is where it will end, at this final judgment. Since death is ended, Hades, that follows death, is also finished. There is no more need for this waiting place—judgment day is here. For the righteous, death will now exist no longer. It is destroyed or overcome and life is all that is left for the child of God.

| 15. And if anyone's name was not found written in the book of | life, he was thrown into the lake of fire. |

15. This is the last group of those who rallied against God. "As there is a second higher life, so there is also a second and deeper death. And as after life there is no more death, so after that death there is no more life."[55] The literal meaning of death is separation. When the spirit is separated from the body, the body is dead. When we sin and separate ourselves from God, we are spiritually dead. Here we view those who will be separated from light, life, and God for eternity. This is eternal death. This is a vision of the truth. It is imperative that we have our names written in the Lamb's book of life. This is the reason why!

QUESTIONS ON CHAPTER 20

1. What might the angel "coming down from heaven" signify?

2. What is the "great chain"?

3. What are 4 appellations for the evil one?

4. What do they mean?

5. How long would Satan be bound? How is he actually bound?

6. Explain the term "thousand years" as it is used in this chapter.

7. Who were the ones beheaded because of the testimony?

8. Who are those who have not worshipped the beast?

John's Revelation

9. How long did they reign with Christ?

10. What is the first resurrection?

11. Who are "the rest of the dead"?

12. What is the second death?

13. What is the situation of one who has a part in the first resurrection?

14. What will happen to Satan after the 1,000 years?

15. Who is "God and Magog"?

16. How long will the torment of Satan go on?

17. Which dead stood before the "great white throne"?

18. What books were opened?

19. What is "Hades"?

20. What does it mean that "death and Hades" were cast into the fire?

21. Who else went with them?

22. What is this great scene?

> **Revelation 21**
>
> 1. Then I saw a new heaven and a new earth; for the first heaven and the first earth passed away, and there is no longer *any* sea.
> 2. And I saw the holy city, new Jerusalem, coming down out of heaven from God, made ready as a bride adorned for her husband.

THE REVELATION
chapter 21

INTRODUCTION:

"In a series of visions beginning in chapter 12, the seer beheld the birth of the man-child; the assault on the church by the dragon's agents; the trials of the church; the waging of the great war; the destruction of the harlot city, the beast, and false prophet; the final conflict with Satan and his destruction; the passing of the present order; the final judgment on mankind; and the punishment of the wicked. From this arrangement of the visions, it is logical that the next scene in order would portray the final glory of the church as it comes to rest with God beyond time. This appears to be the design of the revelation before us."[56]

1. We saw the heavens and earth pass away in 20:11. We understand this term "heaven and earth" to mean a new place of existence as well as a new order of things. "No longer any sea," to be in harmony with the rest of the book, implies that society is gone with its constant unrest and tossing to and fro. In this chapter, John is presented with a *vision* beyond the final day of judgment. Remember he is not seeing actual reality, but a picture that signifies what things will be like.

2. As the old order had its holy city, Jerusalem, so also does the new. This new city coming down from God in heaven shows itself to be of heavenly origin, a spiritual creation, Hebrews 11:10; 13:14; Revelation 3:12. This city is the bride spoken of in 19:7-8. She is arrayed in white linen (righteous acts of the saints) and is ready to be presented to her husband (the Lamb) without spot, wrinkle, blemish, or any such thing (Ephesians 5:25-27). This holy city, this new Jerusalem, this bride of Christ that John sees is the church, glorified! These first

> 3. And I heard a loud voice from the throne, saying, "Behold, the tabernacle of God is among men, and He will dwell among them, and they shall be His people, and God Himself will be among them,
> 4. and He will wipe away every tear from their eyes; and there will no longer be *any* death; there will no longer be *any* mourning, or crying, or pain; the first things have passed away."
> 5. And He who sits on the throne said, "Behold, I am making all things new." And He *said, "Write, for these words are faithful and true."

two verses show us the purified church ready to begin eternity with the Savior.

3. In 13:6 and 15:5, we saw the tabernacle in heaven in view. The tabernacle was the dwelling place of God's glory among the people (Exodus 40:16-34) under the old covenant. The word "tabernacle," used as a verb, means to dwell or abide; "the word became flesh and dwelt (tabernacled) among us...," John 1:14. All this points to the idea that now, in this vision, God is dwelling among men. "His people" here refers to saints from all ages. This is borne out by the fact that "people" (singular, NASB) is actually "peoples" (plural, KJV). His people come out from among all the peoples of the earth in every place and in every time. In heaven all will dwell together with God. Let us lay emphasis on the fact that God will dwell *with* and *among* His people. The common idea that God will be in heaven while the saints are elsewhere in a place prepared for them is false. They will be together *with* God according to this vision. This idea also disputes the teaching of the so-called Jehovah's Witnesses. It is their contention that earth will be made into a paradise dwelling place for men. We repeat—the message of this verse is that God will dwell *with* men, not over them still.

4. Along with the old heavens and earth, in passing away go sin and the results of sin, i.e., tears, death, mourning, crying, and pain. All these are in some way resultant from sin and disobedience incongruous with the joy of eternal life with Deity.

5. Whether the Son or the Father speaks from the throne, it is difficult to say, but no matter...it is God. Because of verse 7, I tend to believe it is the Father who speaks, but the claim made in verse 6 is made in 1:8 and 22:13 by the Son. It really matters not for this is truth and the words are faithful to be believed in. The things to be written could possibly include all of verses 1-8.

6. "Alpha and Omega" is the same as "the beginning and the end." These are the first and last letters of the Greek alphabet. We could think of this as "all in

6. Then He said to me, "It is done. I am the Alpha and the Omega, the beginning and the end. I will give to the one who thirsts from the spring of the water of life without cost.
7. "He who overcomes will inherit these things, and I will be his God and he will be My son.
8. "But for the cowardly and unbelieving and abominable and murderers and immoral persons and sorcerers and idolaters and all liars, their part *will be* in the lake that burns with fire and brimstone, which is the second death."
9. Then one of the seven angels who had the seven bowls full of the seven last plagues came and spoke with me, saying, "Come here, I will show you the bride, the wife of the Lamb."
10. And he carried me away in the Spirit to a great and high mountain, and showed me the holy city, Jerusalem, coming down out of heaven from God,

all" or "everything" or "completeness." As God through Jesus provided spiritual water in this life (John 4:10; 7:37), so He will provide the water of life in the next also (22:1)—not just a drink, but a river.

7. This is the same promise made to everyone who overcame in the seven letters.

8. Most of those named are in easily understood classifications. We might note the first ones named, however, the "fearful" (KJV) or "cowardly" (NASB). There is no place in the Lord's army for cowards or those who are timid and fearful. In the Old Testament army of Israel, cowards were sent home. "Sorcerers" were those devoted to magical arts mainly concerned with *gaining control over others.* Often this was done with deceit and/or drugs. Condemned in this grouping are astrologers, fortunetellers, palm readers, those that deal with and those that use various types of drugs and potions. Modern drug use today would be condemned by the word translated drunkenness as well as by this term. Notice that contrary to men's ideas about such things, *all* liars are condemned. We tend to put a premium *on* large lies and "little white lies," one being more heinous than the other. God, however, puts a premium on truth. All liars are condemned.

9. This could be the same angel of 17:1 that showed John the judgment of the harlot. That would be quite a contrast and quite in line with the presentation of visions to the apostle.

10. In a former vision John was looking for a lion and saw a Lamb. Here he is looking for a bride and instead sees a city. John is not seeing this city a second

> 11. having the glory of God. Her brilliance was like a very costly stone, as a stone of crystal-clear jasper.
> 12. It had a great and high wall, with twelve gates, and at the gates twelve angels; and names *were* written on them, which are *the names* of the twelve tribes of the sons of Israel.

time, but instead is repeating himself as he is about to go into greater detail.

11. Keep in mind that this is a vision. Many turn to this passage as a beautiful description of heaven, but his city came *down out of heaven,* so it cannot be heaven. This city is the "bride of Christ" or the *church*. Note once again verses 3, 9, and 10. The city is adorned as a bride in verse 3. The city *is* the bride in vv. 9-10. In 19:7-8, the bride was the church—without spot or blemish. Therefore, we repeat, the bride *is* the city and the city *is* the church. There seems no good reason in this context to think that this city represents the place where saints will live, i.e., heaven. If these precious building materials represent anything, they tell how precious the church is in God's sight, how expensive the church is since it was purchased with the blood of Christ, and how valuable are the souls that make it up, 1 Peter 2:5. God's glory fills it, for He dwells in it, Ephesians 2:22; 3:21. She shines like a jasper stone (diamond). In 4:3, we noted that this stone represented holiness and purity. It does the same here, except it is representing these qualities in the people of God instead of God Himself.

> 13. *There were* three gates on the east and three gates on the north and three gates on the south and three gates on the west.
> 14. And the wall of the city had twelve foundation stones, and on them *were* the twelve names of the twelve apostles of the Lamb.
> 15. The one who spoke with me had a gold measuring rod to measure the city, and its gates and its wall.
> 16. The city is laid out as a square, and its length is as great as the width; and he measured the city with the rod, fifteen hundred miles; its length and width and height are equal.
> 17. And he measured its wall, seventy-two yards, *according to* human measurements, which are *also* angelic *measurements*.

12-13. The wall indicates security and being at peace (great and high wall) while the gates are gates having the names of and are for the entrance of the twelve tribes or spiritual Israel. These gates are on all four sides of the city so that entrance can be had from all directions, that is, wherever the saints come from.

14. The foundation of the church was laid by the twelve apostles, Ephesians 2:20; 1 Corinthians 3:10. There is no disharmony in naming twelve tribes when we know there were actually thirteen, just as there is no disharmony in naming twelve apostles when we know there were actually thirteen. Twelve seems to be the number of the people of God. Whether it is apostles or tribes, twelve represents *all* of them without naming any or them or leaving out any of them.

15. John measured the church on earth with an ordinary measuring stick in 11:1, but the glorified church in heaven is measured by an angel with a golden measuring rod.

16. When John and the angel measure the city, he finds that it is foursquare, a cube, like a huge "holy of holies." The measurements of the city whose length, width, and height are all the same is probably given to us to stagger us. Remember this is the church, not a real city, twelve thousand furlongs (KJV) = 1,500 miles (NASB). For a comparison of size, consider that it is about 1,500 miles from Washington, D.C. to Amarillo, Texas or from New Orleans, Louisiana to Bismarck, North Dakota. Are these actual measurements? How could they be? This is not an actual city—it is a representation of the church. Is the devil really a dragon with a tail that knocks the stars from the sky and a mouth that pours forth a river? Of course not. That vision represents him to us, however. Likewise, this vision represents the church to us.

> 18. The material of the wall was jasper; and the city was pure gold, like clear glass.
> 19. The foundation stones of the city wall were adorned with every kind of precious stone. The first foundation stone was jasper; the second, sapphire; the third, chalcedony; the fourth, emerald;
> 20. the fifth, sardonyx; the sixth, sardius; the seventh, chrysolite; the eighth, beryl; the ninth, topaz; the tenth, chrysoprase; the eleventh, jacinth; the twelfth, amethyst.
> 21. And the twelve gates were twelve pearls; each one of the gates was a single pearl. And the street of the city was pure gold, like transparent glass.
> 22. I saw no temple in it, for the Lord God the Almighty and the Lamb are its temple.

17. One hundered and forty-four cubits = about 72 yards. Notice that the city and the wall are measured in twelves. That is 144 cubits (12 x 12) and 12,000 furlongs (12 x 1,000). Twelve is considered by many to be the number of God's people (see verse 14). Consider twelve tribes (even though there was thirteen), twelve apostles (though there was thirteen once again), and twelve gates with twelve angels and twelve foundation stones on the holy city, which is the bride of the Lamb (the church or God's people). The phrase "according to the measure of a man, that is of an angel" (KJV) means these are human measurements in the hands of an angel. The NASB reads much the same if the added words are taken out. They seem to change the thought.

18. Diamonds and gold so polished it appears as glass make up the material of the wall and the building materials of the city.

19-20. This is a naming of the most precious stones known to the world at that time, many of which are unidentifiable at this time due to names and customs changing. The picture of immeasurable wealth and value comes ringing through loud and clear.

21. Imagine a gate made from a single pearl. This demonstrates that this is a vision of something, not an actual picture. The street, that is the material the street was made from, also consists of that strange polished gold we found earlier. It is so pure and reflective as to give the appearance of glass.

22. This fulfills the promise of 3:12 for the entire interior of the city is one great sanctuary for worship. There is no physical place to go to get to God here for He lives here, i.e., inhabits this place with the people.

23. And the city has no need of the sun or of the moon to shine on it, for the glory of God has illumined it, and its lamp *is* the Lamb. 24. The nations will walk by its light, and the kings of the earth will bring their glory into it. 25. In the daytime (for there will be no night there) its gates	will never be closed; 26. and they will bring the glory and the honor of the nations into it; 27. and nothing unclean, and no one who practices abomination and lying, shall ever come into it, but only those whose names are written in the Lamb's book of life.

23. The glory of God filled the tabernacle and the temple under the old covenant, on earth, and now it lights the church in heaven permanently. This glory and light is in each one.

24. Whatever glory was in the earth and possessed by kings is now laid at the feet of "Him with whom we have to do." These kings and nations are those from every nation who have come to God, Isaiah 60:3; 52:15.

25-26. See Isaiah 60:11. This is the same promise of glory and honor to come to God's people as He made to Israel. No night, no shut gates, no fear, no danger. Nothing but glory and light and life in this city of God.

27. See 20:12. No danger, no criminal enters this city. This city is the church glorified, cleansed, and presented without spot to the Lamb. Every blemish has been removed and the feast is here.

John's Revelation

QUESTIONS ON CHAPTER 21

1. What was the first heaven and earth that passed away?

2. What had happened to the sea?

3. What did John see coming down out of heaven?

4. What was her appearance?

5. What did this vision represent?

6. What does the word "tabernacle" mean?

7. What does it mean that the "tabernacle of God" was among men?

8. What things were taken away with the first heaven and earth?

9. Explain "Alpha and Omega."

10. Who had a part in the lake of fire?

11. What is the second death?

12. Who or what is the "bride of the Lamb"?

13. When John looked for a bride, what did he see?

14. What is the significance of the number '12'?

15. Why are the apostles' names written in the foundation stones?

16. What is the significance of the city's size?

17. What does the gold and precious stones tell you?

18. Why was there no temple in this city?

19. Why was there no sun or moon to shine?

20. When are the gates open to this city?

21. Who is never allowed to enter?

John's Revelation

Revelation 22	On either side of the river was the tree of life, bearing twelve *kinds of* fruit, yielding its fruit every month; and the leaves of the tree were for the healing of the nations.
1. Then he showed me a river of the water of life, clear as crystal, coming from the throne of God and of the Lamb,	
2. in the middle of its street.	3. There will no longer be any

THE REVELATION
chapter 22

INTRODUCTION:

The first five verses of this chapter are a continuation of chapter 21 and the description of that holy city, new Jerusalem.

1. Whether this "water of life" is water that possesses and gives life, or whether it is life itself is no matter of importance. What should stand out here is that the *source* of life is the "throne of God and the Lamb." Note Ezekiel 47:1-12; Joel 3:18; and Zechariah 14:8. Once again we see the idea presented, not of just a drink, but an entire river of life-giving power available. Evil men wanted blood and took the blood of saints. God gave them blood to drink. He drowned them in blood up to the horse's bridles and pouring from the winepress of His wrath. They got more than they expected. Likewise, the godly here receive more than they expect, not just a drink, but a river.

2. "In the middle of the street" shows where the river ran and seems to illustrate its availability to any who are in the city. "Tree (singular) of life" is used here collectively to imply many trees, perhaps a species of tree all of the same kind (i.e., life). "Twelve manner of fruits" (KJV), and "twelve kinds of fruit" (NASB), is more accurately rendered by the ASV as "twelve crops of fruit." There is only *one* kind or manner of fruit, but it is borne continually. The picture we see then is that <u>all</u> life (water and trees) comes from God as well as all spiritual healing (leaves on the trees). These blessings are available in abundance to those who have a citizenship in this city.

3. We can also easily be reminded of the Garden of Eden in this vision. In Eden there was a garden, a river, the tree of life, man's disobedience and separation

> curse; and the throne of God and of the Lamb will be in it, and His bond-servants will serve Him;
> 4. they will see His face, and His name *will be* on their foreheads.
> 5. And there will no longer be *any* night; and they will not have need of the light of a lamp nor the light of the sun, because the Lord God will illumine them; and they will reign forever and ever.
> 6. And he said to me, "These words are faithful and true"; and the Lord, the God of the spirits of the prophets, sent His angel to show to His bond-servants the things which must soon take place.
> 7. "And behold, I am coming quickly. Blessed is he who heeds the words of the prophecy of this book."
> 8. I, John, am the one who heard and saw these things. And when I heard and saw, I fell down to worship at the feet of the angel who showed me these things.

from these, and a curse in death and separation from God. We have seen a river with trees on both sides, a garden, the tree of life, eternal communion with God, no separation, and no longer any type of curse. No sin, therefore, no death or anything abominable. Man is reconciled and the plan is complete. The throne is in the midst of the holy city. How His servants will serve Him is not and has not been revealed. Suffice to say it will be glorious and uninterrupted.

4. In this life, no man has seen God's face. That will be one of our rewards in heaven. This may be the close, personal relationship that will be available. His people will be identified clearly by His name. Since a person's name represents, in the Scriptures quite often, not "who" a person is, but his character or "what" he is on the inside, it is a singular honor to wear the name of God and shows a kinship between God and His people. They are similar in nature, dare we say, one is in the image of the other?

5. See 21:23-25. Notice the progression from reigning a thousand years with Him in this life to reigning forever and ever at that time.

6. "He" is probably the angel that was speaking to John. The visions are over and the angel is closing this book to the churches in the name of the Lord. "These words" are the words of this book. "Shortly take place" is from *tacheos* (Gk.) which indicates "speedily," "quickly," or "shortly." This agrees with the time period given in other passages for the fulfillment of this book. Please note 1:1, 3 and 22:10. It also disagrees with the futuristic interpretation imposed upon these writings. (See Special Study #1.)

9. But he *said to me, "Do not do that. I am a fellow servant of yours and of your brethren the prophets and of those who heed the words of this book. Worship God." 10. And he *said to me, "Do not seal up the words of the prophecy of this book, for the time is near.	11. "Let the one who does wrong, still do wrong; and the one who is filthy, still be filthy; and let the one who is righteous, still practice righteousness; and the one who is holy, still keep himself holy." 12. "Behold, I am coming quickly, and My reward *is* with Me, to render to every man according to what he has done.

7. Whether this is God speaking of His coming on Rome in judgment, or Jesus speaking of His final coming at the last day, commentators are divided. I lean toward the former since that has really been the primary focus of the book. Also because of verse 10. (See Special Study #2.) His point, however, is noteworthy, i.e., to heed the words of the book, take warning, make correction, or choose sides.

8-9. John adds his testimony to the book stating its truth and then makes the same mistake that he made before, 19:10. It is hard to blame him for falling in worship to the nearest spiritual being after all that he has "experienced" in these visions. Nevertheless, he receives the same admonition.

10. This book was not to be "sealed," i.e., closed up, hushed up, or unrevealed. It was to be sent to the churches as a message of encouragement. The reason being that the time of the subject matter of the letter was not far in the future, but was to happen soon, if not immediately. See verse 6. (See Special Study #1.)

11. The speaker is not commanding or condoning unrighteousness but is addressing himself to the progression of sin and holiness. The one who sins "still" is the one who continues in it. He "waxes worse and worse" (2 Timothy 3:13), while the one who is holy draws closer and closer to God. The point is that we should be aware of what we are so that we can develop towards holiness.

12. According to the word "reward" (wages, payment for action), he could be speaking of the reward rendered at any coming in judgment by God or to the final judgment. Because of the emphasis on speed in this passage (22:6, 7, 10, 12, 20), I still tend to believe that this is the judgment on Rome he is primarily speaking of. However, the following verses show that the final judgment is also

> 13. "I am the Alpha and the Omega, the first and the last, the beginning and the end."
> 14. Blessed are those who wash their robes, so that they may have the right to the tree of life, and may enter by the gates into the city.
> 15. Outside are the dogs and the sorcerers and the immoral persons and the murderers and the idolaters, and everyone who loves and practices lying.
> 16. "I, Jesus, have sent My angel to testify to you these things for the churches. I am the root and the descendant of David, the bright morning star."
> 17. The Spirit and the bride say, "Come." And let the one who hears say, "Come." And let the one who is thirsty come; let the one who wishes take the water of life without cost.
> 18. I testify to everyone who hears the words of the prophecy of this book: if anyone adds to them, God will add to him the plagues which are written in this book;

in some way on his mind. (See Special Study #2.)

13. Jesus is identifying Himself with Deity and the completeness of Godhood.

14-15. This is simply a contrast concerning those who are willing to die for the testimony of the Lamb and those who God identifies as wicked. We wash our robes through obedience.

16. Jesus adds His authorship to the closing of the book here.

17. The Spirit speaks and says "come" through the word. The bride is the church as a whole and being the "pillar and ground of the truth" she also speaks and says "come." "The one who hears" is the individual member of the church who has already heard and comes himself and turns to others and invites them with, "Come." The invitation is for all to come and heed the gospel of Christ. To read and heed is to avoid the judgments illustrated in this book.

18-19. This book has as its authors, Father and Son. It is Scripture and is to be treated as Scripture, with all respect, neither leaving anything out nor presuming to add to what God has said.

20-21. Jesus adds a last word of testimony to the fact that He *is coming* and John answers, "Amen" or so be it.

John's Revelation

> 19. and if anyone takes away from the words of the book of this prophecy, God will take away his part from the tree of life and from the holy city, which are written in this book.
> 20. He who testifies to these things says, "Yes, I am coming quickly." Amen. Come, Lord Jesus.
> 21. The grace of the Lord Jesus be with all. Amen.

QUESTIONS ON CHAPTER 22

1. Where does the river of life proceed from?

2. What does this imply?

3. What is noted about the tree of life?

4. What similarities do you see with the Garden of Eden?

5. Is there any significance in this?

6. What's in a name?

7. Who are the Lord's bondservants?

8. When were these things going to take place?

9. What mistake did John make?

10. How did the angel identify himself?

11. What was John to do with the message of this book?

12. What do "robes" represent here?

13. How are they washed?

14. What is outside the city?

15. How is the invitation to salvation offered?

16. What is the penalty for adding to God's word?

17. What is the penalty for taking away from God's word?

John's Revelation

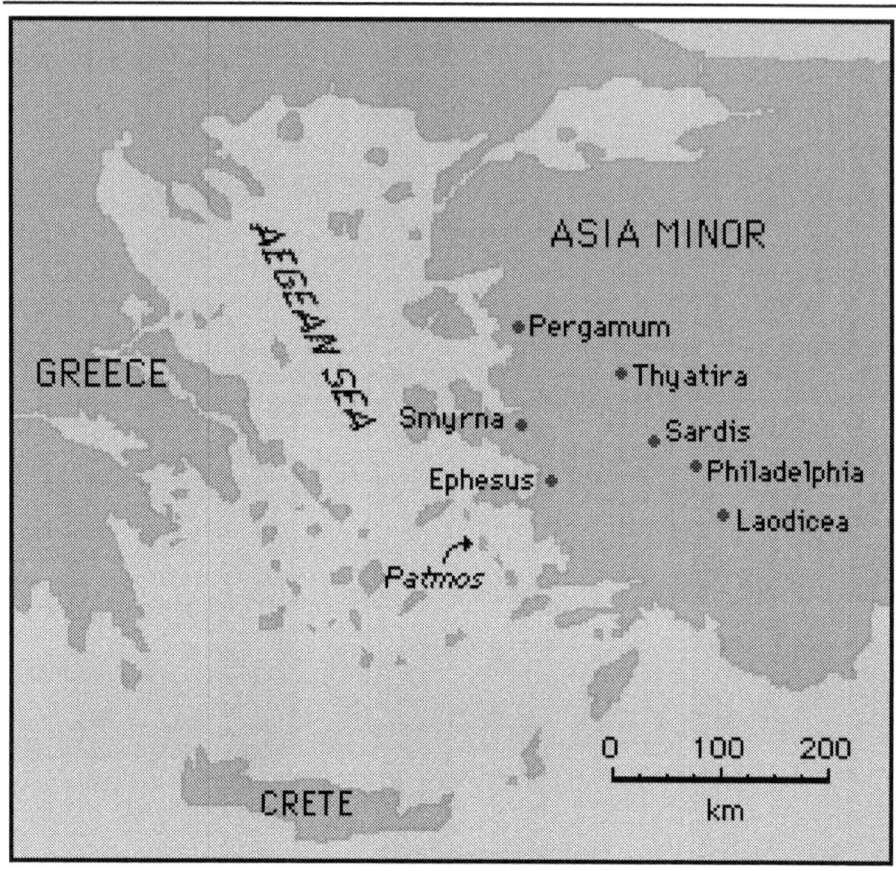

SPECIAL STUDY #1
THE TIME OF FULFILLMENT FOR THE REVELATION

One of the major factors leading to a misunderstanding of the Revelation is a misunderstanding of when the prophecies were to be fulfilled. In the first verse of the first chapter we are given insight as to the time period involved, if we will but read and accept it. The explanation for the book is that the things revealed therein "must shortly take place" (NASB). Taken at face value, John was being told that these things were about to happen in the near future—not 19 centuries later.

This is confirmed by the statements in verse three that the ones who read, heard, and took heed to (i.e., understood and acted upon) the words of this book would be blessed (i.e., happy or fortunate) because "the time was near." Verse four is specifically addressed to "the seven churches that are in Asia." How would "the seven churches" be blessed by reading and understanding a prophecy that was not to take place for almost 2,000 years? It would have absolutely no application for the very ones to whom it was addressed. Once again, however, if we will just accept what the Lord says, we are told that "the time was near" for these prophecies to be fulfilled.

Along with the two occurrences above of the Lord stating the nearness of the events about which John writes, we should also point out Revelation 3:11 where He assures the church in Philadelphia that He was "coming quickly." At the least this would be faint encouragement and at the most this would make Him a liar if He were not in fact going to come soon. He said it plainly and the question left seems to be, do we believe him or not? Shall we deny His words in order to force the book to apply to situations 19 centuries in the future? It would seem more reasonable to believe the words of our Lord and place the blame for misunderstanding on men. Part of the blame must lie with the fact that we often limit the "coming of the Lord." When the terms "day of the Lord" or "Lord's coming" are used we often give consideration only to His return at the end of time, i.e., judgment day. The fact is that there have been many "comings" of the Lord and the context must determine for us which "coming" is being spoken of. (Please see Special Study #2, the "Comings" of the Lord.) Jesus' words here can be understood clearly when we understand that the "coming" under discussion here is the "coming" in vengeance upon Rome during the lifetime of these first century Christians, their children, and their grandchildren. He was promising those Christians that He would "come quickly" and He did!

As the book draws to a close, there are five more references to the nearness of the Lord's return. In chapter 22:6, we read that this message of Revelation was sent to show to His "bond-servants" (Christians) the "things which must shortly take place." Again we ask the question —If the prophecies of the book were not going to "shortly take place," why say so? And if they had no application for those early, suffering Christians to whom they were addressed, why prophecy at all? The explanation is that the book did have application for them and promise for Christians of all ages. And it speaks of events which were surely going to come to pass in a short time and which are now history.

Three times the Alpha and Omega, Jesus Christ, assures the readers of the book (the ones to whom the book was addressed) that He was "coming quickly," 22:7, 12, and 20. He was coming in wrath and judgment upon Rome and He was coming to relieve the faithful.

The last reference we will make is in 22:10 where John is told, "Do not seal up the words of the prophecy of this book, for the time is near." For John to "seal up" the book would have meant for him to tell no one what he saw. This is forbidden, however, with the indication that John is to share the message of the visions. It is a Revelation, not a Covering! He is to send it out to "the seven churches of Asia." The reason given is because "the time is near." They needed the information contained therein for encouragement to steadfastness. If the fulfillment was not for almost 2,000 years—why say it was "near."

GOD MEANS WHAT HE SAYS

The objection might be raised, "What is 'near' to God?" or "What does 'come quickly' mean in eternity?" After all according to 2 Peter 3:8, isn't one day as a thousand years and a thousand years as one day with God?

The answer to this oft-used objection has two parts.

> **1.** 2 Peter 3:8 is not some sort of slide rule or eternal alarm clock that can be used to figure out God's activities in time and eternity. Many forecasters of the Lord's second coming have tried to establish a date upon which He could be looked for based upon equations figured out with this passage as an equivalent. They have all been destined to failure because that is a misuse of this passage. In the context of 2 Peter 3, this verse is just telling us that God is not held to time as man is. The fact under discussion here is the Lord's return and the admonition is for

Christians not to grow weary—because the Lord will return. But we are not to try to hold Him to some sort of time limitations. This is exactly what some are doing when they try to apply this passage to establishing a time when the Lord 'must' return. Our ideas of time do not apply when God is performing His own will according to His own purpose.

2. The second part of the answer has to do with how God communicates with man. Is it reasonable to suppose that God who created man, and knows him better than he knows himself, would use terms and phrases that confuse men? In communicating any message, one usually uses the language that best gets his meaning across. Divine communication is no different. In other words, God means what He says.

Ezekiel prophesied that the day of "doom" was "near" to the inhabitants of the land of Israel in Ezekiel 7:7. In 7:8, God says that He would "shortly pour out" His wrath. What did God mean here by the terms "near" and "shortly"? Jerusalem fell for the third time and was destroyed in about 586 B.C., less than 6 years later.

Zephaniah also prophesied the "great day of the Lord" was "near and coming very quickly" in Zephaniah 1:14. This was the same day of punishment that Ezekiel spoke of, occurring in 586 B.C.E., less than 50 years after the prophecy.

Isaiah prophesied that the "day of the Lord" was "near" for Babylon in Isaiah 13:6. The Babylonian Kingdom fell in less than 200 years.

When John preached "...the kingdom of heaven is at hand," he meant it. The kingdom was actually near; in fact in about 3 years it was established in Jerusalem. In Matthew 4:17, when Jesus preached the same message as John, He meant it. The establishment of the kingdom was really "at hand" or near, as already noted.

When the Lord communicates to man, He uses language that the men understand. If He says something is going to happen soon, He means that in a short time that event will take place. That "short time" has been illustrated at times to be less than 3 years and as long as a couple hundred, but those who take the prophecies of the Revelation and try to apply them over 2,000 years later when the Lord plainly says that the time for those things was "near" and that He was "coming quickly" wrest the scriptures to their own destruction.

CONCLUSION:

To summarize the above then, we are stating that the time of fulfillment for almost all of the Revelation was in those early centuries. This is based upon the fact that...

A) Eight times in the book reference is made to the time of fulfillment and that time was "shortly" (1:1; 22:6), "near" (1:3; 22:10) and "coming quickly" (3:11; 22:7, 12, 20).

B) God means what He says. Whenever God has used this type of terminology with men, it has meant that the prophesied event was actually going to take place soon—not 2,000 years (or more) in the future.

SPECIAL STUDY #2
THE "COMINGS" OF THE LORD

One idea that is often difficult for people to grasp is the fact of the Lord coming more than just once. This has led to no end of misunderstanding as believers have sought to apply the meaning of the final coming of our Lord at the end of time to all New Testament scriptures speaking of His coming, for example Matthew 24:30. Likewise, much false doctrine has been encouraged by taking Old Testament scriptures dealing with the Lord's coming and applying them to what is commonly referred to as the "second coming" of Christ. The truth of the matter is that the Lord has "come" many times in history and the Revelation is just dealing with one of those "comings," not the final one when time will end. Let me explain.

The Lord's coming is often referred to as the "day of the Lord." Notice how many "days" the Lord has had.

1. The prophet Obadiah speaks of a "day of the Lord" which was drawing near. Obadiah 15, 8. This "day of the Lord" takes in the time in which God would repay Edom for the hardship and mockery heaped on Israel through that nation's past. Note that history does not give us a single date for the downfall of Edom—but every prophecy came true over a period of time so that eventually the nation was destroyed and the people disappeared from history. The "day" of the Lord then was a period of time in which the Lord came in vengeance on this nation.

2. In Joel 2:1, the prophet speaks of a "day of the Lord" that was "coming." According to v. 11 it would be a "great and very awesome" day. This day of the Lord's coming was prophesied around 835 B.C.E. and is a prophecy of punishment upon Judah (carried out by the Babylonians) if they would not correct themselves.

3. Amos 5:18-20 speaks of Israel "longing for," i.e., looking forward to the "day of the Lord." Amos asks the question, "Why?" He then explains that it was going to be a day of darkness and gloom with no light. The reason for this is given in the preceding and following verses. Israel hates good and loves evil. They have become unjust and irreligious. This prophecy was given about 758 B.C.E. and there can be little doubt that the Lord's coming here was a coming in vengeance upon Israel, specifically carried out by the Assyrian nation.

4. Isaiah 13:6 describes the day of the Lord as a day of destruction from the

Almighty. Verse one identifies the focus of this destruction as Babylon. This great day that would come with fury, burning anger, and extermination (according to verse 9) came in 539 B.C.E. when Babylon was invaded. Verse 17 correctly prophesies that it is the Medes whom God would stir up against Babylon to do His will and destroy this proud and beautiful society.

5. In about 730 B.C.E., Micah said that the Lord was "coming forth from His place," Micah 1:3. In the language of the prophets, Micah tells how the mountains would be tread down and melted and the valleys would split. Is he speaking of the end of time? Not at all. Further reading will show that it is Israel and Judah that the Lord is threatening with wrath. Their sins of idolatry (Israel) and false worship (Judah) had earned God's wrath. The Lord was going to "come" and set the matter right through discipline.

6. In about 630 B.C.E., Judah is around 90 years short of her humiliation at the hands of the Babylonians. The prophet Zephaniah warns expressly that "near is the great day of the Lord, near and coming very quickly," Zephaniah 1:14. He goes on to say that this would be a day of trouble, distress, wrath, destruction, desolation, darkness, gloom, clouds and thick darkness. This occurrence of the Lord's coming refers, once again, to the terrible tragedy of Jerusalem and the Temple being destroyed at the hands of the Babylonians.

7. Ezekiel chapter 7 speaks of a "day of the wrath of the Lord," in verse 19. This "day of the Lord" was to be a day of doom and disaster (verses 5-7) as well as being referred to as "the end." This "day of the Lord" was the Babylonian invasion of Judah with the resulting fall of Jerusalem for the third and final time in 586 B.C.E.

8. Around 430 B.C.E., it is Malachi who is the prophet speaking of the Lord coming once again. In Malachi 3:2, the prophet speaks of a "great and terrible day of the Lord" that was going to come. Before it came, however, Elijah the prophet was going to be sent to warn the people. We are not left to wonder about this as in Luke 1:17 an angel tells the priest Zacharias that his son was this prophesied forerunner. John the baptizer was the one who was to speak in the Spirit and power of Elijah. Matthew 11:10-14 and Matthew 17:12 also verify this. We are almost 2,000 years past this forerunner of the "day of the Lord." He could not be a forerunner for us. When was the Lord's coming? It was at no other time than the destruction of Jerusalem at the hands of the Romans in 70 A.D., just about forty years after John. Once more the Lord's coming is a day in which He pours out His wrath in judgment and settles scores.

9. My last illustration of this meaning applied to the Lord's coming is in Matthew 24. In verses 27, 30, 37, and 39 Jesus makes reference to His "coming." It would be sudden, in power and glory, obvious to men and surprising to many even up to their deaths. Certainly this sounds on the surface as if He could be speaking of His return at the end of time. The truth, however, is that the final judgment day is not under discussion at all here. Instead He is speaking of a day of wrath and judgment to be poured out upon Jerusalem and the Jewish people. This chapter is in the context of the disciples' questions of verse 1—when would the temple be destroyed? When would come the end of the age? Matthew 24 is the answer to these questions and the answer that our Lord gave was "when Jerusalem is destroyed by the Romans!" Parallel readings in the other gospels will verify this interpretation.

CONCLUSION:

Our conclusion then is that in order to harmonize the Revelation with the rest of scriptures, we must keep the idea of the Lord's coming in context. Down through history there has been <u>many</u> judgment days and the Lord has come <u>many</u> times. He came in judgment on Sodom, Gomorrah, Tyre, Sidon, Edom Egypt, Assyria, Babylon, Jerusalem, and others. In the Revelation, when He speaks of His quick coming, He is speaking of coming in judgment upon Rome. In this payment of vengeance upon a corrupt society that had raised itself up to fight against and persecute the children of God, the early Christians could find encouragement, hope, and confidence that their cause would overcome.

In the language of John, we hear the prophetic language of God's judgment from ages past. In the message of the book, we too can gain confidence that our God is a living God who hears the cries of His people and will not forsake them, but instead repays those who harm them many times over. We see the cause of Christ as a righteous and victorious cause. And taking this view one is able to see through the emotional, modern day interpretations proclaiming eminent doom, a one-world government, bar-codes tattooed on people's hands, an earthly future kingdom, etc., etc., etc., commonly proclaimed by today's sensationalists.

God bless your study.

SPECIAL STUDY #3
EPHESUS

Tradition and old legends have Ephesus first being founded by female warriors known as Amazons and named as the city of the Mother Goddess. It changed locations several times but was founded a second time by Androclus, the son of Codrus, King of Athens. It is dated back past 1200 B.C.E. and thus was ruled by Persia, and Alexander the Great, as well as Rome. By 129 B.C.E., ancient sources show the city with a population of 200,000.

Ephesus was a city favored by both land and sea. It was a seacoast city 3 miles from the west coast of Asia Minor and opposite the island of Samos. It had an artificial harbor providing access to the largest ships and was linked by major roadways to all the chief cities of the province. The soil in this area was fertile, the climate temperate, and with its access both to the interior and to the sea, the city was blessed with religious, political, and commercial development. We might add here, however, that the truly great days of Ephesus were past by the end of the first century. Because of the deforestation of surrounding hills, the harbor was already silting in and clearing operations to keep it open were the continued project of city rulers for decades. During the time of the apostle Paul, the city was still a major center of its day, but the bell was tolling and in a couple centuries Ephesus would pass from existence. As Paul spent 2 years here (Acts 19:10) teaching in the school of Tyrannus, all Asia heard the word of the Lord. It was an excellent field of labor for the apostle.

Ephesus and Pergamum, the capitol of Asia, were the 2 great rival cities of the province. Whereas Pergamum was the center of Roman government and religion, Ephesus, being more accessible to commerce and the home of the goddess Diana, became the chief city of the province.

Connected to the early culture of the city and untraceable for us today was the temple of Diana or Artemis. This temple was burnt and rebuilt seven times, each time on a scale grander and larger than before, eventually leading to its placement as one of the seven wonders of the world. The last temple was built upon a foundation that was reached by a flight of 10 steps. The building itself was 425 ft. long and 220 ft. wide with 127 pillars supporting the roof, each 60 ft. high. About 220 years were spent in its last construction, being finished about 100 years before Christ. It was looked upon in that time, as noted, as one of the wonders of the ancient world. Pilgrims brought wealth into this temple from all over the world and in time the temple came to own valuable lands, controlled the fisheries, and its priests became bankers of enormous revenue. The temple was, in addition to being a great bank and place of worship, a museum where the best paintings and statues were preserved. It was also well known for the orgiastic feasts and temple prostitutes that characterized the worship of Diana. It was a safe haven for criminals, since none could be arrested for any crime within bowshot of its walls. Because of this there sprang up around the temple a village of thieves, murderers, and other criminals. A large number of artisans were employed by the temple to manufacture images of the goddess and it is probably this group that Paul ran afoul of in Acts 19:25ff. When Paul visited the area, the temple of Diana probably represented the greatest single source of income for the city. In addition to the souvenirs, providing food, shelter, and care for the multitude of pilgrims that came to the temple was a profitable trade for Ephesus.

In 269 A.D., Ephesus and the surrounding countryside was devastated by the Goths. In 381 A.D., by the order of emperor Theodosius the temple was closed down and for centuries it was abandoned and served as a source for building materials. In 401 A.D., it was torn down by St. John Chrysostom.

Paul first visited this city on his 2nd journey in Acts 18:19-21 and returned while on his 3rd journey in 19:1-10. While there he taught in the synagogue (19:8-10) as was his custom, in the school of Tyrannus (19:9), and in private homes (20:20). His teaching here for over 2 years was complete and all encompassing (Acts 20:26-27) as he even brought to maturity elders in this congregation (20:17). Tradition says that the apostle John was one of the elders here in his later years. The foundation laid here testifies of strength if we recount that Christians met in this city for hundreds of years following, while the great temple of Diana went downhill. The temple ended as the city did centuries later, in ruins and uninhabited. The city has now been excavated for almost 100 years and most remains come from the later Roman period.

SPECIAL STUDY #4
SMYRNA

Smyrna is a large, ancient city on the west coast of Asia Minor at the head of a gulf reaching 30 miles inland. With a good harbor and standing at the head of a major highway into the interior, early it became a large trading center. The city was founded approximately 1000 B.C.E. and destroyed about 580 B.C.E. by the King of Lydia. Being rebuilt no sooner than 300 years later, it was ceded in 133 B.C.E. to the Romans. The Romans subsequently built there a judiciary conventus and a mint. In Roman times, it is said to have rivaled Ephesus and Pergamum. Its streets were wide and paved, its coinage old, its buildings handsome, and it was praised for its schools of science and medicine. It claimed a theatre to seat 20,000 and temples to Zeus and Cybele, as well as to the Caesar Tiberius. The city laid claim to be the birthplace of the poet Homer and built a shrine to his honor. The city vied with Ephesus and Pergamum for the title of Foremost City in Asia. Streets and buildings extended up from the bay up the sides of surrounding hills. Fountains flowed from the city's aqueducts and cultural life was encouraged with a library, gymnasiums, baths, and a stadium. Smyrna was also one of the seats of the sinister Caesar-cult, which caused much damage to the church, even going so far as to have legislation on the books against the church. It was a powerful city in the Roman scheme of government since it had worshipped the spirit and the beast of Rome since about 195 B.C.E.

Several early writers speak of the church fathers in Smyrna with high praise. One of the early fathers, Polycarp, was martyred here where his grave is still shown. It is said that the Jewish sentiment here was more antagonistic to the spread of Christianity than even the Romans—they being the ones who martyred Polycarp early in the second century, even going to the extent of gathering wood for his fire on the Sabbath day.

The hilltop of Smyrna was surrounded by a diadem of porticos, giving the appearance of a crown. Several writers of the early centuries referred to this "crown of Smyrna" as beautiful and shining (Apollonius of Tyana, Aelius Aristides, etc.). The "crown of Smyrna" seemed to have been a recognized image of rhetoric in that day. This is probably the source of John's reference to a "crown of life." It was a comparison of one crown to another, which would make an effective picture to the people living in this city.

The city is still a large city in Asia with a population of about a quarter million. Its modern name is Izmir, a Turkish corruption of its ancient name. The large ancient harbor and stadium are filled in, but because of its good modern harbor, its climate, and the railroad, the city still prospers.

SPECIAL STUDY #5
PERGAMUM

Pergamum (or Pergamos) was an old Greek city that existed at least since the 5th century B.C.E., but became important during the Hellenistic age about 323-350 B.C.E. when it became host to the Attalid dynasty with their fortress and palace. It became the capitol of the Roman province in 129 B.C.E. and during its Roman period the population was estimated at about 200,000. It was located in the Caicus Valley about 15 miles from the sea in the old Roman province of Asia (do not confuse with the continent nor with Asia Minor). Pergamum sought Roman protection early and therefore became a seat of Roman government early on. This lasted for about 4 centuries with the city reaching its highest point of power about 190 B.C.E.

One of the most renowned structures in the city was the altar to Zeus. Over 40 ft. high with a base more than 100 feet square, it was another of the seven wonders of the ancient world. In addition to its large theatre, stadium, and gymnasium, there were also beautiful temples to Zeus, Dionysus, Athena, Hera, Demeter, and Asklepios. In the worship of Zeus he was referred to as "Zeus the Savior." This would have been particularly offensive to Christian minds.

In connection with the temple dedicated to Asklepios there was a School of Medicine and travelers came from all over the world to sleep in its courts. It was said that while sleeping there, cures and remedies for ailments were revealed to the priests in dreams. As one would expect, deception was commonplace. The worship involved not only healing, but snake handling. One coin discovered shows the Emperor Caracalla before a giant serpent giving that peculiar salute that Hitler's Nazis brought back in a later day. Once more, the presentation of serpents in worship has been considered by many to be something peculiarly offensive to Christians. The modern day twin serpents on the pole is said to have its origination here.

There were also 3 temples dedicated to Roman emperors and the Caesar-cult here. The "two-edged sword" which would remind one of Rome is probably a reference based on the strength of the cult here and its resulting oppression of the church. Corinth had the immorality of Aphrodite's worship to contend with and Thyatira had the economic pressure of its labor guilds—but nowhere was the confrontation more blatant and frightening than here where Christianity and Caesar-worship came face to face.

It is here that Antipas was martyred (Revelation 2:13), the first Christian to be put to death officially by the Roman state. Tradition says he died by burning inside of a brazen bull. Also mentioned as being present here are the Nicolaitans. These might have been those Christians who were trying to find a compromise between Christianity and the overwhelming influence of the pagan deities.

It is here that a parchment for writing was developed, called in the Greek, pergamenos. This was made necessary when Ptolemy Philadelphus forbade the export of papyrus from Egypt to Pergamum, because he was fearful that his library in Alexandria would be overshadowed. It is said that the great library in Pergamum held 200,000 manuscripts. Alexandria truly was the only library that was greater. The modern town still exists under the name of Bergama. It is built among the ruins of the ancient city but is far less in size.

SPECIAL STUDY #6
THYATIRA

Thyatira, which name means "sweet savor of labor," was a wealthy town in the north part of Lydia in the Roman province of Asia. It was located on the River Lycus. The city was originally founded as a border garrison between two major powers and for centuries held strictly to that role. There was not a great deal of natural defense to its geographical location on flat ground, but being forced into the role of military importance, the city could not help but develop a sense of military strength and ability built around individual valor and readiness. This attitude also dominated the commerce and religion of the city for centuries. The earliest settlers of the town adopted as their god a local hero, shown in inscriptions as a warrior on horseback with a battle-ax. The military attitude of the place is probably addressed in verses 26-27 where Christ is explained as being the one with authority to "rule" and "break in pieces." This town was never a major metropolitan area since it was located on none of the Greek trade routes; however, it was a busy commercial center in its day.

Temples located in this city were those dedicated to the ancient sun god Tyrimnos (Apollo) as well as to the goddess Boreatene and Sambethe, a local and lucrative oracle in the fortune telling business. Other deities worshipped here were Aesculapius, Bacchus, and Artemis. It was in the name of Apollo that games were instituted here. His worship was joined to that of the emperors who each, like him were identified as a son of Zeus. This may be why Christ identified Himself here as having eyes like a flame of fire and feet like burnished bronze. This sun-god-emperor worship and an emphasis on female deities and female led religions, as well as the strong trade guilds may explain some of the compromise that seemed apparent in the church in this city. Only the temple of Apollo, an ancient church, and a colonnaded road remain today of the ancient city.

Paprhys, a martyr about 250 A.D., is said to have been from Thyatira.

As noted above, Thyatira was especially noted for its well organized trade guilds even to the point of their mention in ancient records concerning this city. Every artisan belonged to a guild and every guild was an incorporated organization possessing property, acquiring contracts, and wielding great influence. There is evidence of unions of wool-workers, linen-workers, makers of outer garments, leather-workers, tanners, and bronze-smiths. Two powerful guilds were the coppersmiths and the guild of the dyers of which Lydia (Acts 16:14) was probably a member. The purple colored material that this guild sold is now identified by the dye called "Turkish red." The guilds were closely associated with pagan feasts and immoral religious practices, so as such they became powerful opponents to Christianity. This was intensified as many in the early church taught that no Christian could be a member of any guild. The reference to "fine brass" used only here in the New Testament has been suggested as relating to one of the guilds in Thyatira known for its brass work.

The modern city goes by the name Akhisar, "The White Fortress," named by the Turks and the population is around 22,000. It is little more than a large village railway stop of the Manisa-Soma Railroad. It is 9 hours, on the old Roman Road, from Sardis.

SPECIAL STUDY #7
SARDIS

Sardis is a city easily dating back to the Medo-Persian Empire and possibly founded about 1200 B.C.E. during the time of the judges in Israel. The name of the city comes from the stone sardius, a semi-precious stone, orange red in color, but reflecting a deep red when light is passed through it. It is one of the oldest cities in Asia Minor. The city was often considered impregnable because of its situation on a mountain with the River Pactolus flowing at its base as a moat. The acropolis was built about 1500 feet above the plain on a ridge of 5,800 foot Mt. Tmolus and said ridge was considered extremely difficult to reach and thus an extremely safe and secure place for the populace. Through their failure to watch, however, the cliff under the city had been scaled twice and the city taken by stealth. Tradition has it that the first time it happened it was a result of a Lydian soldier who dropped his helmet over the wall. He scaled down the cliff to retrieve it and was observed closely as he returned to his post. The enemy promptly climbed up the same way. Something to be said here about giving one's enemies the tools to defeat you.

Gold and silver minted coinage had its origin here, the earliest form of which was made of electrum, an alloy of gold and silver. The river was known for its rich flow of precious metal from the mountains. The city was also an economic stronghold of the wool industry.

The city was noted for its fruits and wool as well as for its temple to the goddess Artemis, known as Diana to the Romans. This goddess was the goddess of the hunt, the moon, and fertility and her temple here is one of the largest of the Greek temples, being more than double the size of the Parthenon. Also located here was the temple of Cybele, the great Mother, whose worship consisted of sexual orgies, hysteria, and mutilation in the form of self-castration. Today only two columns from that temple are all that stand.

In John's day, the city would have been about 120,000 in size. Like Corinth, Sardis developed a name of contempt, even on pagan lips. Its citizens were notorious for loose living and luxury loving. The name Sardis became a byword for slack and effeminate living. Although it had begun as a frontier town, it became a city of decadence. It was also another seat for Caesar-worship. When desiring funds to build a temple to Caesar here, the envoys are recorded as speaking long and loud of the city's past glories and history. In 17 A.D., Tiberius assisted in rebuilding the city after a terrible earthquake and some scholars feel that from this time forward the emperor cult gained great power. The city, as well as the church there, had a name or reputation for being alive—but was really dead.

The works undone (city defenses not seen to), the thief in the night (city taken by surprise when soldiers scaled the cliff walls), the reputation that was undeserved (all glory was past glory), all should have been well understood by wise and observant Christians in the church in that city. Today the city on the ridge is a ruin and nearby stands a small village by the name of Sart. The legends of Midas and King Croesus of Sardis are about all that lives on.

SPECIAL STUDY #8
PHILADELPHIA

This city is located on the Cogamus River in Asia Minor, 105 miles from Smyrna and 28 miles southeast of Sardis. Being founded 189 B.C.E., it is not so ancient a city as others in Asia Minor, but it did quickly become an important and wealthy trade center. Its public buildings and temples were magnificent enough so that the city has received the title of "Little Athens." It has been destroyed by earthquakes several times and has been continuously beset by tremors. The practice of running out of the city for fear of falling walls must have been a familiar one to the Philadelphians. There may be reference to this idea in 3:17 when the promise of the Lord is safety and security. His people will not have to "go out anymore" once they receive their reward.

There were enough Jews in this area that a synagogue is recorded as being built here. The ground in the area is extremely fertile and an excellent wine was produced here about which the Roman poet Virgil wrote.

The modern city goes by the name Alashehir and is still considered a "Christian" town, speaking in terms of the early century. It boasts a licorice factory that is the single greatest source of income for the people in that area, and is best reached by rail from Smyrna.

SPECIAL STUDY #9
LAODICEA

Laodicea is a city of Asia Minor in the province of Phrygia, about 50 miles from Philadelphia, within sight of Colossea. The city's history really began in the third century B.C.E. when it was renamed by the Syrian king, Seleucus II in honor of his wife Laodice. In 60 A.D., the city was almost completely destroyed by an earthquake, but the citizens possessed such wealth that they refused Roman aid and rebuilt the city themselves. Perhaps these things are the basis for our Lord's comments in Revelation 3:18. The Laodicean church received the sharpest rebuke for being infected with the worldly prosperity of the city. Today the ruins of three theatres, a stadium, sarcophagi, and a gymnasium speak eloquently of a glory in that place that has long since passed. The aqueduct that piped water to Laodicea carried water that was rich in calcium that caused the pipes to clog. It is noteworthy that the aqueduct was designed with vents covered by stones that could be removed periodically for cleaning.

Laodicea was known in Roman times for the fine black wool of its sheep, which was considered high-grade, glossy, soft and dark. At least four different kinds of garments were made from this wool and marketed all over the world. The city also manufactured sandals, and a Phrygian powder for the eyes, which was manufactured in tablet form. The city had a renowned School of Medicine and

John's Revelation

in fact this treatment for the eyes was a specialty they were famous for. Laodicea was well know for its extensive banking operations. Her bankers negotiated with the whole world. Its coins and inscriptions show evidence of the major form of worship going to Zeus, as well as Aesculapius, Apollo and the emperors. The city was inhabited by Greeks, Romans, and an influential and wealthy Jewish colony. One writer comments that outside the city were tepid mineral springs, which, if one drank from them, would make one vomit. An interesting fact, if true, that would sound quite clear to the citizens of this church and city.

Epaphras may have been the one to bring the gospel to Laodicea (Colossians 1:7) though little is known. Mentioned as bishops in the early church here, by tradition only, were Nymphas in whose house the church met (Colossians 4:15) and Diotrephes (3 John 9) of preeminent fame.

Today the city is a ruin by the name of Eski Hissar and has long served as a quarry to a neighboring town. Three ruins of early Christian churches can be seen there and that is about all that is left to be seen of the ruins.

SPECIAL STUDY #10
PREMILLENNIALISM
IN THE BOOK OF REVELATION

Those that look to Revelation chapter 20 as a proof-text to Premillennialism must see several things in it that are *not present*. They must see...

1) The second coming of Christ.
2) A bodily resurrection.
3) Christ reigning literally on the earth.
4) The literal throne of David, set up in Jerusalem.
5) The city Jerusalem, in Palestine.
6) The conversion of the Jews.

There are so many different accounts of this millennial reign that it would be fruitless to name only one, but most of them include the above named parts. Suffice it to say that a theory that is dependent upon a certain passage as proof for all its main tenants, when the passage makes *no mention of any of them*, cannot be right. If we know the truth about the thousand year reign, that is all that we need to know to resist error. We refer the reader to our comments on 20:6 as to the actual teaching here of Jesus' thousand year reign. The truth is that Jesus' reign began in the first century and is still continuing. Any who would deny this deny both the Messiah of Old Testament prophecy and the Christ of the New Testament, King of Kings and Lord of Lords.

In addition to the above problems with a premillennial interpretation, these theorists put themselves into a unique position of having to deny other plain Bible teaching in order to prop up their doctrine.

For example...

THEY MISUNDERSTAND GOD'S PROMISES

Most premillennialists begin with the assumption that not all of God's promises to Abraham have been fulfilled. They acknowledge the three promises recorded for us in the book of Genesis. God promised Abraham that He would:

1) make of his seed a great nation (Genesis 12:2; 13:16; 15:5),
2) give him a great land (13:14-18; 15:7ff), and
3) bring forth a blessing to bless all nations from his seed (12:3).

It is the premillennialists contention that the land promise was never fulfilled, thus the great importance placed on Israel getting its land in 1948 and subsequent encouragement for U.S. involvement to make sure they kept it. This contention of an unfulfilled promise flatly contradicts the scriptures that teach and show us all those promises were fulfilled with Israel centuries ago. See Exodus 19:6; Joshua 23:14; 2 Chronicles 9:26; and Acts 3:25-26.

THEY MISUNDERSTAND THE KINGDOM

In teaching their "future kingdom" ideas, they must deny plain Bible teaching concerning the true kingdom of God. Daniel 2:44 is a prophecy that God would set up His eternal kingdom in the days of Rome. The Premillennialists must make God fail in this because he is still looking for the kingdom to come, centuries after Rome has fallen. In Mark 9:1, Jesus said that some standing there would still be alive to see the kingdom come. Once more the millennial advocate must either make Jesus' words null and void, or there are some extremely old people alive today, still looking for His kingdom.

It is impossible to be a king without a kingdom. When one loses his throne, he is no longer a king. Premillennialists dethrone Jesus in that they are looking for Him to rule someday in the future. They want His mediating power as a priest now, and they want Him as a king later. In doing so, they deny Zechariah 6:12-13 that identifies "the Branch" (Christ, the Nazarene) as a "priest-king," holding the two offices simultaneously. You simply can't have one without the other. The New Testament writer verifies this in Hebrews 7:1-17 when he identifies Jesus as being a "priest forever according to the order of Melchizedek." Melchizedek was a "priest-king" in the days of Abraham. Hebrews 5:5-10 identifies Christ as being designated by God, according to this same order; therefore, Jesus Christ also is a "priest-king." He is a priest now (Hebrew 3:1) and He is a king now, ruling over heaven (Matthew 28:18), the whole earth (Psalms 2), and His kingdom (Colossians 1:13; Revelation 1:6) the church.

THEY MISUNDERSTAND THE CHURCH

Most advocates of the premillennial theory hold to the idea that the church is some kind of substitute arrangement that Christ gave because He was not able to set up His kingdom as He had planned, instead being killed by the Jews. In addition to making God a liar by defeating His prophecies, as we have already noted, these people now make Christ a failure because men defeated His purpose. Once more this also denies plain Bible teaching on the church. In Matthew 16:18-19, Jesus states His intention to build His "church." The Premillennialists fail to understand that the church and the kingdom are the same. In this passage Jesus uses the term interchangeably. In Ephesians 3:8-11, Paul teaches that:

1) God was making known His wisdom to rulers and authorities in heavenly places, *through the church,* and
2) that this was in accordance with His eternal purpose in Christ Jesus.

The church is not a substitute arrangement of any kind. Christ did not fail in His task. He plainly stated that He had accomplished all that the Father had given Him to do. The church was in the eternal purpose or mind of God from the beginning and Jesus intended to build it. That's why God prophesies of an eternal kingdom to be built (Daniel 2:44), and Jesus built the church. God prophesies of His temple to be built (Zechariah 6:12-13) and the church is called the temple of God (1 Corinthians 3:16). Once more we repeat—the church and the kingdom are one.

Premillennialism denies too many other Bible passages to ever be considered truthful, and when this is considered along with the first thought in this study, it ought to become obvious that this religious theory should be rejected, not only in the apocalypse, but also in all other passages of scripture where its proponents try to go to find evidence.

SPECIAL STUDY #11
WHAT ABOUT TOTAL ANNIHILATION?

Some labor under the impression that when one is cast into the lake of fire he will be totally consumed or annihilated and that will be all there is. The Bible continues to affirm, however, that torment will continue forever. It will not be over in a moment. In 14:10, the smoke of torment (pain, severe distress of body and mind) from those who worship the beast goes up *forever and ever*. In 20:10, their torment goes on *day and night, forever and ever*.

In Matthew 25:41, 46, eternal punishment is contrasted with eternal life. Both life and punishment are described by the same term—eternal. To know how long the punishment will last, let us simply ask how long the life will last? Notice also in 7:15 and 14:11 that one group before the throne serves him "*day and night*" while the other group "has no rest *day or night.*" Whatever it means in one place it also means in the other. If there is total annihilation for the wicked, the Bible does not speak of it. This is just another example of men not being willing to accept God at His word.

Luke 16:19ff is probably one of the clearest examples of Jesus' teaching on the matter. Here is an account of a man who dies and finds himself in torment. There is no annihilation, no destruction, or unconsciousness. There *is* awareness, pain, regret, desire, fear, and pleading. There is also the indication of no respite. All these things are in perfect accord with the picture presented in all the passages listed in the first paragraph. Lest someone respond (like Jehovah's Witnesses have been known to do) that this is "just a parable," please note...

1) Jesus never calls it a parable.
2) If it is a parable, does that mean we should not believe it? Should we not believe all Jesus' teaching done in parables?
3) The definition of a parable is an account that could easily be true, i.e., it has all the facts and requirements of a true story. (For example there are no talking dogs, fairy godmothers, or magic elves.) It is not a fable. That leads us to the conclusion that this account in Luke 16 of torment and rest is literally true.
4) Would our Lord use an untruth, a misrepresentation of fact, to teach truth? If there were no "torment" would Jesus use this picture to teach something? The answer is as obvious as the question is senseless. Of course not. This is no parable and torment is real.

SPECIAL STUDY # 12
THE CAESARS AND PERSECUTION OF THE SAINTS

The following material was presented to me by a brother in one of the congregations where I taught this material. I have included it here for the purpose of perhaps helping the student to be more familiar with the events taking place in the Roman Empire around the time of the writing of this book.

the author

CHRISTIANITY VERSUS RULERS OF THE ROMAN EMPIRE

compiled by Mac Payne

The first 300 years of Christianity found the Christians in conflict not only with the Jews and local magistrates of providential governments, but also with the very rulers of the Roman Empire. The persecution of the church began in the city of Rome in A.D. 64, but eventually spread into the entire known world. Although there were periods of tolerance or lesser persecution, there were many periods of severe trial for the early faithful.

The times of persecution began as a political ploy by Nero, then was attributed to prejudice, refusal to accept the Caesars as deity, refusal to worship the national gods of the Roman Empire, and suspicion of being subverters and possible enemies of the empire, until merely calling oneself a Christian was illegal and itself worthy of being sought out and put to death.

Through it, however, the church continued to grow, and it might be noted that one of the worst periods for the church seems to have been between A.D. 253 and about A.D. 300, when there was no persecution and Christians even rose to high offices within the empire. Apparently, being a "Christian" was in vogue, and many weak and wealthy were attracted to the church, only to defect when persecution again arose. Hailey's commentary provides a quote that states that this period of time was more dangerous to Christian virtue than the severest of persecution, and that the internal condition of the church was corrupt and filled with hypocrisy, covetousness, and hatred.

The information herein was gleaned from REVELATION, AN INTRODUCTION AND COMMENTARY by Homer Hailey, and THE REVELATION OF JOHN by William Barclay. To provide a historical background, both commentators quote from writings of ancient authorities, historians, and contemporaries of the early Christians. It is provided here simply as reference material for the time period.

Rulers of the Roman Empire:

Augustus (B.C.E. 27 - A.D. 14) Allowed worship of Julius (his predecessor) to continue. Also, allowed temples and altars to be erected in the providences in his honor. Made no attempt to enforce worship of himself. (Mentioned in Luke 2:1.)

Tiberius (A.D. 14-37) Actively discouraged Caesar worship. (Spoken of in Luke 3:1 and is the Caesar of Acts 25:11.)

Caligula (A.D. 37-41) Madman. Described as cruel and the most debased of men. Insisted that he be worshipped as divine and attempted to impose this requirement upon the Jews.

Claudius (A.D. 41-54) Reversed the policies of the insane Caligula, but expelled the Jews from Rome (Acts 18:2). This expulsion was likely because of the uproar caused by "one Christus" (Christ), according to some ancient historians.

Nero (A.D. 54-68) Enjoyed being worshipped. First, because he was disliked and secondly, for his life style, he was accused of responsibility for the fire that destroyed or damaged three-fourths of Rome in A.D. 64. He diverted attention from himself by using Christians as scapegoats. This beginning of Christian persecution was politically motivated, and likely limited to Rome itself. (Explaining the Christians, one early historian is quoted as telling of the crucifixion of "Christus" under Tiberius, at the hands of Pilate, and the spread of "the mischievous superstition" to Rome.)

Galba, Otto, and Vitellius (A.D. 68-69) No Caesar worship recorded and with the shortness of their reign (lives, once in office), it appears that no confrontation with the Christians was raised.

Vespasian (A.D. 69-79) No Caesar worship and no direct confrontation with the Christians.

Titus (A.D. 79-81) No Caesar worship or persecution of Christians. Possibly poisoned by his brother, Domitian.

Domitian (A.D. 81-96) Demanded to be worshipped and receive divine honors. Described by Barclay as a devil and cold-blooded. Hailey says "In Domitian, the spirit of Nero was reincarnated..." and that men of nobility were put to death on the slightest pretext. Any subjects of the Roman Empire who would not address him as Lord God were likely to be put to death, although exile seems to have been a favorite punishment also. (This is likely when the apostle John was banished to the Isle of Patmos.)

Nerva (A.D. 96-98) Humane, considerate. Rescinded some of Domitian's more intolerable laws, ended policy of exiling, and returned former exiles to their homes. (This is likely when John was returned to Ephesus.)

Trajan (A.D. 98-117) Noble ruler, possibly the best that Rome had, but because Christianity was considered an illegal religion, and because of a Jewish uprising put down in A.D. 115, there was a general persecution of Christians, and martyrdom of their faithful leaders, although no official edict was published. The Jews stirred up trouble for the Christians.

Hadrian (A.D. 117-138) Somewhat tolerant toward Christians, in that they were not to be hunted, magistrates were not to condemn Christians because of local prejudice, and false accusers were to receive heavy penalties.

Antoninus Pius (A.D. 138-161) Very religious in his worship of national gods of the Roman Empire. Known for clemency and lenient administration, but had little sympathy toward Christians because, to him, they represented a secession from the religion of the state. To the delight of the Jews, many Christians were martyred. There are references to the Jews ignoring the Sabbath to "as usual" eagerly help gather wood for the fire that was Polycarp's sentence.

Marcus Aurelius Antoninus (A.D. 161-180) Because Christian's would not worship the Roman gods, they were considered disloyal to the state. Official policy drifted toward intolerance, and Christians were being sought out for persecution.

Commodus (A.D. 180-192) Persecution eased somewhat.

Septimus Severus (A.D. 193-211) Sporadic persecution of Christians. They were looked upon as the lowest members of society. Christians were blamed for earthquakes in Asia Minor, and in 202 A.D., Severus issued the first official edict outlawing conversion to Christianity and providing heavy penalties. Christians were beaten, burned, and beheaded.

According to Hailey, the three rulers from 235-253 A.D. "declared open war against Christianity" in an attempt to annihilate it and restore worship of the Roman deities. Following this was a period of peace, followed by yet another time of terrible persecutions.

FOOTNOTES

1. W.E. Vine, <u>Expository Dictionary of New Testament Words</u>, 1984.
2. John T. Hinds, <u>Revelation</u> (Nashville: Gospel Advocate, 1974), p. 12, Intro.
3. Frank Perigo, <u>Study Notes on Revelation</u>, Intro.
4. William Hendriksen, <u>More Than Conquerors</u> (Grand Rapids: Baker Book House, 1979), p. 101.
5. Perigo, p. 19.
6. Homer Hailey, <u>Revelation: An Introduction and Commentary</u> (Grand Rapids: Baker Book House, 1979), p. 168.
7. Jim McGuiggan, <u>Revelation</u> (Lubbock: Montex, PC, 1976), p. 80.
8. Ibid, p. 81
9. Ibid, p. 81.
10. Hailey, p. 175.
11. Hendriksen, p. 105.
12. Hailey, p. 185.
13. Willie Wallace Speck, <u>The Triumph of Faith</u> (Athens: CEI Bookstore), chapter IV.
14. Weldon E. Warnock, <u>Revelation: A Message From Patmos</u> (Bowling Green: Guardian of Truth, 1985), p. 52.
15. Hailey, p. 189.
16. Ibid, p. 190.
17. Ibid, p. 190
18. Hendriksen, p. 122
19. Vine
20. Joseph Henry Thayer, D.D., <u>Thayer's Greek-English Lexicon of the New Testament</u> (New York: Zondervan, 1963).
21. Hailey, pp. 196-199.
22. Ibid, p. 200.
23. Ibid, p. 201.
24. Ibid, p. 209
25. Hendriksen, p. 141.
26. Hailey, p. 215.
27. Ibid, p. 221.
28. Ibid, p. 222.
29. Ibid, p. 223.
30. Warnock, p. 60.

31. Hailey, p. 233.
32. Ibid, p. 237.
33. Ibid, p. 239.
34. Ibid, p. 244.
35. Ibid, p. 245.
36. Ibid, p. 273.
37. Ibid, p. 274.
38. Ibid, p. 279.
39. Ibid, p. 285.
40. Ibid, p. 293.
41. Ray Summers, <u>Worthy Is the Lamb</u> (Nashville: Broadman Press, 1951), p. 179.
42. Hailey, p. 296.
43. Perigo, p. 46
44. Hailey, p. 321.
45. Ibid, p. 336.
46. McGuiggan, p. 231.
47. Hailey, p. 342.
48. Ibid, p. 349.
49. Perigo, p. 57.
50. Hailey, p. 376.
51. Ibid, p. 379.
52. Ibid, p. 386.
53. Ibid, p. 391.
54. Ibid, pp. 396-397.
55. <u>Alford on Revelation</u>, pp. 735ff.
56. Hailey, p. 404.

BIBLIOGRAPHY

Jenkins, Ferrell. The Old Testament in the Book of Revelation. Temple Terrace: Florida College Bookstore, 1972.

Howard, V.E. and Hines, J.L. Study of Revelation. West Monroe Central Printers and Publishers, 1967.

Warnock, Weldon E. Revelation: A Message From Patmos. Bowling Green, Guardian of Truth Foundation, 1985.

Speck, Willie Wallace. The Triumph of Faith. Athens: C.E.I Bookstore.

McGuiggan, Jim. Revelation. Lubbock: Montex, PC, 1976.

Eusebius. The Nicene and Post-Nicene Fathers, Vol. 1. New York, Parker & Co., 1890.

Hendriksen, William. More Than Conquerors. Grand Rapids: Baker Book House, 1949.

Orr, James, ed. International Standard Bible Encyclopedia. Grand Rapids: Wm. Eerdmans Publishing, 1956.

Lindsey, Hal. The Late Great Planet Earth. New York: Zondervan 1970.

Revelation in the Pulpit Commentary. Grand Rapids: Wm. B. Eerdmans Publishing Co., 1962.

Summers, Ray. Worthy Is the Lamb. Nashville: Broadman Press, 1951.

Thayer, J.H. Thayer's Greek-English Lexicon of the New Testament. New York: Zondervan, 1963.

Perigo, Frank. Study Notes on Revelation.

Crawley, Bob. Study Outline on Revelation.

Harkrider, Robert. Revelation, Outlines and Questions. 1979.

Ogden, Arthur. The Avenging of the Apostles and Prophets. Louisville: Ogden Publications, 1985.

Elkins, Tice. The Sounding of the Seven Trumpets. Austin: Firm Foundation Publishing House, 1942.

Pack, Frank. The Revelation, Vol. 1 & 2. Austin: Sweet Publishing Co., 1965.

Patton, Herschal E. Revelation in Outline. Huntsville, Alabama.

Hinds, John T. Revelation. Nashville: Gospel Advocate Co., 1974.

Zerr, E.M. Bible Commentary. Marion: Cogdill Foundation Publishers, 1954.

Wiersbe, Warren W. Be Victorious. Wheaton: Victor Books, 1985.

The Doctrine of Last Things: Florida College Annual Lectures 1986. Temple Terrace: Florida College Bookstore, 1986.

Stanley, Arthur. Lectures on the History of the Eastern Church. New York: Charles Scribners' Sons, 1871.

Mosheim, John L. An Ecclesiastical History, Vol. 1. 1849.

Brumback, Robert H. History of the Church Through the Ages. Mission Messenger, 1957.

Hayes, Carlton J.H. and Moon, Parker Thomas. Ancient and Medieval History. New York: MacMillan, 1935.

Fisher, George Park. History of Christian Doctrine. New York: Charles Scribners' Sons, 1923.

Norton, Fredrick Owen. The Rise of Christianity. Chicago: University of Chicago Press, 1924.

Keller, Werner. The Bible as History. New York: William Morrow & Co., 1956.

Newman, Albert Henry. <u>A Manual of Church History</u>. Philadelphia American Baptist Publication Society, 1899.

Hailey, Homer. <u>Revelation: An Introduction & Commentary</u>. Grand Rapids: Baker Book House, 1979.

Vine, W.E. <u>Expository Dictionary of New Testament Words</u>. 1984.

John's Revelation

More Bible workbooks that you can order from Spiritbuilding.com or your favorite Christian bookstore.

Inside Out
Studying spiritual growth in bite sized pieces

Night and Day
Comparing N.T. Christianity and Islam

Church Discipline
A quarter's study on an important task for the church

Compass Points
Foundation lessons for home studies or new Christians

We're Different Because...
A workbook on authority and recent church history that ought to be taught regularly

Communing with the Lord
A study of the Lord's Supper & issues surrounding it

Marriage Through the Ages
A quarter's study of God's design for this part of our life

Parenting Through the Ages
Bible principles tested & explained by successful parents who are also a preacher, elder, grandparents, and foster parents

1 & 2 Timothy and Titus
A commentary workbook on these letters from Paul

From Beneath the Altar
A workbook commentary on the book of Revelation

The Parables, Taking a Deeper Look
A relevant examination of our Lord's teaching stories

The Minor Prophets, Vol. 1 & 2, with PowerPoint CD and Teacher's Manual
Old lessons that speak directly to us today

Esteemed of God, Studying the book of Daniel
Covering the man as well as the time between the testaments

Transitions - Moving Through the Twenty-Somethings
A relevant life study for this changing age group

More Bible workbooks that you can order from Spiritbuilding.com or your favorite Christian bookstore.

Reveal In Me...
A ladies study on finding and developing one's talents
**I Will NOT Be Lukewarm,
with Powerpoint CD**
A ladies study on defeating mediocrity
The Gospel of John
A study for women, by a woman, on this letter of John
Snapshots, Defining Moments in a Girl's Life
How to make godly decisions when it really matters
Sisters at War
Breaking the generation gap between sisters in Christ
The Path of Peace
Relevant and important topics of study for teens
The Purity Pursuit
Helping teens achieve purity in all aspects of life
Romans, with Powerpoint CD
*Putting righteousness by faith on an understandable level,
for teens through adults*

AUTISM, In the Eye of the Hurricane
What do you do when your child is diagnosed as autistic, the specialists are expensive, and the outlook is that nothing can be done? This is the story of one courageous couple that has set the medical community back on its heels. With faith and hard work they present a story of hope for those touched by this storm, helping their autistic son to move from permanently handicapped to the status of gifted learner.

www.ingramcontent.com/pod-product-compliance
Lightning Source LLC
Chambersburg PA
CBHW071657090426
42738CB00009B/1555